Foreign Direct Investment and Development

Launching a Second Generation
of Policy Research

Avoiding the Mistakes of the First,
Reevaluating Policies for Developed
and Developing Countries

Theodore H. Moran

PETERSON INSTITUTE FOR INTERNATIONAL ECONOMICS
Washington, DC
April 2011

Theodore H. Moran, nonresident senior fellow, has been associated with the Peterson Institute since 1998. He holds the Marcus Wallenberg Chair at the School of Foreign Service in Georgetown University. He is the founder of the Landegger Program in International Business Diplomacy at the university and serves as director there. In 2007 he was invited to join the Director of National Intelligence Advisory Panel on International Business Practices. In 1993–94 he was senior adviser for economics on the Policy Planning Staff of the Department of State. He returned to Georgetown University after the North American Free Trade Agreement and Uruguay Round negotiations. In 2000 he was appointed counselor to the Multilateral Investment Guarantee Agency of the World Bank Group. In 2002 he was chairman of the Committee on Monitoring International Labor Standards of the National Academy of Sciences. He is a consultant to the United Nations, governments in Asia and Latin America, and international business and financial communities. His books include *China's Strategy to Secure Natural Resources: Risks, Dangers, and Opportunities* (2010), *Three Threats: An Analytical Framework for the CFIUS Process* (2009), *Harnessing Foreign Direct Investment for Development: Policies for Developed and Developing Countries* (2006), *Does Foreign Direct Investment Promote Development?* (coedited with Magnus Blomstrom and Edward Graham, 2005), and *Foreign Investment and Development* (1998).

**PETER G. PETERSON INSTITUTE
FOR INTERNATIONAL ECONOMICS**
1750 Massachusetts Avenue, NW
Washington, DC 20036-1903
(202) 328-9000   FAX: (202) 659-3225
www.piie.com

C. Fred Bergsten, *Director*
Edward A. Tureen, *Director of Publications, Marketing, and Web Development*

Typesetting: Susann Luetjen
Printing: Versa Press, Inc.
Cover photo: © Kybele—Fotolia

Printed in the United States of America
13   12   11   5   4   3   2   1

Library of Congress Cataloging-in-Publication Data

Moran, Theodore H., 1943–
 Foreign direct investment and development : launching a second generation of policy research : avoiding the mistakes of the first, reevaluating policies for developed and developing countries / Theodore H. Moran.
  p. cm.
 Includes bibliographical references and index.
 ISBN 978-0-88132-600-0
 1. Investments, Foreign--Government policy. 2. Investments, Foreign--Government policy--Developing countries. I. Peterson Institute for International Economics. II. Title.

 HG4538.M67 2011
 332.67'32--dc22

                                        2011006938

To

Rob, James, and Grace

Harlow and Nessa

Contents

Tables

Box

Preface

Foreign direct investment (FDI) and its role in development is an important area of research at the Peterson Institute. Ted Moran has been a key contributor to our repertoire of studies in this area. His past contributions include *Foreign Direct Investment and Development* (1998), *Parental Supervision: The New Paradigm for Foreign Direct Investment and Development* (2001), and *Does Foreign Direct Investment Promote Development?* (2005) coedited with Magnus Blomstrom and the late Edward M. "Monty" Graham. Alongside Ted's work is Monty Graham's *Fighting the Wrong Enemy: Antiglobal Activists and Multinational Enterprises* (2000), which touches on many of these issues. On a personal note, Ted and I—with Tom Horst—provided an early perspective on FDI in the extractive sector, and FDI in developing countries, in *American Multinationals and American Interests* (1978).

This volume is the culmination of Institute investigations of the relationship between FDI and development. More than one-third of world trade today takes place in the form of intrafirm transactions—that is, trade among the various parts of the same corporate network spread across borders—and the bulk of technology is transferred within the confines of integrated international production systems. This means that FDI and the operations of multinational corporations have become central to the world economy at large.

Nowhere is this more important than for developing countries. But as Ted Moran argues in this path-breaking new volume, foreign direct investment is not a single phenomenon. FDI has such different impacts in the extractive sector, infrastructure, manufacturing and assembly, and services—and presents such distinctive policy challenges—that each broad category of FDI must be treated on its own terms. Indeed, past studies that have aggregated all FDI flows together to try to find some unique relationship to host-country growth or welfare have led to unreliable substantive findings and, sometimes, mistaken policy conclusions.

Moran examines each of the principal forms of FDI, extracts the best from previous analysis, and offers new findings and perspectives about how benefits from FDI in each sector can be enhanced and potential damages limited or eliminated.

To avoid "resource curse" outcomes from FDI in the extractive sector, Moran would fill loopholes in anticorruption regulations and plug gaps in the rules governing OECD versus Chinese, Russian, and Indian investors. To enable a new generation of infrastructure agreements, he would redesign investor-state arbitration procedures. To combat sweatshops, he shows how international supply chains might transfer premium prices for consumers into decent wages for lowest-skilled workers.

But most FDI in manufacturing and assembly does not flow to lowest-skilled operations. By far the majority of manufacturing FDI flows to medium-skilled industrial sectors—transportation equipment, industrial machinery, electronics and electrical products, medical devices and the like—rather than to garments, footwear, and toys, and the weighting toward more skill-intensive FDI activities is speeding up over time. The ratio of FDI in higher to lower skill-intensive activities was roughly 5:1 in1989–91 but approximately 14:1 in 2005–07 (latest data available).

The implication is that the potential benefit of manufacturing FDI to host economies in developing countries is many times greater than contemporary trade-and-investment models portray, because multinational corporations can help hosts upgrade and diversify their production-and-export base. The process of using FDI to diversify and upgrade production-and-exports, however, does not come about simply by reforming "doing business" indicators and letting markets work on their own. Important market failures and other impediments must be overcome by host-country authorities, backed by assistance from the World Bank/International Finance Corporation and regional development banks, as well as by nongovernmental organizations (FDI) and corporate social responsibility advocates.

Indeed Moran suggests using FDI to upgrade and diversify the production-and-export base as the new frontier for developing countries, especially when this is accompanied by creation of backward linkages and supplier relationships deep into the host economy. He shows how to identify vertical and horizontal externalities, as well as export, labor-market, and labor-institution externalities, and offers practical guidance on how to promote them.

FDI is by no means a panacea for development. But FDI effectively deployed across the extractive, infrastructure, manufacturing, and services sectors can help promote broad-based economic and social welfare and increase host-country rates of growth. Moran shows that the greatest contributions from foreign investors derive from their well-structured, well-regulated core activities. He identifies policies that can best enhance the benefits, while avoiding negative side-effects—policies for host governments, home governments, and multilateral lending institutions. Finally, he urges the NGO and corporate social responsibility communities to refocus their agenda toward enhancing how multinational corporations go about conducting their main-line operations, rather than merely urging them to "give back" more via greater corporate philanthropy.

The Peter G. Peterson Institute for International Economics is a private, nonprofit institution for the study and discussion of international economic policy. Its purpose is to analyze important issues in that area and to develop and communicate practical new approaches for dealing with them. The Institute is completely nonpartisan.

The Institute is funded by a highly diversified group of philanthropic foundations, private corporations, and interested individuals. About 35 percent of the Institute's resources in our latest fiscal year was provided by contributors outside the United States.

The Institute's Board of Directors bears overall responsibilities for the Institute and gives general guidance and approval to its research program, including the identification of topics that are likely to become important over the medium run (one to three years) and that should be addressed by the Institute. The director, working closely with the staff and outside Advisory Committee, is responsible for the development of particular projects and makes the final decision to publish an individual study.

The Institute hopes that its studies and other activities will contribute to building a stronger foundation for international economic policy around the world. We invite readers of these publications to let us know how they think we can best accomplish this objective.

C. FRED BERGSTEN
Director
March 2011

1

Introduction

The stage is set to launch a "second generation" of research on the impact of foreign direct investment (FDI) on host economies in the developing world. As documented in the pages that follow, this second generation is distinguished by research that is more careful, thorough, and sophisticated than earlier investigations. It identifies "first-generation" research that remains credible and builds on it but often reveals that there are serious and sometimes fatal flaws in these previous studies.

The results of this new wave of research have profound implications for developed- and developing-country policymakers, multilateral financial institutions, national aid donors, international labor organizations, civil society groups and nongovernmental organizations (NGOs), and the corporate social responsibility community.

FDI flows come in at least three—and probably four—separate forms: FDI in extractive industries, FDI in infrastructure, and FDI in manufacturing, plus the underresearched field of FDI in services. Each form presents such distinctive policy challenges for developing-country host authorities, and generates such diverse impacts on the developing host economy, as to undermine the usefulness of any research that does not disaggregate the FDI flows.

At least four quite different inquiries arise from even a first-glance examination of the question of whether FDI contributes to host-country development. First, does FDI in the extractive sector generate substantial government revenues that are managed in a fiscally sound manner (no "Dutch disease") with reasonable transparency and lack of corruption (no "resource curse")? Second, does FDI in infrastructure provide reliable electricity, water, and other services to businesses and households with appropriate sharing of foreign exchange and demand-fluctuation risk? Third, does FDI in manufacturing raise the productivity of host-country economic activities, make the host competitive in new sectors, and generate externalities that benefit local firms and workers? And fourth, does FDI in services (as well as the nonservices sector) "crowd in" or "crowd out" indigenous investment, and which outcome is more beneficial for host-country development?

Despite the standalone importance of each of these lines of inquiry, investigations commonly referred to as "benchmark studies" of the impact of FDI on the host economy invariably use aggregated data combining all four categories for FDI flows and stocks, as do most other investigations. The casualty list is long: Balasubramanyam, Salisu, and Sapsford (1996); Borensztein, de Gregorio, and Lee (1998); Bosworth and Collins (1999); De Mello (1999); Haveman, Lei, and Netz (2001); Reisen and Soto (2001); Hermes and Lensink (2003); Choe (2003); Carkovic and Levine (2005); Blonigen and Wang (2005); and Lensink and Morrisey (2006).[1]

The use in these studies of aggregate data is like asking whether or not the FDI tree produces fruit punch (apples, oranges, bananas, and pears)? Or, more to the point, using aggregate data is like trying to find the common relationship between the impact of FDI on the oil industry of Nigeria (where the outcome depends on policies related to the resource curse and Dutch disease), the impact of FDI in the electrical power industry of Indonesia (where the outcome depends on policies related to the mismatch between foreign currency obligations and local revenue), the impact of FDI in the electronics industry of Malaysia (where the outcome depends on policies related to backward linkages and vertical spillovers), and the impact of FDI by Wal-Mart in the retail service sector of Mexico (where the outcome depends on policies related to the crowd-in/crowd-out investment debate).

Similarly, efforts to model FDI as a homogenous phenomenon and test with data that combine diverse kinds of FDI have to be restructured. These studies include the foundational works of Helpman (1984), Carr, Markusen, and Venables (1998), and Feenstra (2004), all of whom appear to be character-

---

1. Balasubramanyam, Salisu, and Sapsford (1996) use data from the United Nations Convention on Trade and Development (UNCTAD) consisting of aggregate flows of FDI into individual host countries. Borensztein, de Gregorio, and Lee (1998) use data from the Organization for Economic Cooperation and Development (OECD) that tally gross FDI originated in OECD member countries into developing economies on a yearly basis. Bosworth and Collins (1999) use balance of payments data from the International Monetary Fund (IMF) that divide capital flows into aggregate FDI, portfolio investment, and other financial flows (mostly bank loans). De Mello (1999) and Haveman, Lei, and Netz (2001) also use the IMF's aggregate FDI statistics. Reisen and Soto use gross FDI inflows from World Bank national accounts data. Hermes and Lensink (2003), Choe (2003), and Carkovic and Levine (2005) also use World Bank data on gross inflows. Blonigen and Wang (2010) use annual aggregate FDI flows, added together by decade, using the same inputs as Borensztein, de Gregorio, and Lee (1998). Lensink and Morrisey (2006) use both the OECD data used by Borensztein, de Gregorio, and Lee (1998) and World Bank data on the FDI/GDP ratio.

Table 1.1   FDI in developing countries
(billions of dollars)

Sector	Flows, 2005–07	Stock, 2007
Extractive sector	31	223
Manufacturing and assembly	114	917
Infrastructure	32	319

Notes: These figures do not include the large and amorphous foreign direct investment (FDI) in services, except electricity, gas, water, and telecommunication services (aggregated here within infrastructure).

Source: UNCTAD (2009, annex tables A.1.4 and A.1.6).

izing multinational enterprise activities as engaging solely in multiplant manufacturing FDI while subsequently using aggregate data to check their models.[2]

All three (or four) forms of FDI are large in absolute terms and relative to each other. The flow of FDI into the extractive sector and infrastructure is more than half as large as FDI into manufacturing and assembly, as is the stock (table 1.1). None of the three can be subsumed within another category, nor can the distinctiveness of each be ignored. Who would continue to honor results from a database of which one-third of the observations can easily be shown should be left out for the purposes of the study (with an even higher proportion of rejected observations if FDI in the entire service sector is included as part of the data universe)?

The idea that FDI has some generalized positive or negative impact on host-country growth does not make sense. More importantly, phrasing the question this way obscures what may be very different kinds of effects, and muddles what are very distinctive policy challenges.

To illustrate that this is not merely a methodological issue, one need only review the much-cited foundational study "How does foreign direct investment affect economic growth?" by Borensztein, de Gregorio, and Lee (1998). Their investigation concluded that FDI is an important vehicle for the transfer of technology, contributing relatively more to growth than domestic investment. But they found that the higher productivity of FDI holds only when the host country has a minimum threshold stock of human capital. Their dataset for FDI flows covered all FDI originating in OECD member countries that was invested in developing economies on a yearly basis. As a result, they mixed FDI in the extractive and infrastructure sectors with FDI in manufacturing and services. Their findings include what they call the "puzzling" observation that there is a negative coefficient for the FDI variable in most specifications for

---

2. Markusen and Maskus (2001) assert that they use annual sales volume of nonbank manufacturing affiliates for their estimation results, but then refer to the annual sales data collected by the US Department of Commerce's Bureau of Economic Analysis (BEA). The annual sales data collected by the BEA are for all nonbank affiliates, not just manufacturing affiliates.

countries with a low level of human capital, implying that FDI makes a negative contribution to growth (Borensztein, de Gregorio, and Lee 1998, 126).

Their sample includes 69 developing countries, but it is not possible to tell which countries are included or which have the lowest level of human capital, except to note that a distinctive proportion come from sub-Saharan Africa. If some fraction of these include host countries where the largest FDI flows are in extractive industries, with rent-seeking, corrupt leadership,[3] this may explain the low or negative contribution to productivity in the host economy, not the low stock of human capital.[4] Such a discovery would help reconcile their findings with abundant evidence elsewhere that FDI in manufacturing can in fact have a major positive impact on host economies with very low levels of human capital. The pages that follow document a positive relationship between manufacturing FDI and productivity increases in the host economies of Mauritius, Madagascar, Kenya, Bangladesh, El Salvador, the Dominican Republic, and Lesotho—to give but a few examples—during periods when measures of average schooling, absolute poverty, and per capita GDP were all extremely low.

A naïve reader of the "core" article by Borensztein, de Gregorio, and Lee might conclude that little priority should be assigned to either providing assistance to the poorest countries to enable them to attract low-skilled manufacturing FDI or ensuring that the poorest countries have access to developed-country markets for manufacturing FDI exports. The reader of the analysis in the present volume, on the other hand, would conclude just the opposite. In short, dissecting the relationship between type of FDI by sector and the impact on the host country is crucial not just for analytical reasons but to inform policy choices for host authorities and the array of governmental and nongovernmental players cited earlier.

Asking whether FDI makes a positive contribution to "development" involves multiple separate economic investigations and multiple areas in which economic and social externalities (positive and negative) are inextricably intertwined. The relationship between economic outcomes and governance and environmental outcomes is particularly close for FDI in extractive industries and infrastructure, but is often important for FDI in manufacturing and services as well. Within FDI in manufacturing and assembly—writ large, to include agribusiness and horticulture—and FDI in services, there are quite distinctive kinds of contributions to investigate. FDI in manufacturing and FDI in services may increase the efficiency with which a host country does

---

3. See the discussion of the "resource curse" in chapter 2.

4. See the section in chapter 4 on spillovers and externalities for analysis of the competence of local businesses as a limiting factor for the generation of horizontal or vertical spillovers from manufacturing FDI to indigenous firms. The investigation of this crucial relationship between the skill intensity of FDI investor operations and the skill intensity of potential local suppliers is quite different from assessing whether FDI in manufacturing (or services, infrastructure, or natural resources) can have beneficial impacts on the host economy when the median level of human capital is low.

what it already does, with or without horizontal, vertical, and export externalities. Or, FDI may have transformational qualities, bringing entrepreneurship externalities, overcoming "idea gaps" (Romer 1992, 1994), generating "self discovery" (Hausmann and Rodrik 2003), and contributing to the "what-you-export-matters" effect by diversifying and upgrading the production base of the host economy. FDI may offer compensation and training premia, along with labor market externalities and (an underresearched outcome) labor-institution externalities. FDI may—or may not—augment the rate of host-country economic growth.

The evidence examined in this volume identifies 12 principal channels through which FDI can have a positive or negative impact on the real income, standard of living, and growth rate of the host economy (box 1.1). The analytics and evidence surrounding these channels are examined in detail in the chapters that follow, culminating in chapter 7 (as well as in the implications for policy in chapter 9).

Not only are the potential impacts of FDI varied and diverse, but host efforts to secure those potential benefits (and avoid potential damage) require particular kinds of policies to improve market functioning, supply public goods, set standards, and overcome idiosyncratic types of market failure.

Following this introductory chapter, this volume opens with two chapters that summarize the evidence on how FDI in the extractive sector and in infrastructure might impact the host economy, and what kinds of policies are most effective in maximizing the benefits and minimizing or eliminating negative effects. Here the need for external forces to help ensure good governance, protection of the environment, transparency in revenue flows, and prevention of corruption is particularly apparent. Each of these initial chapters—on FDI in the extractive sector and in infrastructure, respectively—reveals important gaps and loopholes in the contemporary policy agenda, and shows how anticorruption laws must be rewritten (including the US Foreign Corrupt Practices Act), how dispute settlement procedures must be reshaped, and how requirements of the Extractive Industries Transparency Initiative must be modified to raise standards for OECD investors while bringing Chinese, Russian, and other non-OECD investors into common compliance.

Chapter 4 then devotes more extensive attention to the need for a new generation of research on the relationship between manufacturing FDI and host-country development. It exposes disqualifying flaws in the first generation of econometric investigation, and shows how second-generation researchers are avoiding these mistakes and moving into new territory. It unravels puzzles in the search for spillovers and externalities, and shows how difficulties can be overcome. It demonstrates how firm survey data and industry case studies can be integrated with econometric investigation to pinpoint the channels through which spillovers take place and so assist in the design of host-country policy.

The chapter provides important new evidence on the types of activities and jobs and the level of wages associated with multinational manufacturing investment. It documents how carefully coordinated campaigns involving

Box 1.1 The 12 principal channels through which FDI impacts development

Channel 1   FDI in the extractive sector: resource rents to fund host-country economic and social expenditures; environmental and governance externalities (positive or negative).

Channel 2   FDI in infrastructure: cheaper, more reliable, expanded access to electricity, water, sewage, telecom, transport; environmental and governance externalities (positive or negative).

Channel 3   FDI in manufacturing and assembly:[1] more or less efficient use of host-country resources and greater or lesser real income generated in the host economy (as measured by economic or social cost/benefit analysis of individual projects).

Channel 4   FDI in manufacturing and assembly:[2] horizontal spillovers and externalities.

Channel 5   FDI in manufacturing and assembly: vertical spillovers and externalities.

Channel 6   FDI in manufacturing and assembly: horizontal and vertical export externalities.

Channel 7   FDI in manufacturing and assembly: compensation premia and training premia.

Channel 8   FDI in manufacturing and assembly: labor market externalities; labor institution externalities.

Channel 9   FDI in manufacturing and assembly: diversification of the production and export base; expansion along the extensive frontier; entrepreneurship externalities, "ideas" (Romer 1992, 1994), "self-discovery" (Hausmann and Rodrik 2003), and contribution to the concept that "what you export matters."

Channel 10   FDI in manufacturing and assembly: upgrading of the production and export base from lower-skill-intensive to higher-skill-intensive activities; expansion along the extensive frontier; entrepreneurship externalities, "ideas" (Romer 1992, 1994), "self-discovery" (Hausmann and Rodrik 2003), and contribution to the concept that "what you export matters."

Channel 11   FDI in services: improve the productivity of specific service sectors; horizontal and vertical spillovers and externalities.

Channel 12   FDI and higher or lower host economic growth rates.

---

1. Channels 3–10 (FDI in manufacturing and assembly) include FDI in agribusiness and horticulture.

2. Channels 4–10 (FDI in manufacturing and assembly) could include FDI in the extractive sector and infrastructure.

international and local labor groups and NGOs can combat sweatshop abuses and under certain (limited) circumstances raise the wages of the lowest-skilled workers. However, the chapter offers uncontested but surprising contemporary data to show that the predominant thrust of manufacturing FDI is not toward lowest-wage sectors like garments and footwear, but instead flows—by a factor of 14 to 1—into middle-skilled activities like auto parts and electronics, where wages and benefits are two to nine times greater than what lower-skilled plants pay. The chapter concludes by separating the genuine policy choices that confront host authorities and the broader pro-poor sustainable development community from today's false debate about FDI and development that is filled with outdated, ill-considered, and counterproductive policy advice.

Chapter 5 takes a first look at new research on FDI in services—a large and vital area where research is just in its infancy—while chapter 6 builds on this to offer a fundamental critique of the debate over FDI crowding out or crowding in domestic investment. After examining three of the most prominent cases of trade-and-investment liberalization in specific sectors of host economies, chapter 6 provides a heretical demonstration that, at least initially, crowding out is not only likely to be inevitable but desirable. Trade and investment liberalization unleashes Schumpeterian winds of creative destruction that rearrange sector dynamics in ways that simple measurements of the amount of capital invested fail to capture entirely.

Chapter 7 examines how FDI can have transformational qualities to diversify and upgrade the production and export base of a host country. But important market failures and unappreciated coordination externalities prevent structural transformation from taking place easily or naturally. The chapter identifies the most important constraints to using FDI for structural transformation and the most successful approaches to overcoming them. From this vantage point, the chapter examines the value of the benefits from trade and investment liberalization and shows that conventional models underestimate the ability of FDI to place a host economy along the frontier of best practices in a given industry and to maintain the host at the frontier with real-time improvements in technology, management, and marketing. Drawing on the preceding analysis in this volume, the chapter shows what is needed for more accurate models and estimations. Do these potential benefits justify subsidies for FDI? The chapter shows how the standard economic calculus of whether to provide incentives for FDI is almost useless for real-life host authorities, and undertakes the tricky task of providing an alternative approach.

Chapter 8 reverses perspective and looks at FDI and globalization from the point of view of home economies in the developed world, particularly the United States. It reviews allegations and evidence that FDI exports jobs and siphons off capital from the home economy, and investigates whether the globalization of industry via FDI comes at the expense of firms and workers at home or, instead, complements and strengthens developed-country economic activity.

It scrutinizes new assertions—such as those by Paul Samuelson and Lawrence Summers—that multinational investment might relocate technology once monopolized by developed countries to developing economies in a manner that damages the welfare of the firms, workers, and communities left behind. Noting the comment by Paul Samuelson (2004, 144) that "All of us Yankees, so to speak, were born with silver spoons in our mouths," the chapter examines the evidence for whether multinational corporations (MNCs) might be taking those "silver spoons" and delivering them to "non-Yankees" in China, India, and other parts of the developing world. The chapter provides an in-depth look at contemporary evidence of exactly how outward investors from the developed world are—or are not—transforming the indigenous production base in China.

Chapter 9 draws policy conclusions for developed and developing countries, multilateral financial institutions, international labor organizations, civil society groups and NGOs, and corporate social responsibility advocates. Developing-country authorities face tasks that are much more selective and difficult than just saying "yes" to foreign investment. Developed countries and multilateral financial institutions will be surprised at how far they fall short in helping FDI to generate optimal benefits for developing countries. International labor, civil society groups and NGOs, and corporate social responsibility advocates will discover that they can contribute more to broad-based sustainable development if they reshape their agenda around the main-line activities of MNCs—as laid out here—rather than simply demanding that investors "give back" more to workers and communities. To be sure, there is nothing inherently wrong with corporate philanthropy, but the transformative power of MNCs comes through carefully constructed extractive industry, infrastructure, manufacturing, and services investments as laid out in the pages of this volume.

Finally, chapter 10 extracts lessons for the next generation of policy research and identifies obstacles and market imperfections in the international economics discipline that continue to hinder the most valuable and useful research from being undertaken.

2

FDI in Extractive Industries

In the annals of development literature, a rich natural resource base was originally considered a valuable asset, and the arrival of foreign firms with capital and technology to invest in extractive industries offered welcome benefits to the host country. In the contemporary period, the presence of oil, natural gas, diamonds, gold, copper, iron ore, coal, nickel, bauxite, and other minerals is more likely to be characterized as a "curse," with foreign investors accused of complicity in host-country corruption, authoritarian rule, and civil strife, as well as of being responsible for environmental damage, suppression of indigenous peoples, and the more mundane overvaluation of the exchange rate (Dutch disease).

What is the impact of FDI in extractive industries on a host developing country? Pursuing an answer to this question here establishes the framework for each of the sections to follow—there is no single outcome associated with FDI in extractive industries. Instead, the impact from FDI in natural resources can be quite positive, or extremely negative, depending on the policy framework of the host government and the broader institutional setting within which FDI takes place. In other words, the impact depends on a broader institutional setting over which the external multinationals themselves may exercise some considerable influence, for good or ill.

The Resource Curse and Dutch Disease

The history of FDI-led exploitation of mineral resources in the Democratic Republic of the Congo and of oil in Nigeria, Angola, and Equatorial Guinea, among other places, paints a vivid picture of misappropriation of extractive industry revenues (Shaxson 2007, Le Billon 2005, Bannon and Collier 2003).

FDI in extractive industries has propped up dictatorial regimes, fueled rebellions and civil wars, undermined reformers, and buried indigenous businesses in highly distorted rent-seeking activities. Corruption and lack of transparency have often been the norm, whether in family-run domination of revenues as in Equatorial Guinea, or cascading levels of revenue diversion as in Nigeria, where more than $1 billion has been lost each year until recently.

Evaluating the comparative economic performance of countries over time, Sachs and Warner (2001)—following in the tradition of Auty (1994)—present gloomy findings of an aggregate nature, arguing that resource-rich countries tend to suffer from lower growth rates than other less well-endowed nations. Are such dismal outcomes inevitable?

In reviewing the historical record, subsequent investigations point out that the Sachs-Warner-Auty low-growth correlation is very sensitive to the time period chosen and find many examples of individual countries that have fared well.[1] The country experiences of Botswana, Chile, Argentina, Colombia, Peru, Brazil, Indonesia, Morocco, and Malaysia—alongside Australia, Canada, Norway, Sweden and the United States—reveal a positive contribution from exploitation of abundant natural resources, without large-scale corruption and institutional failure being the inevitable result.

Before the financial crisis erupted in 2008, government revenues in Botswana from taxes on production of diamonds, copper, and nickel reached more than $1.8 billion on an annual basis and flowed through to fund education, health, and infrastructure projects with a high degree of transparency, accounting for some 40 percent of total public expenditures. In Chile, the comparable figure from taxes on privately owned copper production alone was $6.5 billion, or 14 percent of all government outlays. Between 2003 and 2008, output from the largely foreign-owned extractive sector climbed above 62 percent of all exports from Peru, 44 percent from Tanzania, and 42 percent from Ghana.

The relevant question for contemporary developing- and developed-country authorities, as well as for multilateral lending agencies and international civil society groups and NGOs, is how to promote FDI in the extractive sector in ways that strengthen good governance as well as generate economic growth.

The cluster of problems captured under the rubric of Dutch disease arises when rapid expansion in the oil or mineral sector draws resources from other parts of the economy, raises wages, and causes the currency to appreciate (Roemer 1985; Lewis 1989; Brahmbhatt, Canuto, and Vostroknutova 2010). The boom in natural resource exploitation reduces the competitiveness of other domestic industries, prevents diversification, and leaves the country vulnerable when oil or mineral production tails off. Here again the empirical record of exposure to the "disease" is mixed, and the actual outcome depends

---

1. See Lederman and Maloney (2003), Wright and Czelusta (2004), Collier and Goderis (2007), Stevens (2003), and Brahmbhatt and Canuto (2010).

on public-sector restraint in allowing the economy to overheat, and on prudent expenditure of the revenue buildup (Davis and Tilton 2005, Davis 1995). Over long periods of time, both Chile and Indonesia, for example, husbanded resource receipts for use in countercyclical fashion and deployed them to build infrastructure, strengthen human capital, and support the growth of new economic activities—quite at variance with the pessimistic predictions of the Dutch disease model (ICMM 2007, Glassburner 1988). In Botswana, successive governments sterilized mining revenues, invested a portion abroad almost every year, and smoothed out social expenditures on infrastructure and health (such as coping with the AIDS epidemic) (Jefferis 2009, Norberg and Blomström 1992, Criscuolo 2007). Botswana's foreign exchange reserves are equivalent to about 80 percent of GDP and have enabled the country to earn an investment-grade credit rating from Moody's and Standard & Poor's.

As for the ultimate fear of economic collapse when the resource base runs out, the last half century shows only one case—Tunisia—in which the country experienced what might be considered a collapse of extractive-sector exports (Davis 1995). Like Chile and Indonesia, farsighted devotion of resource revenues to modernize Tunisian infrastructure and upgrade the skill level of the workforce allowed a relatively successful post-natural-resource transition.

The literature reveals no single path or magic ingredient that leads to comparatively efficient, corruption-free administration of natural resource industry revenues. In Botswana, the beef-exporting tribal elites demanded trustworthy national stewardship of mineral tax receipts, from independence onward, in order to generate expenditures on roads, vaccines, veterinary offices, and fences to serve their needs (the Lomé Convention gave them access to the high-priced European Union market) (Criscuolo 2007, Good 1992). Governments and civil service gained a reputation for being largely noncorrupt and reasonably efficient (Acemoglu, Johnson, and Robinson 2003; Good 1994). The Transparency International Global Corruption Perceptions Index awards Botswana the highest mark in all Africa in its most recent surveys (Transparency International 2009). In Chile, left-wing, right-wing, and centrist political leadership all ensured accountability for revenues generated in the copper industry.[2] World Bank and Transparency International control of corruption indicators have consistently placed Chile at the top of Latin America (Transparency International 2009).

If the consequences of FDI in extractive industries are highly contingent on the policy environment within which the investment takes place, what steps can host-country authorities and the other players involved take to ensure a more favorable outcome? Fighting corruption and ensuring transparent revenue flows is the place to start.

---

2. General Pinochet's personal corruption involved arms sales, not misappropriation of copper revenues. See US Senate (2004).

Combating Corruption and Ensuring Transparent Revenue Flows

Until 1997, bribery and corrupt payments were considered a normal part of doing business in the developing world, and many developed countries allowed payoffs for favorable treatment to be deducted from income as a routine business expense (Center for Global Development 2010). The United States was the exception, making the payment of bribes abroad a crime through the Foreign Corrupt Practices Act (FCPA) of 1977. Then, in 1998, the Organization for Economic Cooperation and Development (OECD) adopted the Convention on Combating the Bribery of Foreign Public Officials in International Business Transactions, which requires member states to pass domestic legislation criminalizing corrupt payments. It came into force the following year. OECD members perform peer-review audits of each others' legislation and make recommendations to improve performance. By 2010, 37 of 38 parties to the OECD convention had completed Phase II audits.

But FDI in extractive industries—as well as FDI in infrastructure, as examined in the next chapter—is rated in the Transparency International Bribe Payer's Index as the sectors (along with defense and construction) where corrupt payments are most likely to take place. There are two reasons for this: First, significant gaps have been discovered in both the OECD convention and the FCPA that enable companies from OECD countries to provide what by any commonsense definition must be considered bribes without fear of criminal prosecution; and second, FDI in oil and minerals from non-OECD members (such as China, Russia, and India) has pushed vigorously into the developing world.

What are the gaps in the OECD convention and associated national anticorruption legislation, including the US FCPA, and how can they be filled?

Home-country legislation written to comply with the OECD convention forbids any investor from that state from paying a foreign government official to obtain favorable treatment or securing an exception to host-country laws and regulations. So does the US FCPA, adding a prohibition against payments to political parties or their administrators as well as to public officials. Both the OECD convention and the FCPA also ban payments to "third parties" if the payment takes place at the direction (or with the agreement) of the official and/or ultimately ends up in the possession of the official (OECD 2007, 2008).

What became clear over the course of the 1990s with FDI in both extractive industries and infrastructure is that some OECD-based companies were obtaining investment concessions and favorable treatment to operate their projects by forming partnerships with family members, business associates, and personal friends of the leaders of developing-country host governments (Wells and Ahmed 2007, Moran 2006). The parent multinationals loaned capital to these special partners to enable them to take equity positions in the partnerships, and then paid them a dividend more than adequate to service the debt (thus covering all interest payments while allowing them to pocket additional funds each year over the life of the loan). These special partners put no resources of their own at risk, had no responsibility to pay back the loans if the projects were unsuccessful, and performed no discernible services to justify their partnership status other than enabling the investor to win the concession and enjoy favorable treatment. In some cases, the dividends to cover the interest owed, plus extra money, began to flow to the partners even before the projects came on line, let alone began to operate profitably.

From a technical financial point of view, these partnerships constituted "deferred gifts"—the loan for the equity being paid off over time—plus an extra payoff (the difference between the dividend and the debt service) to be pocketed by the special partner on a monthly or semiannual basis. These arrangements were more damaging than if the foreign investor had simply deposited a bribe to a family member, business associate, or personal friend of the leader in an offshore bank account, since the partner had a long-term interest in ensuring that the favorable treatment, lax regulation, or absence of host-country oversight lasted throughout the lifetime of the project. International oil companies in Equatorial Guinea set up partnerships with spouses of children of the ruling family and other favored business associates (US Senate 2004). International investors elsewhere found sons, daughters, military associates, and golfing buddies.[3]

The reason these partnerships did not place investors in legal jeopardy is that the payoff did not flow to the officials directly, nor was there any evidence—at least no paper trail—that the payments were made at their direction or even with their explicit agreement. US, European, and Japanese companies employed these kinds of partnerships. In the case of US companies, some international investors vetted the arrangements with independent legal counsel, and then duly reported them to US government agencies, including the Securities and Exchange Commission (SEC) and the Overseas Private Investment Corporation (OPIC). When Louis T. Wells, Jr. asked the US Department of Justice why an Indonesian partnership involving the daughter of the president did not violate the US FCPA, he received an email response: "[W]hether a series of payments, or a loan, or a deferred gift would be a violation of FCPA would depend upon whether it occurred at the direction of the official, or other public official, and whether some form of benefit inured to the official."[4] There was no direct evidence that equity shares financed by the foreign company for President Suharto's daughter benefited him directly.

---

3. According to the Approved Judgement of the Honourable Mr. Justice Cooke between Kensington International and the Republic of Congo in the High Court of Justice, Queens Bench Division, Commercial Court, Royal Court of Justice, Strand, London, November 28, 2005. See Wells and Ahmed (2007).

4. Email from Philip Urofsky, Special Counsel for International Litigation, Fraud Section, US Department of Justice, to Louis T. Wells, Jr., August 6, 2002.

The route to closing this loophole is for the OECD Anti-Corruption Working Group to adopt the widely accepted OECD Guidelines for Multinational Enterprises as the new standard for permissible/impermissible behavior, and to issue an "interpretive statement" that Phase III examination of members will incorporate this standard.[5] The OECD guidelines state that "enterprises should not, directly or indirectly, offer, promise, give, or demand a bribe or other undue advantage to obtain or retain business or other improper advantage. Nor should enterprises be solicited or expected to render a bribe of other undue advantage. In particular, enterprises should not offer, nor give in to demands to pay public officials or the employees of business partners, any portion of a contract payment. They should not use subcontracts, purchase orders or consulting agreements as a means of channeling payments to public officials, to employees of business partners or their relatives or business associates."[6] These guidelines do not make prohibition of payments dependent upon whether they occur at the direction of, or with the consent or agreement of, the public official.

OECD Phase III audits to confirm that member countries' antibribery legislation conforms to the guidelines will be slow, but the signal to international investors from OECD states about what will make them liable to prosecution in the future will be clear. To ease acceptance of this new perspective, OECD-headquartered companies arguably have understood, at least in principle, that they should be in compliance with these OECD guidelines as quoted above for decades.

If these loopholes are eliminated for OECD investors, how can a level playing field be created in which non-OECD investors, such as those from Russia, China, India, and elsewhere, become subject to similar constraints on the use of corrupt payments?

Creating a level playing field will be a formidable undertaking, but a trend has emerged in investor-state arbitrations that may contribute to success. Independent tribunals have shown themselves to be increasingly reluctant to enforce contracts where there is credible evidence that such contracts were secured by corrupt means (Center for Global Development 2010). It would have a forceful deterrent effect if international investors from non-OECD states were to face the prospect that they might not be able to have their billion-dollar property rights recognized by tribunals operating under provisions of the International Centre for Settlement of Investment Disputes (ICSID) or the United Nations Commission on International Trade Law (UNCITRAL) at any point over the life of their projects if those projects were secured via corruption. Outside powers cannot dictate how investor-state panels behave, and arbitrators do not have to consider precedents set by other tribunals (there is no stare

---

5. Hearings of the OECD Working Group on the Convention on Combating Bribery of Foreign Public Officials in International Business Transactions, Paris, June 16, 2008.

6. The OECD guidelines are available at www.oecd.org (accessed on February 1, 2011).

decisis). But strong endorsement of this trend by OECD member states would reinforce the likelihood that panels would refuse to enforce contracts obtained by corrupt methods; at the least, this possibility would alter the calculation on the part of investors who might otherwise be counting on arbitrators to uphold their property rights when those rights are subject to dispute.

Alongside reforms of OECD laws against corruption and more selective enforcement of contracts by arbitral panels, a key ingredient to ensure favorable outcomes from FDI in the extractive sector is enhanced transparency for revenue streams. Securing this objective has become a model for demonstrating that extramarket forces are required to enable developing countries to enhance the gains and avoid damages from FDI. At the urging of civil society groups such as Publish What You Pay and Transparency International, the British government established the Extractive Industries Transparency Initiative (EITI) at the World Summit on Sustainable Development in Johannesburg in 2002. An Oslo-based independent institution supported by most OECD states, the EITI has as its operating concept for investors in the oil, gas, and mining industry to publish all payments they make in any given country, and for host governments to publish all payments they receive, in a form that can be understood, examined, and reconciled by independent auditors, citizens, and parliamentarians.[7] As of mid-2010, 32 developing countries in Africa, Asia, and Latin America had signed up for EITI candidate status. The EITI secretariat put in place a program to validate the performance of participating countries, with 19 countries having been scheduled to complete validation before the end of 2010.

To complement the EITI, the World Bank has launched an EITI++ to provide technical assistance for all aspects of resource management, from solicitation of tenders to macroeconomic management of revenues.[8] A World Bank Trust Fund helps fund capacity-building among host officials, legislators, and local civil society entities as do efforts by NGOs such as Publish What You Pay and Revenue Watch. Transparency International, Oxfam, and Global Witness, among others, help keep watch over outcomes (Ravat and Ufer 2010, World Bank 2010).

Developed-country governments and multilateral lending institutions— including the Inter-American Development Bank (IDB), Asian Development Bank (ADB), African Development Bank (AfDB), and European Bank for Reconstruction and Development (EBRD), as well as the World Bank—can play a powerful role in promoting developing-country participation in the EITI, since host-government and international investors often seek public-sector guarantees, finance, and political-risk insurance for extractive industry projects. The ADB endorsed the EITI on February 28, 2008 and the IDB on August 5, 2009. The EBRD claims to support the EITI, but its Energy Operations

---

7. See EITI website at www.eiti.org (accessed in April 2010).

8. See EITI++ at http://web.worldbank.org (accessed on February 1, 2011).

Policy (successor to its Natural Resources Operations Policy) does not mention or discuss the EITI with regard to EBRD programs in Russia or in any other member state.[9]

As shown by preparations for exploitation of new oil discoveries in Ghana, the need for external help to ensure effective host-country governance over the extractive sector is not limited to the poorest states—an observation that will be important later in discussing whether the World Bank and regional development banks continue to have a role to play in middle-income developing countries. The government of Norway and the IMF, World Bank, and Oxfam, among others, helped Ghana over the course of 2010 to prepare for management of oil income.

But, as argued earlier, to be effective, international companies of all nationalities—including those that originate in states not known for vigilance about corrupt payments—must be included. Some 41 of the largest oil, gas, and mining companies have committed to support the EITI, but most still oppose company-by-company reports of payments to the government (they want only anonymous aggregation of revenue flows to prevent scrutiny of their particular fiscal contributions). This issue has been brought to a head by the passage of the US Dodd-Frank Wall Street Reform and Consumer Protection Act that President Barack Obama signed into law in July 2010. This act includes a provision that requires oil, gas, and mining companies registered with the SEC to publish how much they pay to foreign countries and the US government in their annual reports.

Many US companies argue that this reporting requirement will put them at a competitive disadvantage in relation to investors of other nationalities. Ken Cohen of ExxonMobil argues that "[t]he amendment requires U.S.-listed companies to essentially turn over the competitively negotiated terms of their proprietary contracts to all foreign competitors who don't have U.S. SEC reporting requirements—providing no protection for confidential information. At a time when the U.S. is concerned about international competitiveness, this would create a new competitive disadvantage."[10]

Proponents of the reporting requirement counter that the concern about competitive disadvantage is overblown. The Publish What You Pay Coalition states that the SEC requirement "will apply to hundreds of companies, including 90 percent of the world's largest internationally operating oil and gas companies, as well as eight of the world's ten largest mining companies. The Hong Kong stock exchange, which carries a number of Asian majors, enacted similar rules this year and the International Accounting Standards

---

9. See Energy Operations Policy at www.ebrd.com (accessed on June 21, 2010).

10. Ken Cohen, "A Less than Transparent Approach to Transparency in Congress," ExxonMobil Perspectives blog, July 14, 2010. www.exxonmobilperspectives.com/2010/07 (accessed on February 1, 2011).

Board (IASB) is considering a rule change to make disclosure of payments to governments standard in the 110 countries which use IASB rules."[11]

The Revenue Watch Institute reiterates the point: "Of the 32 largest internationally active oil companies, 29 are registered with the SEC or have other SEC reporting requirements and would be covered by the new law. Eight of the world's 10 largest mining companies are also registered with the SEC and could be covered, too."[12]

Moreover, all oil, gas, and mining companies that operate in the United States make comparable disclosures to the Interior Department every month. And some extractives companies already publicly disclose all payments made to foreign governments as a normal part of doing business—including US-based Newmont Mining, Canada-based Talisman Energy, and Norway's Statoil. All extractives companies in countries implementing the EITI already make public their payments to the governments of these countries. Companies need to keep accurate books and records to comply with foreign and US tax filing requirements and the FCPA, among other measures.

The concern about potential competitive disadvantage caused by individual company-by-company reporting can be matched against the empirical record. The Extractive Industry Transparency Reports published in Ghana, Guinea, Liberia, Mongolia, and Nigeria all identify how much each company pays in income taxes, royalties, bonuses, and other payment streams. BP has chosen to disclose the company's individual EITI reports in Azerbaijan, even though EITI findings are published there only in aggregated form. Anglo American discloses payments to governments in the 12 countries that host the company's largest operations.

Sefton Darby analyzed survey data related to individual company disclosure and found instances that document commercial disadvantage are extremely minor or nonexistent (Sefton 2009; Ravat and Ufer 2010, 3–4). EITI reporting does not require disclosure of proprietary data such as geological information or the operational costs and profitability of individual operations. It is extremely difficult to glean commercially useful information, such as profitability of individual operations, simply by looking at payments to government. Not one company involved in disaggregated payment disclosure has subsequently had its contract cancelled or renegotiated as a result.

But some resource investors that do not register in the United States may nonetheless be able to achieve competitive advantage through their ability to make unreported payments associated with their extractive industry concessions. This presents an opportunity to the world community. The logical conclusion is just the opposite of what conventional industry wisdom asserts: Company-by-company reports will ultimately benefit the most conscien-

---

11. See the Publish What You Pay website at www.publishwhatyoupay.org (accessed on October 29, 2010).

12. See Revenue Watch Institute website at www.revenuewatch.org (accessed on October 29, 2010).

tious investor by forcing all participants (including those from Russia, China, India, and elsewhere) to provide transparency on an equivalent basis. In their own self-interest, socially responsible investors should support company-by-company reports. Socially responsible investors can also play a powerful role in persuading new hosts to join wholeheartedly in the EITI process. Working together, international extractive companies and their home governments—led by the United States—should work to make the EITI mandate that all EITI-compliant countries require individual company-by-company reporting, instead of opposing this.

The best outcome from this SEC reporting requirement would be to set in motion the same sequence that followed the original passage of the FCPA (hopefully more rapidly). US investors at first objected to being put at a competitive disadvantage by the FCPA, but then—when Warren Christopher became secretary of state and orchestrated the effort—pushed for adoption and ratification of the OECD Convention on Combating Bribery. International corporate support for all EITI countries to require individual company-by-company reporting would force non-OECD investors to comply, thereby leveling the playing field for OECD and non-OECD investors alike.

Promoting FDI, Ensuring Contract Stability, and Assisting Host Tax Collection

FDI in extractive industries enjoys a more extensive history of official support from home-country governments and multilateral lending agencies than FDI in any other sector in part because of the long-standing needs of wealthy countries for external sources of petroleum and minerals, the political-economic clout of the investors in home-country decision making, and a well-recognized market failure that Raymond Vernon (1971) first called the "obsolescing bargain." This bargain reflects abrupt changes in negotiating strength between foreign companies and host authorities over the lifetime of FDI in the extractive sector. Natural resource investors begin with quasi-monopolist control over the expertise and capital required to find and develop hydrocarbons or other raw materials, without which developing-country hosts are virtually incapable of knowing (let alone exploiting) the extent of their subsoil wealth. At the same time, natural resource investors face substantial risk and uncertainty about what oil or mineral reserves can be found and whether untried sites might ultimately prove profitable. International natural resource investors insist therefore that their initial concessions and contracts be favorably structured to reflect their powerful position and to compensate them (and their financial backers) for the associated risk and uncertainty.

Host authorities agree to frontloaded favorable treatment for foreign investors—even if there is no corruption involved—because the alternative is often to do without the investment. However, as soon as international companies commit capital, and if the projects turn out to be successful, the bargaining relationship changes profoundly. Investment is sunk in the ground (and ports and pipelines) and risk and uncertainty dissipate. Once launched, the foreign investor cannot credibly threaten to withhold crucial inputs or withdraw. In contrast to FDI in manufacturing and assembly, where foreign firms maintain negotiating strength vis-à-vis host authorities by controlling technology and marketing (see chapter 4), in extractive industries and infrastructure host authorities are in a position to take advantage of the "hostage effect" and unilaterally change the terms of the initial investment contracts. If they do not, their rivals or successors will.

This propensity to alter contractual terms is sometimes referred to as "opportunistic behavior" on the part of host officials, but Vernon (1971) recognized the dialectic as a more basic structural flaw that private parties are not able to correct on their own. International investors try to compensate for later vulnerability by making initial contract terms yet more favorable; this makes subsequent demands for readjustment something of a self-fulfilling prophecy.

Extractive-sector investors have gone so far as to conclude that there is "an inverse relationship between the generous fiscal incentives offered to investors and the stability of the fiscal regime. Where low tax rates are offered to attract investment, it tends to be more likely that subsequent political pressure results in a realignment of fiscal regimes in later years, when mining operations become productive. This has led to many companies emphasizing that from their perspective, the *optimal* level of taxes does not equate to the *minimum* level" (ICMM 2009, 57, emphasis in original).

Private political-risk insurers can offer breach-of-contract coverage to ensure that foreign investors are compensated when their initial agreements are unilaterally changed. But such coverage is costly, and the revelation that a particular project is insured may mean that the investor is singled out to be squeezed.

As in other forms of strategic negotiation, the inability of host governments to make credible commitments that they will honor their promises constitutes a fundamental market failure (Schelling 1966, Williamson 1985). Instability in contract terms—even if no formal nationalization takes place—leads to suboptimal levels of investment from the point of view of both investors and hosts, and the world community more broadly.

This market failure provides a rigorous justification for national and multilateral guarantees, finance, and political-risk insurance. Host governments sign an agreement with the World Bank Group (including the International Finance Corporation [IFC] and the Multilateral Investment Guarantee Agency [MIGA]), the ADB, IDB, or AfDB, or with public-sector agencies such as the US Overseas Private Investment Corporation (OPIC) or the UK Export Credits Guarantee Department, specifying that investment disputes will be submitted to binding international arbitration, and the decisions respected by the host, or else the guarantor can pursue the host for remedy. Since developing-country governments do not want to damage relations with these institutions, the coverage the latter provide is much more potent than what commercial political-risk insurers present. Beyond offering compensation to the investor, national and multilateral political-risk insurers supply deterrence against the workings of the obsolescing bargain. A host government in a developing country becomes capable not just of making credible commitments about its own treatment of a foreign investment contract but also of tying the hands of its successors. FDI flows to high-profile, valuable, long-term projects become greater than would otherwise be feasible—especially oil, mining, and infrastructure.

But while failure in contract markets provides an authentic rationale for public-sector intervention, such intervention puts national guarantee agencies like OPIC or multilateral guarantee agencies such as the World Bank in the position of helping to enforce the highly favorable contractual terms initially demanded by international investors long after the early risk and uncertainty have dissipated. These public agencies have historically eschewed providing advice to host authorities about the structure or terms of the contracts demanded by multinational natural resource companies, arguing that these are private and confidential business matters between the parties. Today, it is becoming increasingly evident that the interests of developing countries—and, arguably, of the international investors themselves—would be better served if official guarantee agencies were to provide more advice and assistance about the apportionment of risk and the sharing of revenues from oil, natural gas, and mineral projects over long periods of time.

In the extractive sector, the most important contractual issues involve not just the rate of taxation but the structure of how taxes are calculated, whether via royalties or income taxes (Otto et al. 2006). A royalty consists of a per-unit levy on production ($10 per barrel of oil, 20 cents per pound of copper) or a percentage of the market price of production (10 percent of the market price for oil or copper). The royalty structure is business-unfriendly in that the investor must pay the royalty from day one of production (before capital is recovered), and must keep paying whether the operation is showing a profit or a loss. The royalty tax structure raises per-unit cost of production, discourages investment in more risky or uncertain circumstances, reverses comparative advantage (lower-cost sites become higher-cost sites), encourages early cutback of production (otherwise commercially feasible reserves become noncommercial), and promotes undesirable engineering practices (the investor removes high-grade deposits and leaves low-grade deposits in the ground). In the petroleum sector, production-sharing agreements have all of these adverse royalty characteristics.

Host authorities nonetheless favor the use of royalties for reasons of historical legacy (a royalty is what an operating company owes the landlord for exploitation of the subsoil around the world) and simplicity of calculation. The royalty structure avoids the threat that international companies will use transfer pricing—an unavoidable feature of the income tax structure—to deprive the host of what rightfully is owed.

An income tax subtracts costs of production from sales revenues to calculate company profit, and then applies the income tax rate to the profit (say,

30 percent) to determine what is owed to the host. The income tax structure is business friendly in that the company pays only when it is making a profit. This structure encourages continued production in any given country, or site, to the point where marginal extraction cost equals market price. Depending on host-country accounting regulations, the investor usually recovers most capital via accelerated depreciation and payoff of loans before showing a profit or being liable for income tax.

Host authorities object to the income tax structure because international investors pay little or no tax in the early years of project life. The host authorities abhor the specter of international companies manipulating transfer prices to avoid paying the taxes they otherwise would owe—a multinational natural resource company may sell oil to its own refinery in Rotterdam or mineral concentrate to its own refinery in Japan, may borrow capital from its own financial center in Panama, or may purchase bookkeeping services from parent headquarters at prices calculated to shrink the profit reported to the host.

In principle, transfer pricing can be dealt with in a straightforward manner: The international company is required to show that the price received or paid in an interaffiliate transaction is approximately comparable to what would be received or paid in a comparable transaction among unrelated parties, with the burden of demonstration on the company. In practice, transfer pricing can become quite complicated in the details, but with training of local tax officials and with services purchased from recognized accounting firms, host authorities in the developing world can be equipped to deal with transfer pricing just as tax collectors in Canada, Australia, or the United States do. In Liberia, for example, the mineral development agreement initially negotiated by Mittal Steel allowed the parent investor to use for tax purposes a price paid for Liberian iron ore that was exported to Mittal affiliates, potentially depriving the government of substantial revenues (Global Witness 2006). International experts brought in by President Ellen Johnson Sirleaf amended the contract to reflect the arm's-length rule, leaving taxation to be based on the international market price of iron ores of the same grade (Global Witness 2007).[13]

There is growing recognition that both host-country and international-investor interests would be served by more active multilateral assistance in the design and negotiation of contracts in the extractive sector.[14] The regressive royalty structure has been a principal reason why many developing countries did not participate more fully in the commodity boom of 2002–07, which in

---

13. See also Publish What You Pay, "Liberian Legislature Passes the Liberian Extractive Industry Transparency Initiative Act," press release, June 11, 2009, www.publishwhatyoupay.org (accessed on February 1, 2011).

14. Daniel Dumas, Head of the Economic and Legal Section of the Commonwealth Secretariat, presentation at Extractive Industries Week, a conference on "Improving Extractive Industries Benefits for the Poor," World Bank, Washington, March 4, 2009. The Commonwealth Secretariat has been a pioneer in helping developing-country authorities design oil and mineral codes and negotiate with international investors.

turn has contributed to the reaction against private ownership in the extractive sector in Latin America, Africa, and Asia (Christian Aid 2007, Donnelly and Ford 2008). Leaders of the international corporate community, in turn, have indicated that they would be receptive to more progressive income tax rates—perhaps even excess-profits taxes—if these would contribute to greater contract stability.[15]

To be sure, multilateral efforts to give developing-country negotiators confidence that a shift toward income taxes would serve their populations' long-term interests most effectively will not eliminate all sources of tension. The income tax structure means host authorities receive few revenues early in the life of even highly successful projects (ICMM 2006–07). In Chile, the top 10 foreign-owned mining companies paid taxes of $2.1 billion from 1991 to 2003, in comparison to the two state-owned mining company payments of $9.7 billion, despite greater production and lower costs, largely because they subtracted accelerated depreciation on new properties (six of the 10 paid no income taxes during this 12-year period, and two began to pay income taxes only in 2003). Once the period of accelerated depreciation ended, one foreign-owned mine alone (Escondida) jumped from virtually no income taxes to $423 million in 2004. Similarly, in Peru, the new Antamina copper mine paid no more than $20 million in taxes in 2004, the last year of accelerated depreciation, thereafter climbing to $319 million in 2005.

So it is unlikely that the royalty structure will be abandoned altogether. However, host interests would be best served by help in tilting tax collection as steeply as is politically feasible away from royalties and toward income taxes.

Finally, there is widespread concern among international civil society groups and host-country activists that local communities where mines, pipelines, or oilfields are located will be neglected or shortchanged in the distribution of host-country revenues. There have been notorious difficulties in the delta regions of Nigeria and other parts of Africa. A frequent recommendation is that host countries adopt a revenue-sharing formula to ensure that a portion of tax receipts be dedicated to producing areas.

The empirical record of such earmarking arrangements is quite mixed, however. Budget and tendering procedures at the local level may be quite weak. For example, recent evidence from Peru, where a portion of mining revenues has been given directly to mining communities without central government planning, coordination, or supervision, offers a cautionary picture.[16] Instead of water supply systems, roads, and schools, the local communities now have dozens of new futbol stadiums, usually built without competitive bidding by

---

15. Sir Mark Moody-Stuart, Chairman, Anglo American, presentation at the Resource Endowment Initiative Discussion Panel, Brookings Institution, Washington, June 29, 2006; John Groom, Chair of ICMM's Resource Endowment Initiative and Head of Safety, Health and Environment for Anglo American, "Extractive Industries Week: Improving Extractive Industries Benefits for the Poor," remarks at the World Bank, March 4, 2009.

16. Author interviews, Peru, June 2007. See also ICMM (2008).

associates of the mayor or governor. Chile, in contrast, has achieved significant poverty reduction in the Antofagasta region via efficient centralized budget allocations from Santiago.[17] The desire that producing areas—like those in Nigeria—actually see some benefits from natural resource revenues must be tempered by wariness about the capacity of local communities to handle how to spend what they receive.

Advancing Environmental Standards and Sustainable Development Goals

The participation of rich-country development agencies and multilateral lending institutions in extractive-sector projects can also help ensure that investors and hosts observe best environmental practices and promote other sustainable development objectives.

These agencies and lending institutions categorically refuse to support investments in primary tropical forests or other areas where exploitation would significantly disrupt the ecosystem or jeopardize endangered species. Less risky but still problematic projects are required to prepare an environmental impact assessment, and investors must agree to ongoing environmental audits. Most official supporters now require that regional and local authorities as well as the general public be involved in environmental assessment activities before and over the course of extractive industry operations. Banks representing some 80 percent of the project finance market have signed on to the Equator Principles that state that the projects they lend to will be developed in a manner that is socially responsible and reflects sound environmental management (Likosky 2009). How these principles will be implemented will be bank-specific, and where disputes will be settled is unclear. Unlike in the past, in the contemporary era international investors must prepare life-cycle plans to ensure cleanup of waste sites and postdepletion rehabilitation in order to qualify for national or international backing. In 2010, the World Bank adopted new measures to promote the Global Gas Flaring Reduction Partnership, which is dedicated to helping combat climate change by reducing gas flaring worldwide.

An area where concerns about contract stability as discussed in the previous section and environmental regulation overlap emerges when host countries decide to raise standards or tighten enforcement. International investors may invoke dispute-settlement provisions of free trade agreements to seek damages from stricter environmental regulation. For example, Pacific Rim, a Canadian-based gold mining firm, is suing El Salvador under the Central America Free Trade Agreement for $77 million in costs and hoped-for profits because the company has not received approval to exploit gold ores it has found (Van Harten 2010). The government of El Salvador responds that Pacific Rim has failed to satisfy steps in the investment approval process,

---

17. For evidence from Chile and other countries with mining industries, see ICMM (2009).

including conducting an acceptable environmental impact assessment. On the one hand, international companies that have invested money in exploration do not want to be frustrated when they are ready to move into exploitation. On the other, host authorities will seldom be able to upgrade environmental regulations that apply to all companies if international investors have a privileged position that requires them to be totally compensated for every change that is ever made.

Efforts to ensure transparency and accountability in natural resource revenue flows, and to improve governance, will be at the center of policy recommendations for developed and developing countries in the concluding chapter of this volume—overlapping somewhat with concerns about FDI in infrastructure, but quite distinct from the policy agenda for FDI in manufacturing and assembly.

3

FDI in Infrastructure

The quality of infrastructure—energy, transport, telecommunications, water, and sanitation—affects prospects for economic development in many ways. Whether looking at growth, productivity, or output, 63 percent of the studies carried out between 1989 and 2007 found a positive and significant relationship between infrastructure and the target economic outcome (Straub 2008). For studies focusing exclusively on developing countries, the link between quality of infrastructure and economic performance is stronger than for developed countries.

While there is a considerable degree of diversity among the experiences of countries in Latin America, relatively poor performance in infrastructure in the 1980s and 1990s accounted for as much as one-third of the widening output gap between Latin America and East Asia (Easterly and Servén 2003). In Africa during the 1990s, only about one-fourth of the decline in the continent's share of world exports could be attributed to weak price competitiveness. The remainder derived from nonprice factors, including infrastructure services and the flow of trade information (Oshikoya et al. 1999). Limão and Venables (1999) show that the volume of trade varies closely as a function of transport costs—a 10 percent drop in transport costs expands trade by 25 percent. They estimate that raising a country's ranking in infrastructure services from the 75th percentile to the median (50th percentile) increases the volume of trade by 50 percent. As of 2009, Freund and Rocha (2010) estimate that a one-day decrease in the inland transit time in sub-Saharan Africa increases exports of new products by 7 percent and is equivalent to about a 1.5 percent decrease in all import tariffs of partner countries.

Over the span of history, the functioning of state-owned infrastructure monopolies has varied considerably. In developing and transition economies, however, there have been persistent problems of underpricing of output, nonpayment and theft, revenue shortages and inadequate investment, poor maintenance of facilities, and deteriorating service quality (Kessides 2005). With the exception of Eastern Europe, publicly owned infrastructure companies underserved poor and rural households (Clarke and Wallsten 2002).

Privately owned infrastructure—whether domestic- or foreign-owned—has demonstrated better performance (UNCTAD 2008; Andres et al. 2008, chapter 10). Despite fears that private ownership would deny access to the poor or price infrastructure services beyond reach, evidence from telecommunications, electricity, water, and sanitation sectors suggests that access for lower segments of the population in Uganda, Bolivia, Gabon, and Peru increased with privatization.[1] Poor citizens also gain from higher growth rates and more employment throughout the economy associated with good infrastructure performance; however, they may experience fewer opportunities for direct employment in electric utilities, railroads, and water companies.

Distinctive Public Policy Concerns

The 1990s witnessed an investment boom in infrastructure led by foreign corporations. In 1990, private infrastructure investment equaled no more than $18 billion, but climbed rapidly to a peak of approximately $130 billion in 1997. In Latin America, privatization of existing facilities represented the largest outlays. In East Asia, greenfield power projects were the predominant phenomenon. As discussed later, the Asian financial crisis of 1998 showed that many of the projections upon which investments were made were excessively rosy. By 2006–07—even before the onset of the international financial crisis—private infrastructure investments had dropped to less than half of the higher levels of the 1990s (UNCTAD 2008, figure 3-2; Leigland 2008). Meanwhile, public attitudes toward private ownership of infrastructure soured in many parts of Latin America and Asia (Andres et al. 2008, chapter 1), although by 2010 a rebound in private infrastructure projects had begun to emerge in parts of both regions.

Effective participation of foreign investors in infrastructure projects remains of vital importance to developing countries. In the pages that follow, reliable electricity, water, and telecommunications will repeatedly show themselves to be key components of indicators found in the World Bank's Ease of Doing Business Index.[2] High marks for these services, plus efficient road, port, and airport facilities, are central ingredients for the growth of a robust indigenous business sector in any given developing economy; for the attraction of

---

1. For a summary of the evidence of access for the poor, see Andres et al. (2008), Harris (2003), Nellis, Menezes, and Lucas (2004), and Chong and Lopez de Silanes (2005). For a more cautious assessment of distributional effects, see Estache (2006).

2. The World Bank index is available at http://doingbusiness.org/rankings (accessed on February 1, 2011).

foreign investors in low-skilled FDI operations like garments and footwear; for the ability of individual host countries to move up from these low-skilled FDI operations to middle-skilled FDI operations like electronics, medical products, auto parts, and other industrial products; and for the development of FDI supply chains and backward linkages deep into the host economy.

The public policy preoccupations associated with foreign investment in infrastructure closely parallel those found in the extractive sector. Contract stability is highly problematic, and when foreign infrastructure companies are involved, official political-risk insurance agencies (national and multilateral) become parties to disputes. Foreign investors in infrastructure, like natural resources, rank near the top among those accused of giving bribes and of corruption, just below defense industries and construction (Kenny and Soriede 2008, Kenny 2006, Estache 2006). Special partnerships with family members, business associates, and friends of developing-country leaders have been used by US, European, and Asian investors to secure infrastructure contracts—like natural resource concessions—without running afoul of the Organization for Economic Cooperation and Development (OECD) Anti-Bribery Convention or the US Foreign Corrupt Practices Act. Therefore, in the concluding chapter of this volume, many of the policy recommendations for developed and developing countries and for multilateral financial institutions concerning FDI in infrastructure will overlap with FDI in extractive industries.

But foreign investment in infrastructure—particularly FDI in large-scale power projects—also features distinctive issues that are only now being recognized and grappled with, leading to somewhat tentative conclusions about the appropriate path for policymakers. These distinctive issues require separating political from commercial risk, reforming investor-state arbitration, and avoiding moral hazard.

For help in trying to optimize the benefits from FDI in infrastructure, it is useful to consult the World Bank's infrastructure and law website, which has been designed for government officials, project managers, and lawyers involved in the planning, design, and legal structuring of infrastructure projects, especially projects with private-sector participation (so-called public-private partnership, or PPP, projects).[3] The website was launched in February 2009 with funding from the Public-Private Infrastructure Advisory Fund (PPIAF), a multidonor technical assistance facility that helps developing countries improve the quality of their infrastructure through private-sector involvement. The PPIAF grew out of a joint initiative of the governments of Japan and the United Kingdom, working closely with the World Bank. The multilingual site covers the power, telecommunications, transport, and water and sanitation sectors. Regional consultations, cross-border pairings of regulators, and international training missions play a growing role in capacity building (UNCTAD 2010a).

---

3. See the World Bank website at http://web.worldbank.org (accessed on February 1, 2011.)

Blurring of Commercial and Political Risk and the Need to Reform Investor-State Arbitration

The development strategy community has generally applauded the movement to arbitrate disputes between foreign investors and host governments. Independent arbitral tribunals following the procedures of the International Centre for Settlement of Investment Disputes (ICSID) or the United Nations Commission on International Trade Law (UNCITRAL) represent a channel for disputes to be resolved via the rule of law rather than through crass political pressure of the strong against the weak, overt or covert.

It has become clear since the Asian financial crisis of the late 1990s that foreign investor participation in infrastructure projects requires reappraising which parties should bear the burden of absorbing commercial risks associated with fluctuations in supply and demand for services and with fluctuations in exchange rates, as well as how contracts in this sector should be enforced.

Foreign investment in power, roads, water, sewerage, and telecommunications resembles foreign investment in petroleum and mining in that the foreign investor must sink large amounts of capital up front and then rely on subsequent revenues over a long period of time to justify the initial commitment of capital. But foreign investment in infrastructure suffers from one distinctive feature that complicates the life of such projects immensely—a mismatch between most of the resources that are initially expended in dollars, euros, yen, or whatever foreign currency involved, and the local currency payments that take place over the life of the project. Who should bear these currency risks, and when should failures to satisfy contractual expectations be considered economic or commercial events (inability to pay) as opposed to political events (unwillingness to pay)?

To participate in booming Asian and Latin American markets, foreign investors in the power sector grew accustomed to insisting—as a condition of putting capital into infrastructure—that host authorities commit themselves to supply inputs, or to purchase outputs, and to guarantee the foreign exchange value of payments made in local currency years into the future. In settings where host-country economic expansion seems unending, and forecasts of demand for electricity grow at 8 percent per year (or more) as far as the eye can see, the take-or-pay contracts associated with foreign-sponsored infrastructure projects can appear quite reasonable, even when they guarantee rates of return on the order of 30 percent a year to the foreign sponsors.[4] As the global economy emerges from the international economic crisis in 2010, contemporary power project proposals in China and India replicate the optimistic projections associated with Indonesia more than a decade ago, and may suffer similar effects any time the international economy weakens.

How should the costs of adjustment be apportioned, however, when the underlying assumptions for particular projects prove excessively rosy, or when

---

4. The data on private return-on-investment expectations come from Wells (1997, 10).

economic fluctuations in the world economy move in an adverse direction? Following an odd legal logic, when host authorities find themselves incapable of fulfilling their contracts due to external changes in the international economy, investor-state arbitral panels now typically judge their performance as political acts (unwillingness to behave as promised) rather than commercial acts (inability to behave as promised).[5]

An archetypal case that has drawn intense scrutiny involves the MidAmerica Corporation in Indonesia (Martin and Bracey 2001). MidAmerica sought concessions to build geothermal power projects in Indonesia in the mid-1990s backed by take-or-pay power purchase agreements signed by the state utility Perusahaan Listrik Negara (PLN). The central government of Indonesia had the Ministry of Finance provide a support letter, promising that it would "cause" the national oil and gas corporation (Pertamina) and PLN to honor and perform the obligations they had signed up for with MidAmerica.

Throughout the early 1990s, Indonesian authorities enjoyed a solid record of sound macroeconomic management. But when the Asian financial crisis of 1997 (originating in Thailand) hit the Indonesian economy, the central government in Jakarta had to formulate a tough austerity program as a condition to receive assistance from the IMF, World Bank, and ADB. Within the budget cutbacks, Indonesia placed "under review" those power facilities whose capacity was not needed immediately, including those of MidAmerica. In 1998, when PLN failed to accept and pay for the electricity under contract, MidAmerica took the case to arbitration.

Over the course of 1999, two arbitration panels found PLN in breach of contract, and ordered the government of Indonesia to pay damages in hard currency. The panels took no note of the financial crisis, the demands placed on Indonesia by the IMF and the World Bank, or the country's need to use scarce dollars to import food and medicine. When Indonesia failed to comply, MidAmerica demanded that the Overseas Private Investment Corporation (OPIC) make good on its political-risk coverage, triggering one of the largest claim payments in OPIC's history ($290 million of the total arbitration judgment of $572 million against Indonesia), prompting the US government, in turn, to seek recovery from Indonesia.

This case illustrates the pattern that has emerged in which the line between commercial and political risk becomes blurred (Kessides 2004). Political risk has traditionally been defined as a set of deliberate acts undertaken by host authorities to change the treatment of a foreign investor. Changes in market conditions over which the host country has little or no control that impede the host capability from meeting its obligations fall under the broader category of commercial risk. But according to Berry (2003), more than 90 percent of the political-risk claims paid by Lloyds syndicates in the five years after the onset of the Asian financial crisis arose because a state buyer or supplier was *unable* to make good on its commitments in full and on time. The formal default derived

---

5. For the origins of this interpretation by arbitration panels, see Berry (2003).

from economic misjudgment or overcommitment, not from bad faith or malicious intent on the part of host authorities.

This distinction has not gone unnoticed: National and multilateral guarantee agencies have become acutely aware of the need to redraw the line between political and commercial risk when take-or-pay contracts signed by parastatal agencies in the developing world are denominated in dollars, whereas utility payments by the local populace are made in local currency (private investors are seldom able to hedge local currency risk more than six months or so into the future). These agencies categorically refuse to provide explicit exchange rate protection. But they have abruptly discovered that when they insure these take-or-pay agreements against breach of contract, they implicitly expose themselves to enormous currency risk (Kessides 2004, 179). They have found themselves inadvertently fronting for private investors intent on shifting business risk onto others under the rubric of political-risk coverage. They now realize that international investor-state arbitration is being used to enforce an extremely one-sided distribution of risks in infrastructure projects, with adverse consequences for themselves and for the investment system as a whole, as well as for particular host countries that become parties to disputes.

One approach has been for institutions like the International Financial Corporation, Inter-American Development Bank (IDB), and Asian Development Bank to provide guarantees of infrastructure project debt denominated in local currency (Haddon 2004). The Chilean toll road Costanera Norte borrowed the local-currency equivalent of $260 million on the strength of a guarantee from the IDB in 2003. A wireless telecom company (Société Camerounaise de Mobiles) in Cameroon raised financing from local banks of $45 million on the basis of a guarantee for 25 percent from the IFC and Proparco, a French development institution, in 2002. But these guarantee structures still leave inflation risk to be dealt with by lenders and guarantors, and—since increased costs must be allowed to be passed through to customers—government "performance risk" remains as well.

What can be done to restore the distinction between political and commercial risk, while continuing to encourage FDI in infrastructure? No perfect solution has yet been found, but the outlines of how to proceed are beginning to emerge, as considered next.

Mediation, Work-Outs, and Avoiding Moral Hazard

The challenge for official political-risk insurers and investor-state arbitration panels is to devise a framework for dealing with investment project difficulties that arise out of regional financial contagion rather than from deliberate hostile acts on the part of host authorities. Such a framework could provide a "force majeure" suspension of contractual obligations during a sudden economic collapse, along the lines already visible in normal commercial relationships. In a study of 20 infrastructure projects whose terms had to be changed between 1990 and 2005, Woodhouse (2008) finds that the majority

(11) involved a mutual "work-out" between investor and host aimed at keeping the project viable over the longer term. These 11 all featured some kind of cooperative renegotiation, including restructuring fuel supply provisions, refinancing project loans, or identifying other aspects of the original contracts that could be changed by mutual agreement.

A change in how political-risk contacts are interpreted and arbitrated would have the added appeal of eliminating the element of moral hazard that is evident in the current system. International power companies covered by official political-risk insurance of the vintage in the Woodhouse study—like MidAmerica—behaved differently from those that were not. Investors caught in a regional economic downturn without multilateral or national political-risk coverage against breach of contract engaged in work-outs as outlined above. In Indonesia, for example, Unocal and Jawa Power agreed to a new timetable for bringing their power projects on line as the host economy recovered, in contrast to MidAmerica's exercise of the take-or-pay requirement in order to activate its OPIC claim. Current breach-of-contract coverage simply tempts an investor to walk away from a project once it is clear that the original assumptions were too optimistic. Worse, these policies lead the banks with a portfolio of insured infrastructure loans to withhold authorization for restructuring the original agreement.

A new framework that pushes the parties toward a mutually acceptable work-out would broaden the context within which investor-state dispute-settlement functions (UNCTAD 2010b, Riskin et al. 2009). Instead of focusing exclusively on the most narrow dimension of contract compliance—aimed at making the foreign investor "whole" ahead of every other priority for hard-currency expenditures on behalf of a population in crisis—arbitration could evolve toward a more mediation-like process to determine what is the best outcome for all parties and what best serves the public interest.

4

FDI in Manufacturing and Assembly

Dissecting the possible contributions that FDI in manufacturing and assembly might make to host-country development requires an understanding of what motivates multinational corporations to set up operations, build or acquire factories, and manage plants in the target economy. Unlike trade, rigorous analysis of the dynamics of FDI in manufacturing and assembly is a relatively recent phenomenon and—with regard to developing countries—is still prone to flaws and misconceptions.

What motivates FDI in manufacturing and assembly? When flows of manufacturing FDI began to soar after the Second World War—foreign affiliates of US multinational corporations (MNCs) alone climbed from 7,400 in 1950 to 23,000 in 1966, with a rate of expansion averaging near 10 percent per year—commonsense explanations relating to factors of production did not seem to apply. Perhaps the motivation was related to capital—manufacturing FDI represents a movement of investment from a region of capital abundance to a region of capital scarcity. But this surge of FDI showed capital moving from one region of capital abundance (the United States) to another region of capital abundance (Europe), followed soon enough by the even more baffling flows of cross investment among capital-abundant regions (US FDI into the United Kingdom, Germany, and other states in Europe alongside UK, German, and other European FDI into the United States). Flows of manufacturing FDI to capital-short developing countries were rather tepid. Perhaps the motivation was related to wage levels—manufacturing FDI represents a movement from a region of high wages to a region of low wages. But most manufacturing FDI was moving from one region of relatively high wages to other regions with relatively high wages, with cross investment among high-wage areas again adding perplexity. Flows of manufacturing FDI to the lowest-wage developing countries were hardly noticeable.

The breakthrough in understanding the dynamics of manufacturing FDI originated among a small group of researchers that included Stephen Hymer, Charles Kindleberger, Raymond Vernon, and John Dunning, and was captured in the analytically brilliant but awkward phrase "internalization of intangible assets" (Dunning 1993). Functioning as an alternative to exporting or licensing, FDI represented a strategic effort to maintain or extend the parent's ability to extract oligopoly rents by controlling operations across borders.

Contemporary business school jargon divides this strategic effort into "market-seeking" (horizontal) FDI and "efficiency-seeking" (vertical) FDI, although as shown below these buzzwords overlook what emerged as the most important distinction when MNCs began to establish manufacturing operations in the developing world. One motivation was for the parent to set up plants behind trade barriers in highly protected host-country markets, designed as cash cows to fund MNCs' worldwide operations. A quite separate motivation was for the parent to build plants that were integral to the multinationals' supplier network and designed to make the entire corporation more competitive in international markets.

This distinction provides the key to what kind of inputs the multinational manufacturing firm brings to the host economy, and what kind of contributions manufacturing FDI might make to host-country development. As in the case of FDI in extractive industries and infrastructure, the impact of manufacturing FDI on the host differs noticeably depending on the policy environment established by the host. This variation in outcomes emerged clearly in early attempts to measure the contribution of manufacturing FDI to national income on the micro level, but was overlooked in the first wave of research that used econometric techniques to investigate how FDI affects developing host economies, rendering these early econometric studies unreliable for generalization and misleading for policy.

Impact on Developing-Country Hosts: Early Evidence

Initial attempts to evaluate the impact of FDI in manufacturing and assembly included cost-benefit analyses of individual FDI projects and industry studies from individual developing countries.[1]

Cost-Benefit Analysis of Individual Projects

The first widely recognized study of the impact of FDI on developing-country host economies was conducted by a team headed by Reuber (1973). They analyzed 80 FDI projects in 30 developing countries and for 45 of the projects were able to compare project production costs to production costs of the parent in the home market. In one-quarter of the developing-country affili-

---

1. Throughout this chapter, the analytics applied to what is commonly called FDI in manufacturing and assembly apply equally well to FDI in processed foods and horticulture.

ates, production costs were equal to or lower than in the home plants of the parent; the rest—three-quarters—exhibited higher production costs. All of the projects that were oriented toward export markets fell in the lower-production-cost group. Of the projects that were oriented toward host-country domestic markets, 93 percent were in the higher-production-cost group. The higher production costs could be traced to lofty levels of trade protection, suboptimal scale of production, and expensive local costs of doing business. The Reuber group concluded that, under a wide range of shadow exchange rate scenarios, the protected FDI projects imposed a substantial real resource cost on the host economy.

Following the same tradition of project-by-project analysis, Lall and Streetan (1977) calculated the social rate of return on 147 FDI projects in six developing countries. They found that approximately 60 percent (92 projects) had a positive impact on national income, but 40 percent (55 projects) did not. For all projects in all industries in all countries, a high rate of protection from import competition was the variable that separated the positive from the negative outcome.

More sophisticated cost-benefit analysis of data from a decade later shows the same contrast in FDI outcomes. Encarnation and Wells (1986) examined 50 manufacturing projects submitted by multinational firms to the screening agency of a large developing country, calculating the net impact each would have on the host. This net impact consisted of the contribution to national income minus the costs to the national economy, using world market prices for energy, foreign exchange, labor, and domestic capital to derive the opportunity cost for the host. The authors estimated that a majority of the 50 projects (55 to 75 percent, depending on shadow prices used) would have a positive impact on national income, while a sizable fraction (25 to 45 percent) would not. Most of the results were not a close call; they were either clearly positive or clearly negative. Encarnation and Wells uncovered a perfect rank-order correlation between the positive/negative impact and the amount of trade protection surrounding the project.[2] All eight export-oriented projects generated a positive impact.

To anticipate later discussion of what can be superciliously dismissed as "anecdotal" evidence—and what constitutes robust evidence with safeguards to avoid selection bias—it should be noted that this contrast between FDI in export-oriented projects that enhances host economic welfare and FDI in protected domestic products that does not emerges from microexamination of 242 projects in some 30 developing countries over more than 15 years, a difference in outcome that has been observed in more contemporary cost-benefit analyses as well.[3]

---

2. Projects that received subsidized energy also tended to reduce national income.

3. Wasow (2010) finds that for 35 goods produced by 14 foreign investors with trade protection in Kenya, only in three cases do benefits outweigh costs to the host economy.

Industry Analyses and Case Studies of FDI Used for Import Substitution

The finding that the impact from FDI depends on the extent of competition or protection surrounding the foreign-owned manufacturing operations was not limited to project-by-project cost-benefit calculations. Sectoral or industry studies in individual developing countries that attempted to use FDI for import substitution showed inefficient use of host resources, especially when scale economies could not be achieved. Krueger's (1975) analysis of India's attempts to create a domestic auto industry is a model of such investigation. Foreign investors in the highly protected Indian market all built auto plants much smaller than those located in developed-country markets. This condemned them to low levels of efficiency, with high-priced output, precluding exports as a result. Rather than climbing out of infant industry status, they remained trapped in a vicious circle far removed from the industry frontier: 27 of the 34 assemblers (and their associated suppliers) required ongoing levels of effective protection above 50 percent to remain in business.[4]

Cline's (1987) assessment of the import-substitution "informatics" policies of Brazil, Argentina, and Mexico uncovered many of the same results. Brazil's policy of limiting foreign ownership in the computer industry to 30 percent in designated sectors, imposing heavy domestic content requirements on foreigners, and forbidding foreign ownership in other sectors entirely led to subscale production and generated prices for more sophisticated models that were 2½ to 3 times the international level. With a tariff of more than 100 percent, Argentine computer users paid domestic prices three times the international norm. In Mexico, joint-venture and domestic-content requirements, plus trade protection, also led to boutique FDI plants producing older and more expensive computers, although a parallel market fed by smuggling kept prices 125 to 170 percent of what was available in international markets.

A closer look at the protected operations of foreign investors—from case studies in the automotive and computer industries—revealed that the parent firms not only built subscale plants but employed distinctive production processes to assemble semi-knocked-down and completely knocked-down "kits" of imported parts.[5] These kits were then literally assembled by hand (car bodies welded by hand, computer circuits hand-soldered) in a manner far more

---

4. Eastman and Stykolt (1970, 336–47) offered an early model of why trade protection leads to excessive entry and results in inefficient plant size.

5. See Ngo and Conklin (1996) for an engineering comparison of these semi- and completely knocked-down kits used in auto plants to standard full-scale assembly operations. See Austin (1990) for details about assembly of computer kits in small import-substitution plants. These studies illustrate how market-seeking FDI used for import substitution in protected developing economies was structured differently from the much more sophisticated and beneficial market-seeking FDI in markets open to vigorous domestic and international competition.

primitive than highly automated quality control procedures used in world-class plants.

As a result, manufacturing FDI in these developing-country import-substitution industries did not resemble what was coming to be called "tariff jumping" FDI in which foreign parents built high-performance carbon copies of home-country plants in other developed countries—like Japanese auto investors in Tennessee—with cutting-edge technologies and advanced quality control methods. Similarly, while the phrase "market seeking" might be technically correct to describe the motivation for such investments, the implication that multinational manufacturing corporations were replicating full-scale best practices identical to their most-advanced operations around the globe was not. The miniature plants and small-batch production techniques in FDI plants in developing countries, meanwhile, offered an inherently poor setting to provide the basic skill sets or dynamic learning needed for infant industries to grow to competitive maturity.

The type of protection also impacted the outcome. To build up the domestic industrial base, host authorities typically imposed performance requirements on international manufacturing investors—the most common were domestic-content and joint-venture mandates. However, for most developing economies, domestic-content rules suffered from an inherent flaw: With FDI plants oriented toward protected domestic markets typically smaller than full-scale export-oriented facilities, host-country suppliers providing inputs to meet the rules for domestic content were often themselves unable to achieve economies of scale or use quality control procedures associated with large-batch production techniques.

As for joint-venture requirements, the directive to operate with a local partner (often a local majority partner) produced counterproductive results. Mansfield and Romeo (1980) and Mansfield and Lee (1996) found that parent firms supplied technology to joint ventures in developing countries that was on average one-third older (three to four years older) than technology introduced into wholly owned subsidiaries. Their samples included 65 observations spread across foreign investors in chemicals, drugs, electrical equipment and electronics, machinery, instruments, glass, food, and rubber.

Like joint-venture mandates, host-country requirements to share technology with local firms actually hindered technology transfer into the host economy. Blomström, Kokko, and Zejan (1992) found a negative correlation between host policies that stipulate foreign investors must provide access to the parents' patents, perform research and development (R&D) in the country, or use the most advanced production processes available, and actual technology inflows into the host country. When host authorities impose technology-sharing requirements on Japanese firms as a condition of entry, Urata and Kawai (2000) observe a negative coefficient for intrafirm technology transfer. Contemporary evidence from Eastern Europe and the successor states of the Soviet Union shows that only less efficient foreign investors (relative to other firms in their industry) are likely to choose a joint-venture mode of entry into a country; foreign investors with more sophisticated technologies and marketing skills prefer entry via a wholly owned affiliate rather than a joint venture (Javorcik and Saggi 2010).

The sole performance requirement that showed some signs of success was the obligation to export—and here only if the effect was to induce the foreign investor to build full-scale export-oriented facilities, not merely to send a small number of products from inefficient local plants abroad using trade rents as internal subsidies to make the exports commercially possible. In the late 1970s, Mexico induced the major US auto firms to build world-class engine plants as the first step in turning the economy into an automotive export platform (Moran 1998). Thailand followed the same strategy for diesel engines to power one-ton trucks assembled in Japan.

As noted later in this chapter in the analysis of policy options for host countries, the idea of requiring multinational investors to meet specific domestic-content levels and share technology via joint ventures has continued to hold appeal even as the evidence shows these practices to be counterproductive. The opposite perspective—that MNCs will contribute more to host-country development (including more domestic content and more technology transfer) if they are allowed to operate free of explicit performance requirements—has remained somewhat counterintuitive. Yet this is what the data consistently show. Foreign investors transfer more technology and newer technology via wholly owned (or at least majority-owned) affiliates than when they are required to operate as joint ventures. They also are likely to generate more extensive and more competitive backward linkages without, rather than with, explicit domestic-content requirements. The potential for backward linkages arises because purchase orders from full-sized multinational plants are typically large enough to enable local suppliers to reach minimum economies of scale and to incorporate world-industry-standard production and management techniques.[6]

Industry Analyses and Case Studies of FDI Integrated into the Parent's Global Competitive Strategy

In contrast to the disappointing results when FDI was used for import substitution, industry analyses of FDI manufacturers set up under competitive conditions—often oriented toward export markets—confirmed the positive cost-benefit outcomes along the lines of those found by Lall and Streetan (1977), Reuber (1973), and Encarnation and Wells (1986). But the more closely

---

6. See Rodríguez-Clare (1996) and Alfaro and Rodríguez-Clare (2004) for formal modeling of the importance of increasing returns to scale in determining whether new suppliers of intermediate goods enter the market and variety expands. Their work builds on the insight of Albert Hirschman (1958) that an industry creates a backward linkage when its demand enables the upstream supplier to attain minimum economic scale. The contribution of the foreign investor is measured as a function of the probability that it will pull local industries over this threshold.

the investigators scrutinized what exactly the foreign manufacturing investors were doing at their new plants, the more clearly plant-level studies revealed a new dimension to investor operations.

Early investigations of multinational firms exporting parts and components from Southeast Asia or Latin America conveyed the impression that the parent investors were simply shopping around for sources of cheap inputs. But a closer look at Ford engine plants in Brazil shows they were designed in the 1980s to produce "perfect substitutes" for Ford engines built in Lima, Ohio. By 1990, Texas Instruments assigned quality control responsibility for high-performance electronics products to its wholly owned affiliate in Malaysia. Once Mexico liberalized its informatics policy in 1995—granting IBM the right to operate a wholly owned affiliate as part of the reform—IBM built a factory nine times larger than any other computer plant in Mexico whose output could be incorporated directly into the parent's worldwide sourcing network. In the late 1990s, the General Motors (GM) auto parts plant in Poland was designed to produce high-performance engines, cylinder heads, and gearboxes that were interchangeable with corresponding output from GM facilities in Spain, Austria, and Germany, and the production lines in all four countries could be upgraded simultaneously in real time.

The notion of searching for low-cost parts or assembly sites does not do justice to this degree of integration or to the dynamism of the process. It quickly became apparent that what manufacturing FDI offers to the host is not simply more efficient total-factor-productivity production processes than already exist in the domestic economy. Much more valuable, manufacturing FDI brings the host directly to the cutting edge of the latest technology and best practices in production, quality control, and marketing worldwide in any given industry—a cutting edge that is continuously pushed forward and improved over time as the parent multinational uses its affiliates to reinforce its competitive position in international markets. As will be shown in the final section of chapter 7, these contributions from manufacturing FDI are still not fully captured in contemporary models of dynamic comparative advantage.

As MNCs build supplier networks in the developing world upon which their fate depends, a degree of intimacy develops between parent and affiliate that is far different from the trading of goods and services among independent parties. The empirical details of such close integration come first from industry case studies but are subsequently reinforced by statistical and econometric analysis. For each new generation of disk drives, for example, Seagate or Read-Rite brings more than a dozen process engineers and managers from wholly owned plants in Singapore, Malaysia, or Thailand to meet with product developers at US headquarters 50 days prior to launch, followed two weeks later by 24 production supervisors to get a pilot line up and running (McKendrick, Donner, and Haggard 2000). Then the entire "new product transfer team" returns to Southeast Asia, together with 10 to 20 engineers and managers from headquarters to build the actual production line. This entire crew remains in place to troubleshoot the line until full capacity with low rejection rates is achieved at the developing-country sites. This back-and-forth sequence is repeated for each disk-drive upgrade.

How might this increasingly close relationship between headquarters and the worldwide production network be described? The title of my 2001 book, *Parental Supervision*, tries to capture the spirit of it (Moran 2001). This characterization was originally chosen as a catchy title to report new evidence about the structure of the parent-affiliate relationship. Now it has become clear that "parental supervision" has become an apt—and accurate—portrayal of this dynamic transfer of personnel, techniques, goods, and services within MNC boundaries.

After reviewing these detail-rich examples, it might be useful to recall some principles about research based on case studies, industry studies, and small-number samples, as well as to revisit the precise meaning of the term "anecdotal." Anecdotal means not only that there is a small number of obser-vations about the relationship between two variables but that there is a high probability that a few further observations might overturn any generalization based on the first observations (King, Keohane, and Verba 1994). If, however, the observations about the relationship—as here, between manufacturing FDI and the positive (or negative) contribution to host welfare—come from observations across countries, time periods, and manufacturing sectors, then the relationship can be considered relatively robust, and the likelihood that the next observation will contradict a generalization about the relationship is small. If carefully arrayed to lessen the threat of selection bias, case studies and small-number samples can be used as the basis for rigorous investigation of social phenomena; they cannot and should not be simply dismissed with a pejorative characterization as "anecdotal" (King, Keohane, and Verba 1994).

Beyond that, the confirmation of close parental supervision over wholly owned global production networks does not emerge solely from industry case studies; nor is it limited to the electronics or auto industries as in the examples above. Across 14 sectors as diverse as chemicals, medical products, metal prod-ucts, rubber, food, transportation equipment, and electronics, Ramachandran (1993) finds that the number of parent-company employees sent to a host country to bring a given technology on line, and the number of host-country employees sent to the parent country for training, is significantly higher when the parent has 100 percent ownership than for joint ventures or licensees.

The evidence shows clearly that multinational firms that set up intrafirm supplier links between developed- and developing-country affiliates behave differently in significant ways than those that do not. In an analysis of the relations between US parents and their affiliates in 49 developing countries from 1983 to 1996, Feinberg and Keane (2005) find that knowledge flows, production coordination, reporting links, and other communication chan-nels are more extensive and more active between the affiliates and the parent— and among the affiliates themselves—for those firms that are organized to engage in intrafirm trade than for firms with little or no intrafirm trade. In the case of relations between US multinational parents and their Canadian manufacturing affiliates, Feinberg and Keane (2006) and Keane and Feinberg (2007, 2009) find that factors associated with the intimacy of their interaction—concurrent engineering, just-in-time inventory control, computer-based logistics management, statistical quality control, and total quality management—are (surprisingly) much more important in explaining the growth in trade than either tariff reductions or declines in transport cost.[7]

As will be shown in chapter 7, these intimate parent-affiliate relationships, especially in middle- and higher-skilled FDI operations, do not spring up automatically. The creation of a setting in which these links may emerge requires host-country attention to difficult macro, micro, and institutional reforms, with complex market failures hindering the process. For now, the empirical takeaway is that these thoroughly integrated FDI interactions materialize only when the multinational investor is allowed to operate free of domestic-content requirements, joint-venture mandates, and technology-sharing agreements.

The discovery of the basic distinction between the impact of manufacturing FDI that takes place under reasonably competitive conditions (often oriented toward export markets) and the impact of manufacturing FDI that takes place under highly protected conditions (often aimed at import substitution) turns out to be crucial in demonstrating why the first generation of econometric studies led to faulty generalizations. It is time for a second generation of studies that avoids the mistakes of the first.

Search for Spillovers and Externalities[8]

In the early days of the globalization of industry via the spread of FDI, a central argument of those who favored imposing performance requirements on multinational investors was that if foreign manufacturing investors were allowed to operate freely on their own, without host-country supervision of how they conducted their operations, there would be no spillovers in either the horizontal or vertical direction. Initial evidence did little to assuage such fears.

Horizontal Spillovers and Externalities

In the horizontal direction, MNCs have been unabashed in their determination to maintain control over their most advanced production processes and prevent the emergence of competitors (this was the reason they employed only older technology, as noted above, when they operated with local partners).[9] But there were soon indications that multinational efforts to prevent the

---

7. Keane and Feinberg (2007) offer exemplary use of regression analysis combined with industry and company case studies.

8. The author is particularly grateful to comments and suggestions on this section from Holger Görg.

9. See Gomes-Casseres (1989), Beamish and Delios (1997), Asiedu and Esfanhani (2001), and Javorcik and Saggi (2010).

leakage of technology and the defection of managers, engineers, and workers to indigenous companies were less than perfect. In more advanced developing economies (Singapore, Taiwan, Hong Kong, Brazil, and Mexico), alumni of US and European multinational firms started to appear on the management rosters of local companies (Pack 1997, Katz 1987). Even in poorer developing countries, managers and workers moved from foreign firms to set up parallel operations: Within six years of the beginnings of FDI-led export growth in Mauritius, 50 percent of the capital invested in export processing zones came from indigenous companies founded by owners who had started in foreign firms nearby (Rhee, Katterback, and White 1990, 39).[10] Görg and Strobl (2005) trace the movement of managers from multinational firms to set up their own companies in Ghana; they find that local firms run by owners who worked for multinationals in the same industry immediately before opening their own company are more productive than rivals in the industry.

Besides the relocation of workers and managers, contemporary survey data from Eastern Europe identify two additional channels through which indigenous firms may be able to observe and imitate foreign practices in the horizontal direction: One-quarter of the managers of Czech firms and 15 percent of the managers of Latvian firms in a sample collected by Javorcik and Spatareanu (2005) report that they gained knowledge about new technologies by studying foreign firms as those firms enter their industry. Twelve percent of the Czech managers and 9 percent of the Latvian managers added that they learned new marketing techniques and discovered new sales outlets by scrutinizing the foreigners' behavior.

In general, however, multinational manufacturing investors have tried and continue to try to limit horizontal spillovers as much as possible.

Vertical Spillovers, Backward Linkages, and Externalities

In the vertical direction, early indications of very limited backward linkages soon gave way to evidence that multinational manufacturers in some locales were playing an active role in helping local firms become cheap and reliable suppliers.

Firm-level research on foreign investors in the electronics sector in Singapore reported that US and European firms provided engineering help to indigenous firms to enable them to meet precise design specifications (Lim and Fong 1982). Firm-level research on foreign investors in the telecommunication and semiconductor industries in Malaysia documented how MNCs assigned technicians to suppliers to assist them in setting up large-volume production and quality control procedures (Rasiah 1995). One study of nine Japanese electronics multinationals identified "deliberate transfers" to Malaysian suppliers that took the form of new product and process technologies, product-design

---

10. The authors are explicit in reporting that these new export-processing-zone firms were founded by former employees of the foreign multinationals.

specifications, advice on the use of equipment, and help with the solution of specific technical problems (Capanelli 1997). These types of assistance to local firms would not qualify as a true externality to the host economy if the recipients remained "captive suppliers" to those who provided the help, but in both Singapore and Malaysia the indigenous firms used the knowledge so gained to become "contract manufacturers" to the electronics industry more generally. In the Singapore case, the MNCs introduced local suppliers to affiliates of the same parent in neighboring economies, following which the suppliers began to enter export markets more widely on their own (an export externality analyzed in more detail later).

In the automotive sector, Nuñez (1990) provides survey data showing that within five years after international auto investors began to use Mexico as an export platform, more than half of the 30 largest auto part exporters (excluding engines) were indigenous firms. The Mexican affiliates of US, European, and Japanese auto investors helped these local companies improve quality control to the point where they could qualify as original equipment manufacturers (OEMs). In Thailand, Kohpaiboon (2007, 2009) describes how the multinational automakers assigned technicians to literally take up residence in supplier factories to achieve the same objective. It is important to note, argues Kohpaiboon, that backward linkages and spillovers come in tiers. The first tier of fully certified original equipment manufacturer suppliers includes 287 affiliates of foreign auto parts manufacturers, plus 10 purely Thai-owned firms. Among the latter, a survey of engineers at two companies (Somboon Group and Summit Auto Body) indicated that Mitsubishi had showed the owners how to purchase and install used equipment from Japan and Germany, respectively, to meet Mitsubishi standards. The second tier consists of approximately 1,000 Thai-owned companies that supply the first tier and the primary foreign assemblers. For the second tier, an important spillover consists of foreign help from the buyer with setting up testing facilities to ensure quality reliability.

The evidence of backward linkages and spillovers from foreign investors extends to supporting industries as well as component producers. Seven of the nine largest machine tool companies in Malaysia entered the industry by securing contracts for tooling services from multinational electronics investors: Each of their founders started out as a manager in the foreign purchaser, and 10 percent of the workforce received initial training in the foreign buyer plants (Rasiah 1994). As noted earlier in Singapore, the multinational patrons procured export contracts for the Malaysian machine tool firms from sister affiliates in the region, setting the stage for the Malaysian firms to become independent players in the international market.

Contemporary survey data from foreign investment in textiles, furniture, chemicals, food products, printing, pulp and paper, fabricated metals, and rubber—as well as electrical machinery, communications equipment, and motor vehicles—show that direct assistance between foreigner and supplier takes the form of training, help with setting up production lines, coaching in management strategy and financial planning, advance payment and other kinds of financing, assistance with quality control, and introduction to export markets (Javorcik and Spatareanu 2005).

But the spread of backward linkages has varied greatly across countries and is by no means assured. The extent of local procurement by foreign investors depends, in the first instance, on a business-friendly climate in the host country that allows local firms to grow and prosper. Firms in Mauritius (indigenous as well as foreign) engage in almost twice as much subcontracting as do companies in Madagascar, and more than three times as much as in Senegal or Tanzania,[11] an outcome that Manju Kedia Shah attributes to superior operating conditions across a number of variables in the World Bank's Ease of Doing Business Index.[12] Tax issues also play a role—countries that have a sales tax instead of a value-added tax, for example, find that the former has a cascading effect that stunts the growth of backward linkages.

The nature and extent of subcontracting also depends on how wide the gap is between the capabilities of the local business elite and the sophistication of what is demanded by the foreign purchaser. Kokko (1994) shows that spillovers between foreign affiliates and local firms in Mexico vary as a function of the productivity difference between the two. Kokko, Tansini, and Lejan (1996) observe the same phenomenon in the Uruguayan manufacturing sector. So do Liu, Wang, and Wei (2009) in China. Blalock and Simon (2009) discover a more nuanced outcome: Local firms with larger size and greater absorptive capacity gain more from downstream FDI, but local firms with weaker productive abilities show stronger motivation to adopt new technologies provided by the downstream foreigners. Meyer and Sinani (2009) provide a meta-analysis of capability-gap studies. In all these studies, the analytic focus is on the difference in capabilities between the foreign investor and the potential supplier, as distinct from the mistaken conclusion that FDI is unable to provide benefits to entire host-country economies below some threshold of median human resources (as asserted by Borensztein, de Gregorio, and Lee 1998, discussed earlier).

The development of indigenous supplier networks also depends on the length of time the foreign investors have been resident in the host country (UNCTAD 2001). Giroud and Mirza (2006) show that local input linkages in Malaysia, Thailand, Vietnam, and Cambodia vary directly as a function of the age of the local foreign affiliate. For Japanese multinationals, Belderbos, Capanelli, and Fukao (2000) find that the proportion of local content purchased from both foreign-owned and indigenous suppliers in a host economy is directly related to the length of the Japanese affiliate's operating

---

11. Supporting the higher rate of subcontracting in Mauritius is a policy of having an export processing zone as a legal status rather than a geographical location, so that export-oriented investors can locate wherever in the country is most beneficial for their operations—and by implication most beneficial for supplier operations—rather than in isolated enclaves.

12. Shah (2006, figure 1) and Shah et al. (2005, table 3-2). The World Bank index is available at http://doingbusiness.org/rankings (accessed on February 1, 2011).

experience there. They estimate that each additional year of local operating experience increases the local content ratio by 0.6 percentage points.

The role of reasonably well-developed financial markets is gaining prominence as a necessary (if not sufficient) condition to enable local firms to become suppliers to multinationals. Javorcik and Spatareanu (2005) find that Czech firms supplying foreign investors are less credit-constrained than nonsuppliers. While some of these suppliers may be financially privileged via supply contracts, Javorcik and Spatareanu find that the supplier base is generally less liquidity-constrained before starting up a relationship with an MNC. Indigenous firms with greater access to credit show themselves to be able to self-select into supplier status. Alfaro et al. (2006) provide a formalization of how this process might work, and Alfaro, Kalemli-Ozcan, and Sayek (2009)—using data from 72 countries for 1975–95—show that the benefits for host countries with better-quality financial institutions come in the form of improvements in total factor productivity rather than mere capital accumulation.

Beyond this, some hosts have set up vendor development programs with the goal of promoting backward linkages from foreign investors, with varying degrees of success. Singapore's Economic Development Board (EDB) reimburses the salary of an engineer or manager in each foreign plant who is assigned to act as a "talent scout" to select and assist local firms to become suppliers (UNCTAD 2001, box V.4). As part of its Local Industry Upgrading Program (LIUP), the EDB provides capital for indigenous firms to buy equipment recommended by foreign investors, to be paid back from purchase contracts awarded by the foreigners. Originally dedicated to building supplier relationships in the electronics sector, the LIUP now covers medical products, petroleum and petrochemicals, marine transportation and logistics, and information technology clusters. Malaysia and Thailand establish secondary industrial zones alongside the major export processing zones, with data banks and "marriage counselors" to support supplier selection. In Malaysia, the Penang state government has a Skills Development Center that organizes its curriculum around specific needs and gaps identified by foreign multinationals in the booming regional electronics complex. Survey data from Slovenia provide a reminder, however, that public matchmaking initiatives in the host country cannot produce results unless the underlying capabilities of indigenous firms match up with the needs of the foreign investors (Bucar, Rojec, and Stare 2009).

Kohpaiboon (2010) argues that the creation of sophisticated high-tech local clusters in developing countries is likely to involve more subtle policy management than simply striving for ever-greater levels of localization. Policies to foster high-tech clusters, he shows, will have to include growing integration of international corporate operations across borders as well. The hard-disk-drive industry in Thailand illustrates both higher levels of localization and higher levels of regional integration. The Thai affiliates of Seagate, IBM, Fujitsu, and Hitachi assumed rising levels of local capability as they moved from following blueprints sent from headquarters to designing production processes in-house and ordering tools, molds, and other equipment to create their new production lines. In this process, they hired a larger proportion of indigenous scientific and engineering personnel as well as skilled production workers in their Thai plants—a progression that is reflected in employment data from the 1980s and 1990s.

Alongside their own plants, the hard-disk-drive affiliates created two tiers of suppliers. The first tier consisted of firms where the joint resolution of problems, trial-and-error procedures, and installation of upgrades had to be customized and completed within a same-day (often 2.5 hour) time limit, necessitating virtual face-to-face interaction. First-tier suppliers were all located in the same host country, and initially consisted almost entirely of foreign (primarily Japanese and US) component producers, although their ranks came to include a growing number of indigenous Thai companies. The second tier of suppliers consisted of firms producing more standardized inputs requiring capital-intensive plants (such as wafer fabrication for read/write heads). Second-tier suppliers might be sister affiliates of the hard-disk-drive producers or locally owned suppliers, but in either case they might be located elsewhere in the region. Because of economies of scale, a wafer fabricator would have a plant in Singapore, Malaysia, or Thailand, but not in all three. The key implication, according to Kohpaiboon (2010), is that cluster formation should not be seen either as complete localization, on the one hand, or as total globalization of supply chains, on the other. Rather, the creation of high-performance clusters will combine important elements of both.[13] These results should inspire caution among policymakers, argues Kohpaiboon, about heavy-handed policy measures that simply favor local sourcing over vibrant cross-border networks.

The development of local supplier chains that become internationally competitive has been largely limited to links with foreign investor operations that are integrated into the parent MNC's global operations. Domestic-content requirements imposed upon foreign firms producing for protected host-country markets can certainly induce local production (Kumar 2002).[14] But the purchase orders from foreigners often do not allow local firms to reach full economies of scale. In the automotive industry, foreign investors met domestic-content requirements by concentrating their local purchases in springs, coils, windows, harness gear, and stamped or molded plastic articles where small batch orders do not drive up costs excessively. Suppliers of complicated components such as axles, transmissions, catalytic converters, and fuel injection and exhaust systems have needed larger orders associated with full-scale foreign assembly operations (usually export-oriented) to achieve efficient

---

13. Kimura (2009) suggests that this phenomenon may be common across manufacturing industries in general.

14. Kumar finds that host countries can increase "localization" by imposing performance requirements on MNCs. However, his assertion that a more restrictive trade and FDI regime "helps in improving the quality or developmental impact for the host country" (p. 52) is supported neither by his data nor by evidence from elsewhere.

production runs. In the electronics industry, indigenous suppliers to protected foreign computer "kit" assemblers used production processes (hand soldering) and materials (aluminum rather than composite casing) far different from the large-batch, automated, high-quality-control operations of suppliers serving world-scale export plants.

For countries with export-oriented FDI strategies, the deliberate nurturing of local supplier networks to bolster the international position of foreign parents has hardly been hidden or obscure. In the 1980s and 1990s, the indigenous industrialization of Southeast Asia represented largely a "contract manufacture" phenomenon among local firms providing inputs to foreign investors in electronics. The growth of national industrial poles in Mexico and Brazil relied heavily on original equipment manufacturers' qualification practices associated with FDI in the automotive sector. The UN Conference on Trade and Development (UNCTAD) gave the title *Promoting Linkages* to the 2001 edition of its *World Investment Report*. The international political economy series of the Princeton, Stanford, Cornell, University of Chicago, Cambridge, and Oxford University Presses featured full-length, refereed country and industry studies that documented supplier development efforts of MNCs.

What is remarkable is that this body of evidence about vertical spillovers and externalities has gone largely unnoticed, or been summarily dismissed, by those who instead have relied on the first generation of econometric research on the relationship between FDI and development. As stated by Rodrik in1999 (and emphasized anew in two of his subsequent studies): "Today's policy literature is filled with extravagant claims about positive spillovers from FDI. These spillovers include technology transfer, marketing channels, superior management, and labor training. Once again, the hard evidence is sobering. Systematic plant-level studies from countries such as Morocco and Venezuela find little in the way of positive spillovers (see Harrison 1996)."[15]

Along those same lines, Lipsey and Sjöholm (2005, 24) argued: "Survey articles have found inconclusive evidence in the literature regarding the most important effects of inward FDI, especially with respect to spillovers." And Hanson (2005) declared: "An abundance of evidence that FDI generates positive spillovers does not exist."[16]

What contrary evidence was so compelling?

By far the most widely cited source—indeed, the sole econometric source on which many policy analysts (including Rodrik and Hanson) based their generalization about the impact of FDI on developing countries worldwide—is the seminal work on Venezuela by Aitken and Harrison (1999), published in the *American Economic Review*. They examined whether foreign equity participation was positively associated with plant productivity in Venezuela (an own-

15. Rodrik (1999, 37). See also Rodrik (2007); and Dani Rodrik, Appel Inaugural Lecture, Columbia University, March 27, 2003.

16. See also Hanson (2001).

plant effect), and found a robust correlation only for small enterprises (less than 50 employees). They then asked what the impact was of rising levels of foreign investment on wholly domestically owned plants in the same industry, and observed that the productivity of the latter declined as foreign ownership increased, which they attributed to a market-stealing effect. They finished by trying to measure the net impact of these two offsetting forces, and concluded that the net effect of foreign investment—positive or negative—was quite small. They found no evidence supporting the existence of technology spillovers from foreign-owned firms to domestically owned firms.

But Venezuela during this period featured what Business International at the time characterized as a rather heavy-handed import substitution strategy (as quoted in Balasubramanyam, Salisu, and Sapsford 1996). Venezuelan authorities imposed both domestic-content and local-partner requirements on foreign firms, and required them to buy and sell dollars at a highly disadvantageous exchange rate. The Venezuelan Department of Foreign Investment restricted repatriation of profits and exercised arbitrary discretion in authorizing foreigners to take majority control in any given investment. When foreigners formed joint ventures, they were forbidden from requiring local partners to respect confidentiality or exercise exclusive use with regard to trade secrets.

The data Aitken and Harrison examined thus originated in a highly distorted setting of the type in which Lall and Streetan (1977), Reuber (1973), Encarnation and Wells (1986), and others found widely divergent positive and negative impacts from FDI at the micro level. The evidence fits well within the framework of subscale plants, inefficient production processes, and highly restricted transfers of older parent technology already familiar in Kreuger's 1975 study of the Indian auto industry and Cline's 1987 investigation of Mexican, Brazilian, and Argentinean informatics policy. The surprise is not that Aitken and Harrison found small or mixed benefits from FDI but that they found any positive benefits whatsoever! Plant-level cost-benefit analysis of these 4,000 to 6,000 operations would probably show most subtracting from host welfare.

To generalize about the impact of FDI on host economies around the world, or about the potential for spillovers in the horizontal (or vertical) direction, Aitken and Harrison would have had to separate FDI oriented toward the protected domestic market from FDI oriented toward exports (if Venezuela had any such FDI), wholly owned FDI (if any) from FDI in majority-owned joint ventures and from FDI in minority-owned joint ventures, and FDI free to source from anywhere (if any) from FDI required to meet domestic-content requirements. Without these controls, it is impossible for the authors—or for subsequent interpreters and surveyors of the literature—to come to reasonable conclusions about the likely impact of FDI on developing economies across the globe.[17]

---

17. Görg and Greenaway published "Much Ado About Nothing? Do Domestic Firms Really Benefit from Foreign Direct Investment?" in 2004, but their title may have been misleading to

The companion piece in this first generation of econometric studies, this time by Haddad and Harrison (1993), proposed to explore the impact of FDI in Morocco after the host had initiated trade and investment liberalization during 1983–85. They found that there was no significant relationship between a larger foreign presence in a sector and higher productivity growth among domestic firms in that sector, indicating an absence of positive spillovers. Foreign-owned firms had higher levels of total factor productivity than domestic firms in the same industry, but the rate of productivity growth among the latter was higher. Holding firm size constant, foreign investors showed no higher levels of labor productivity. As in the Venezuelan case, Haddad and Harrison concluded that foreign investment brought no large or dynamic positive contribution to the host economy.

When the authors varied measures of trade protection, technology spillovers from foreign investors to domestic firms remained insignificant and generally negative. But a closer look at what Haddad and Harrison called Morocco's "trade reform" shows that while quantitative restrictions were phased out during the supposed liberalization years (1983–85), a complicated tariff remained in place, with nominal rates ranging from 17 to 44 percent by sector, and effective rates climbing at each stage of processing. Other observers characterized Moroccan policy of the period studied by Haddad and Harrison as remaining solidly in the import-substitution category.[18]

Over the four-year period (1985–89) investigated by Haddad and Harrison, FDI ownership shares in most manufacturing sectors did not change a great deal: 4 percentage points in scientific instruments, 3 percentage points in machinery, and 3 percentage points in textiles and apparel. Only in phosphate mining (a nonmanufacturing category) did the FDI share rise by a more substantial 7 percentage points. Across the manufacturing landscape, most of the FDI stock during 1985–89 was left over from the period of quantitative trade restrictions and mandatory minority foreign ownership. It is impossible to tell from the Haddad-Harrison data whether some export-oriented FDI projects might have started to spring up during the 1985–89 span, but cost-benefit analysis would almost surely show that most of projects set up in the earlier import-substitution period contained many of the harmful effects already noted. A proper reconstruction of the Haddad-Harrison analysis that did not mix protected inward-oriented FDI with export-oriented FDI—using

---

readers who did not give a close look at their argument. Leaving aside Aitken and Harrison (1999) and Haddad and Harrison (1993)—as recommended here—the 15 papers Görg and Greenaway survey actually include 10 showing positive intra-industry productivity spillovers, with five inconclusive. The authors were critical of these studies on methodological grounds because they used cross-section data that Görg and Greenaway felt were unreliable for drawing policy conclusions.

18. See Balasubramanyam, Salisu, and Sapsford (1996). Haddad and Harrison in fact attribute the higher rate of total factor productivity growth among indigenous firms, in comparison to foreign investors, to the superior ability of the former to maneuver through the continuing warps and controls in the domestic economy.

data from after genuine trade and investment liberalization in the Moroccan economy begun in 1995 led to export processing zone exports that climbed to $3 billion annually by 2008—might well indicate a more positive impact from the new FDI operations. In any case, it would constitute a better basis for generalization about the impact of manufacturing FDI under competitive conditions around the world.

How can the second generation of econometric investigations be structured to avoid these missteps and test for spillovers and externalities in rigorous and generalizable fashion? How might econometric techniques be supplemented, moreover, by other kinds of research so as to identify the channels through which spillovers and externalities take place—a discovery of particular use for the design of host-country policy?

Improving Contemporary Econometric Methodology: Horizontal Externalities

In the horizontal direction, the search for externalities poses some particularly thorny challenges. As the crowding-in/crowding-out debate in chapter 6 will show, the introduction of foreign firms into a host economy is likely to simultaneously produce two diametrically opposed effects on domestic firms in the same sector. On the one hand, the presence of foreign investors offers local companies an opportunity to observe and imitate foreign operations, and to recruit managers, engineers, and workers, while concurrently generating competitive pressure to improve their own performance. On the other, the presence of foreign investors may shrink local companies' market share and drain workers, managers, and capital away from them, undermining local firm performance or driving those firms out of the market. Econometric studies that simply search for a correlation between rising numbers of foreign investors and changes in total factor productivity of local firms in the same industry are going to jumble these two effects together.

Second-generation researchers are going to have to devise means to control for the level of competition across the target industry as well as for the movement of personnel and spread of technology among firms. These tasks are not insurmountable, as researchers investigating the impact of FDI in the horizontal direction in developed countries have shown. Keller and Yeaple (2009), for example, use evidence about the markup rate among firms to control for the change in degree of competition, thereby isolating genuine externalities.[19]

Investigation of the relationship between FDI and the presence (or absence) of horizontal spillovers and externalities in developing countries is beginning to move in this direction as well. For China, Girma and Gong (2008) find that the average state-owned enterprise (SOE) experiences negative intra-industry spillovers from foreign investment in its sector. Since they include

---

19. See also Haskel, Pereira, and Slaughter (2007).

controls for market share (thereby separating out competitive or "market-stealing" effects), they are able to argue that the reverse movement of productive workers out of SOEs to multinationals (multinationals pay an average wage rate 16 percent higher than SOEs) is probably the channel that accounts for the negative impact.

As argued below, the confidence in these statistical relationships—and the identification of the particular channels through which horizontal spillovers take place—would be greatly enhanced if the econometric research were combined with well-structured business survey data along the lines of Javorcik and Spatareanu (2005) and/or with careful industry studies like those of McKendrick, Donner, and Haggard (2000), or of Feinberg and Keane (2005, 2006) and Keane and Feinberg (2007, 2009), as reported earlier.

Improving Contemporary Econometric Methodology: Vertical Externalities

In the vertical direction, the second generation of econometric studies—led by Blalock and Gertler (2005, 2008) and Javorcik (2004)—has fashioned what is becoming the standard method to search for externalities upstream or downstream from foreign investors, while carefully avoiding the mistakes of the first generation. Using data on manufacturing establishments in Indonesia since 1988 collected by region—where FDI operations are predominantly export-oriented—Blalock and Gertler investigate the relationship between the presence of foreign investors and the total factor productivity of domestic firms that are suppliers to or buyers from the foreigners. But the foreign firms may simply be settling in areas where productivity is already high, so the next step is to observe how total factor productivity of the indigenous firms changes as the presence of foreign investors increases. Again, however, there may be some external reason why foreigners would increase their presence as local productivity grows, such as improvements in the business climate. To deal with the possibility that foreign investors are choosing sites where suppliers are particularly productive already, Blalock and Gertler include establishment fixed effects to judge whether the performance of upstream or downstream firms gets even better after the arrival of the foreigners. To deal with the possibility that some external factor is raising the productivity of all firms, they include industry-year and region-year fixed effects to control for changes in conditions affecting all market participants. Finally, to deal with the possibility that suppliers would experience some exogenous improvement that was not part of industrywide or regionwide changes, they employ a simultaneity correction (developed by Olley and Pakes 1996).

At the end of these steps, they find an improvement in upstream and downstream local firms that is significantly associated with the rise in foreign investment and not derived from other factors. The improvement in the performance of these indigenous firms, in turn, results in lower prices, increased output, higher profitability, and increased entry of vertically linked firms.

But does correlation—however careful—actually show causation? What are the mechanisms through which causality takes place? Here Blalock and Gertler do something highly unusual in the economics community and supplement their econometric investigations with survey data from actors on both sides. They report that the foreign investors and the Indonesian local company managers identified specific kinds of uncompensated assistance flowing between the parties, including help with production, quality control, and business management. US and Japanese multinationals reported that they assisted target suppliers to increase efficiency and reliability, moving from small-scale orders to larger regular purchases from local firms that showed promise. In the case of Japanese investors, the usual practice was to introduce successful Indonesian suppliers to other members of the parent company group elsewhere in Southeast Asia, reminiscent of earlier case study evidence about foreigners helping local firms they bought from to get started with exports. But an outcome featuring positive externalities was by no means inevitable or automatic—some Indonesian firms failed to pass muster, some dropped out, and some were abandoned by the foreigners due to subpar performance.

Blalock and Gertler emphasize that they did not attempt to carry out rigorous survey research. While their interviews contain important direct observations of the process of vertical spread of technology and management practices, there would be enormous value added if they had combined their econometric investigations with a well-structured representative survey, including characteristics of respondent firms. This could provide a basis for investigating prerequisites for successful diffusion and identifying channels with larger and smaller impact.

Using many of the same measurement techniques, Javorcik (2004) finds productivity spillovers taking place between foreign investors and upstream domestic firms in Lithuania. Her study avoids the problem of relying on data from a highly protected and distorted host economy because during the period in question (1996–2000) Lithuania was preparing for accession to the European Union and enjoyed an average tariff that was quite low (equal to 3.7 percent). To address the problem that there may be unobserved firm-, time-, and region-specific factors that affect the correlation between firm productivity and foreign presence, she uses time differencing as well as a full set of fixed effects for year, industry, and region. She estimates a separate production function (taking into account the Olley-Pakes correction) for each industry. Since foreign entry into downstream sectors may increase demand for intermediate products, which in turn will allow local suppliers to reap the benefits of scale economies, she introduces controls to provide confidence that the outcome can be attributed to the effects of knowledge spillovers rather than simply to larger-scale economies. She finds productivity spillovers from foreign investors to affiliates with shared local ownership, but no significant relationship with wholly owned affiliates (an outcome she associates with the inclination of the latter to import more intermediate inputs). A one standard deviation increase in the foreign presence in downstream sectors is associated with a 15 percent rise in output of each domestic firm in supplying industries. She separately considers spillovers from export- and domestic-oriented affiliates and finds that in this relatively competitive market setting, both types of FDI generate spillovers to the supplying industries, with no significant difference in magnitude.

Javorcik lacks the direct observation of assistance flowing from foreign investors to local suppliers that Blalock and Gertler provide, however. To substitute for this, she introduces World Bank survey data from neighboring Latvia to adduce that foreign investors in Lithuania may have been providing help to their suppliers (33 percent of the Latvian firms that supplied multinationals reported that they received explicit support of some sort). She concludes that an optimal research strategy would combine a well-structured survey with econometric analysis, and argues, as noted above, that such an approach could identify spillover channels as a function of host-country and investor characteristics.

Export Externalities

The firm-level studies reviewed earlier in this chapter include repeated examples in which US, European, and Japanese multinationals introduce local suppliers to related affiliates in neighboring markets, after which those suppliers begin to sell to independent buyers in those markets and elsewhere in the international economy. This is an important—but rather narrow—observation of an "export externality."

As a more general phenomenon, do growing numbers of foreign investors lead to—and actually help generate—greater exports from other firms in the host economy where the foreigners are located? This is the question that Aitken, Hanson, and Harrison (1997) address in the period after Mexico began to liberalize trade and investment in 1985.

Isolating the relationship between the presence of foreign investors and the export behavior of indigenous firms requires deft analysis, since the natural expectation is that all export behavior will take place where the infrastructure is best, where proximity to borders is closest, or where some other comparative advantage benefits all outward-looking firms. To identify an export spillover from foreign firms, therefore, Aitken, Hanson, and Harrison control for overall concentration of economic activity in a region and for possible region- or industry-specific shocks, so as to eliminate the impact of unobserved fixed factors that might affect the export behavior of all firms. Somewhat surprisingly, their results show that the probability of doing "more than expected" exporting was positively correlated with close-by presence of foreign investors but uncorrelated with close-by concentration of export activity more generally.

This is an extraordinarily interesting and important discovery. But the statistical correlation alone—no matter how well structured and controlled— leaves crucial questions unanswered. Are the host exporters part of FDI supply chains (with spillovers in a vertical direction), or independent of those supply chains and operating in parallel to them (with spillovers in a horizontal direction)? Do host exporters receive direct "export coaching" from foreign firms, or gain new skills indirectly?

A relatively modest effort at gathering survey data, or undertaking case studies alongside the econometric tests, would have tremendous payoff for researchers and for host policymakers alike.

Similarly, Chen and Swenson (2007) show that the presence of multinationals in the same industry is associated with more and higher-quality trade transactions by Chinese firms. Swenson (2008) then finds that the multinational presence is positively associated with the formation of new export connections (greater diversity of products and destinations) by private Chinese exporters between 1997 and 2003. It appears that information spillovers about market opportunities and marketing techniques may drive this result. But the raw data do not permit distinguishing horizontal spillovers from vertical spillovers involving the deliberate buildup of supplier networks. In both studies, firm surveys or industry case studies could help clarify what kinds of foreign investor–local firm interaction are actually taking place on the ground.

A multiple-research-technique approach to investigation could also help with the learning-from-exporting debate. Blalock and Gertler (2004), for example, observe that firms in Indonesia enjoy an increase in productivity of 2 to 5 percent following the initiation of exporting. The timing of the increase indicates that the productivity increase results from learning from exporting rather than representing self-selection of higher-performing firms into export markets. To check whether they were on the right track with this conclusion, Blalock and Gertler interviewed managers in the local plants. The managers reported that purchasers from Japan sent engineers annually to review production methods and provide suggestions that might reduce costs, and that buyers from Germany sent efficiency experts to advise on how best to expand production capacity. These findings reinforce the evidence in the case studies of Lim and Fong (1982) and Rasiah (1994) cited earlier in this chapter, but contrast sharply with those of others who fail to find learning from exporting (Clerides, Lach, and Tybout 1998; Bernard and Jensen 1999; Delgado, Farinas, and Ruano 2002).

Labor Market Externalities

The next section reports evidence of a near-ubiquitous wage premium enjoyed by employees in the plants of foreign investors and uncovers some perplexities in explaining why the wage premium exists.

The question under examination here is how does the spread of foreign manufacturing investment affect the treatment of workers in indigenously owned plants? Does the presence of foreign firms generate labor market externalities that benefit local workers in the host economy more broadly?

The unusually detailed data from Indonesia offer Lipsey and Sjöholm (2004a) an opportunity to investigate quite thoroughly whether the higher wages paid by foreign firms in their own plants lead to payment of higher wages in domestically owned companies. Controlling for labor force characteristics, they find a positive spillover within broad sector classifications at the national level, and a smaller (but still positive and significant) spillover within narrower sector classifications and at the regional level. In another test from Indonesia, Hijzen (2008, chapter 5) shows that inward FDI has a positive effect on the average wage of nonproduction workers in domestic firms in the same industry and region, but he fails to discover any impact on the average wage of production workers.

But why do local firms pay their workers more when foreign investors are present? Is this purely the effect of foreign entry on local demand for various kinds of workers, or the indirect effect of FDI on the productivity of local firms? Or might there be other explanations? Are there host policies that might enhance this effect? Here, once again, is a rich opportunity to conduct survey research to complement the statistical manipulation of data.

Adding another dimension to the potential for externalities, case study research offers interesting evidence of institutional spillovers in the labor markets when the skill intensity of FDI activities rises. As the operations of foreign investors grow more sophisticated—for example, as electronics and auto parts investors build plants in export processing zones and industrial parks alongside garment and footwear assemblers—these operations promote better worker facilities, security, transport, and health and safety standards (even daycare) that apply to all firms (Moran 2002, chapter 3). Although the evidence comes from a small sample, it includes three country histories—the Dominican Republic, the Philippines, and Costa Rica—where the more skill-intensive foreign firms led the way for both passage of regulations at the national level, consistent with International Labor Organization (ILO) regulations, and more effective enforcement of the resulting regulations at the local level, including communal disciplining of violators, in the interest of promoting "labor peace."[20] This process exhibits race-to-the-top dynamics quite at variance with the race-to-the-bottom assumptions in much of the sweatshop literature.

These observations provide the background for a broader examination of the implications of manufacturing FDI for workers in the developing world. Newly accumulated data on multinational manufacturing investment make clear the need for a fundamental reappraisal of the types of activities and jobs carried into the developing world through the globalization of industry via FDI. This is the subject of the next section.

---

20. See Moran (2002). See also the background materials for the US Secretary of State's Award for Corporate Excellence 2009, US Embassy, San Jose, Costa Rica, June 2009.

Painting a New Portrait of Manufacturing Multinationals: Level of Wages, Kinds of Activities, and Types of Jobs

Central to calculating the value of the benefits that FDI in manufacturing might bring to the host economy is an assessment of exactly what level of wages and types of jobs and activities foreign manufacturing investors offer.

As noted earlier, there is abundant evidence that FDI in low-skill-intensive manufacturing and assembly in poorer as well as middle-income countries can have important developmental impacts. Romer (1992) chose Mauritius when it was one of the world's poorest countries as an example where low-skill-intensive FDI could have a transformative influence on the economy. Foreign investors fueled a growth record that ranked Mauritius seventh among the 15 most successful exporters of manufactured products in the world. Before the international financial crisis hit in 2008, Mauritius' manufacturing exports reached more than $1.2 billion (51 percent of all exports), with 413 companies employing 65,000 workers.

The Dominican Republic had per capita GDP only two-thirds as high as Mauritius when the government started to lure FDI into manufacturing and assembly. Before international markets collapsed in 2008, the Dominican Republic's total zone investment exceeded $1 billion, total zone employment was 155,000, and total zone exports reached $4.5 billion (65 percent of all exports). In Kenya, 10 to 15 percent of all formal employment consists of small-hold farmers who become "indirect exporters" of fresh vegetables and flowers via multinational corporate networks (50,000 to 60,000 employed directly and some 500,000 in associated activities related to cut flowers alone in 2008).[21]

Production of garments, footwear, toys, and other such products for export can provide a channel out of rural areas, and out of the informal economy, for hundreds of thousands of workers. In Bangladesh, foreign investors and indigenous subcontractors lobbied against Muslim traditions prohibiting women from working in factories. Today, two million workers, predominantly female, are employed in Bangladesh's garment export sector, earning 25 percent more than the country's average monthly per capita income (USAID 2008).

The number of jobs in low-skilled plants owned by foreign investors or in plants of subcontractors to foreign companies can be quite large (several thousand workers in each plant). This often leaves the impression that low-skilled labor and the prospect of paying the lowest possible wages pull multinational manufacturing investors to the developing world. After all, as multinational firms devise their strategies, they have the advantage: Capital is mobile, and labor is fixed, so foreign investors should be able to ignite a race-to-the-bottom that drives wages as low as possible.

But the data paint a quite different picture.

---

21. Jane Ngige, Kenya Flower Council, "Roses from Kenya Bloom," Management Talk Q&A, August 5, 2009, www.123jump.com/management-talk/Roses-from-Kenya-Bloom/34107 (accessed on February 1, 2011). See also Bell, Milder, and Shelman (2007).

Looking first at how wages in multinational plants compare to wages paid in local companies, survey data consistently show that foreign investors pay more than local firms. In Madagascar, Razafindrakoto and Roubaud (1995) held level of education, extent of professional experience, and length of tenure in the enterprise constant, and found that foreign investors in export processing zones paid 15 to 20 percent more than what workers with similar qualifications received elsewhere in the economy. Data from Latin America and Africa show a similar wage premium (Aitken, Harrison, and Lipsey 1996; te Velde and Morrissey 2003). Lipsey (2006) characterizes as a "universal rule" that foreign-owned firms and plants pay higher wages than domestically owned ones.

Are these wage premiums more pronounced in richer developing countries, and less evident in poorer developing countries?

In fact, the calculations of Graham (2000, table 4.2) show exactly the opposite: As a multiple of average compensation per employee in the host manufacturing sector, compensation per indigenous employee in foreign plants in the manufacturing sector is greater in poorer countries than in middle-income developing countries. In the latter, the ratio of foreign-paid wages to indigenous-firm wages in manufacturing is 1.8; in low-income developing countries, that ratio is 2.0, which is to say, twice as high as average compensation in the host-country manufacturing sector.[22]

What accounts for this foreign-investor wage premium? Perhaps the explanation derives from the fact that foreign-owned plants are typically larger, may use different inputs, and may be located in regions of higher wages overall.

Once again the unusually detailed dataset of plant and worker characteristics from almost 20,000 firms in Indonesia allows Lipsey and Sjöholm (2004b) to separate out the relative influences. Overall they find that foreign investors paid 33 percent more to blue-collar workers and 70 percent more to white-collar workers than did locally owned firms. Controlling for education, MNCs paid more for workers with a given education level than domestically owned firms. Controlling for region and sector, the foreign pay differential showed up as 25 percent for blue-collar workers and 50 percent for white-collar workers. Controlling for plant size, energy inputs per worker, other inputs per worker, and proportion of employees that were female, the wage premium in foreign-owned establishments equaled 12 percent for blue-collar and 22 percent for white-collar workers; that is, the foreign investors were paying their employees more than what might be explained by increased productivity coming from greater inputs per worker and higher efficiency resulting from a larger scale of production.

Lipsey and Sjöholm (2004b) conclude that approximately one-third of the foreign-investor wage premium could be attributed to region and sector and one-third to plant size and use of other inputs, with one-third left unexplained.

---

22. Graham removes salaries for foreign managers and supervisors from these calculations.

Quite at variance with the widespread notion that foreign investors travel to developing countries to "exploit" local workers, or that mobile capital takes advantage of inherently fixed labor, the pleasant puzzle in the data is why multinationals pay local workers more than they apparently need to in order to keep their plants operating efficiently. Perhaps foreign investors provide skill training (unobserved by econometric analysis) that increases worker productivity; or perhaps they want to secure a more stable labor force by limiting turnover. A preponderance of evidence places the worker compensation practices of MNCs in most developing-country sectors squarely in the middle of the "efficiency wage" debate.

Once again, econometric investigation could be powerfully supplemented by survey data and case study analysis. World Bank data show that international investors usually offer more on-the-job training than comparable domestic firms. An unusually detailed case study of export processing zone firms in the Dominican Republic provides an indication of the results (Rhee, Katterback, and White 1990). Eighty-five percent of the workers in the Dominican export processing zones came directly from the country's unskilled labor pool. These workers typically received 2.3 months of on-the-job training, followed by a period of learning by doing for the rest of their first year. For 33 US firms in the Dominican Republic, productivity at the firm level increased 44 percent going into the second year after startup, and 10 percent going into the third year. For 12 Korean, Taiwanese, and Hong Kong investors in the Dominican Republic, productivity at the firm level increased 67 percent going into the second year after startup, and 13 percent going into the third. In a survey of export processing zone workers who achieved the status of skilled worker by the end of the first year, 85 percent of those in US firms and 80 percent of those in Korean, Taiwanese, and Hong Kong firms reported that they had developed their skills exclusively at their current employer at the time of the survey. The researchers concluded that their evidence shows that there are "remarkable private returns to skill formation" and refutes "the usual argument that there is very low skill acquisition in export processing zone firms" (Rhee, Katterback, and White 1990, 18, 22). Additional case studies and survey data could show the extent to which these results can be generalized and whether market forces alone are sufficient to stimulate such in-firm worker training.

Despite the ubiquitous wage premium paid by foreign investors, actual wage levels in low-skilled FDI plants and the plants of their subcontractors may nonetheless be dismayingly low, causing justifiable consternation on the part of external observers. What might be done about this? Trying to find an answer poses genuine quandaries because it is extremely difficult to design policies that intervene directly in labor markets to mandate higher wages without having counterproductive effects on workers.[23] High minimum wages and living wages not tied to relative productivity tend to make exporters uncompetitive. Living wages calculated to support worker families of regional average

---

23. For more analytics, see Moran (2002).

size discriminate against younger, older, and single workers (this outcome is unaddressed, and simply ignored, by many prolabor organizations) (ILO 2008). High minimum wages discourage the hiring of entry-level and other lesser-skilled workers. The only effective public tool to raise the earnings of low-skilled workers—besides training to improve their skills—is some form of a negative income tax or earned-income tax credit (a highly expensive option for developing-country authorities).

One idea that might hold promise is if civil society groups, NGOs, and corporate social responsibility advocates were to insist that international companies producing or selling highly branded or collegiate logo products ensure that lowest-level workers receive what might be labeled a "decent wage"—for example, the prevailing wage per skill level plus a premium of 20 percent. But any such system must be designed to transfer oligopoly rents from the international marketer or retailer (or from consumers) to seamstresses and stitchers, not simply to impose on the lowest-level assembly companies a mandate to pay above-market wages while expecting those companies to absorb the added cost. This kind of transfer mechanism from consumers and company headquarters can be found in Kenya's flower industry: International companies that qualify for "fair trade" certification are obliged to allocate 8 percent of the free-on-board price for flowers to education and health initiatives that are established by a joint worker-management committee. This 8 percent of the flower price is passed on to consumers who choose the fair trade brand. Wages at the plant level are not set by the fair trade system. At one of the largest international exporters, Vegpro, what workers receive depends on individual experience and performance but is nonetheless 15 to 20 percent higher than the national minimum wage for the sector at the entry level and 30 to 40 percent higher for more experienced workers (ILO 2008, 12). In the industry at large, the workers themselves are eligible to participate in a union, and as of 2007, two-thirds were registered members (Bell, Milder, and Shelman 2007).

This approach is consistent with what Harrison and Scorse (2010) found in examining the impact of antisweatshop activism on wages of targeted enterprises in Indonesia in the 1990s. Their data confirmed that rapid increases in the minimum wage during this period led to employment losses for production workers across all sectors in Indonesian manufacturing. Within the textile, footwear, and apparel sector, however, plants targeted by antisweatshop activities—in all likelihood producing branded products—complied with the higher minimum wage more than other manufacturing firms, while raising real production wages an additional 10 to 20 percent as well. The impact of the antisweatshop campaigns did show up in falling profits, reduced productivity growth, and plant closures for smaller exporters in textile, footwear, and apparel, but did not have additional adverse effects on employment in these sectors. Harrison and Scorse suggest that this may be in part due to the fact that labor costs from developing-country factories accounted for only about 4 percent of the total costs of a $90 branded shoe (Nike data).

Combating sweatshop abuses in export processing and free trade zones by preventing health and safety hazards and physical and sexual abuse, and transmitting decent wages for workers in the supply chains of branded products, are notoriously complicated undertakings. The most successful campaigns frequently involve multiple international and local participants, including labor unions, NGOs, and independent auditors and monitors. For example, the struggle to unionize the Hanes TOS Dominicana plant—which produces fabric for t-shirts and is one of the largest textile manufacturers in the Dominican Republic's export industry—lasted from 2006 to 2008. The Worker Rights Consortium (WRC), an independent labor rights monitoring organization founded by university administrators, labor experts, and student activists, launched an investigation of worker complaints in October 2006.[24] The WRC has more than 150 college and university affiliates concerned about garments bearing their collegiate logos. The AFL-CIO's Solidarity Center provided technical and legal support during the unionization drive. After Hanes became a member of the Fair Labor Association (FLA), an NGO with socially responsible companies, universities, and civil society groups on its board, the FLA received a complaint in February 2008 about noncompliance with the FLA Code of Conduct in the area of freedom of association and collective bargaining, and initiated consultations among all the stakeholders.[25] At the end of tough but successful bargaining, Hanes and the union (Syndicato de Trabajadores TOS Dominicana) signed their first collective agreement on August 12, 2008.[26]

In a slightly different application of external pressures, the campaign to help workers at the Legumex fruit and vegetable processing plant in Guatemala was launched by the National Labor Committee (NLC), an NGO formed with backing from organized labor to combat sweatshop abuses. The NLC worked through a local NGO, the Center for Education and Support for Local Development (CEADEL), to ensure that all workers earned at least the minimum wage, received pay for overtime, were enrolled in the Guatemalan Social Security Institute, had protective gear to wear in the cutting areas, and enjoyed new bathrooms and ate in a cafeteria with tables and chairs. On March 18, 2007, the NLC, CEADEL, the US buyer, and the plant management signed an agreement confirming these improvements.[27]

To be sure, even highly coordinated campaigns may encounter determined resistance. Beginning in 2008, the Russell Corporation, owned by Fruit of the Loom, a privately held member of the Berkshire Hathaway portfolio, became the

---

24. The WRC report is available at www.workersrights.org.

25. "Third Party Complaint Regarding TOS Dominicana, Dominican Republic," Fair Labor Association, August 20, 2008, www.fairlabor.org (accessed on February 1, 2011).

26. "Dominican Garment Workers Sign First Contract," AFL-CIO Solidarity Center, August 12, 2008, www.solidaritycenter.org (accessed on February 1, 2011).

27. National Labor Committee, "Harvest of Shame Update: Major Improvements at Legumex in Guatemala," February 28, 2008, www.nlcnet.org (accessed on February 1, 2011).

target of multiple groups due to complaints about labor practices at its Jerzees de Honduras plant. The WRC issued a report in November 2008 asserting that Russell managers had carried out a campaign of retaliation and intimidation against members of the company union Sitrajerseesh, culminating in closure of the plant in January 2009.[28] WRC demanded reopening of the plant and reinstatement of the workers. Major universities including Duke, Georgetown, the University of Wisconsin, and the University of Michigan joined in a boycott of Russell. In May 2009, 65 members of the US Congress wrote to the CEO of Russell expressing concern about labor practices. In June, Russell became the first collegiate licensee to be placed on probation by the FLA for failure to follow through on a remediation plan for the workers.[29] Finally, in November, Russell agreed to rehire the 1,200 former workers and institute a joint union-management training program on freedom of association that would open the door for union representation at all Fruit of the Loom facilities in Honduras. Fruit of the Loom is the largest private-sector employer in Honduras.

"This agreement represents one of the most significant advances for fundamental workplace rights in the twenty-year history of apparel industry codes of conduct," said Scott Nova of the Worker Rights Consortium. "It is hard to overstate the significance of this breakthrough."[30]

After a review of evidence of successful campaigns to improve the treatment of workers, it is odd—but not unusual—to discover international trade union representatives claiming that they should be the sole advocates on behalf of developing-country workers, while denying any legitimacy to NGOs and other civil society labor rights groups.[31] To be sure, local labor unions can in principle have the closest ongoing knowledge of the plight of workers, and their presence can head off the disadvantages of spot checks and erratic (or faked) external monitoring. But the model of independent democratically run trade unions representing the best interests of their membership—as depicted in developed-country debates about the role of trade unions in advancing labor rights (Borjas 2007)—is often at variance with the reality on the ground of politically connected, extortion-prone, clientele-based, corrupt organiza-

28. "Russell Corporation's Rights Violations Threaten 1800 Jobs in Honduras," Worker Rights Consortium, November 7, 2008, http://workersrights.org/RussellRightsViolations.asp (accessed on February 1, 2011).

29. See the Fair Labor Association website at www.fairlabor.org (accessed on August 6, 2009).

30. Maquiladora Solidarity Network, "Historic Victory: Jerzees de Honduras Workers Win Breakthrough Agreement," November 18, 2009, http://en.maquilasolidarity.org (accessed on February 1, 2011).

31. See comments by Ellie Larson, Executive Director, and Mark Hankin, Senior Assistant for Program Development, Solidarity Center, at the labor forum on "The Role of the Labor Sector in Promoting US Foreign Assistance Goals: Lessons Learned to Date," US Agency for International Development, Washington, June 30, 2009. See also Dwight Justice, "Assessing Freedom of Association," presentation at "Quality of Information: Summary of a Workshop," National Research Council, Washington, 2003.

Table 4.1   Manufacturing FDI flows to and stock in lower-skilled versus higher-skilled operations of multinational corporations in developing countries (millions of dollars)

Type of operations	FDI flows (annual average)			FDI stocks		
	1989–91	1999–2000	2005–07	1990	1999	2007
Lower-skilled operations	2,837	3,100	7,487	20,766	46,864	80,545
Higher-skilled operations	13,244	52,800	104,365	137,261	505,928	836,272

Source: UNCTAD (2003, 2009).

tions.[32] International and local NGOs may be more suitable allies for developed-country labor solidarity organizations.

Turning next to types of activities, the data show a well-documented, uncontested outcome that nonetheless will come as a surprise to many: By far the majority of manufacturing FDI in developing countries flows to more-advanced industrial sectors than to the lower-skilled operations, and the weighting toward more skill-intensive investor operations is speeding up over time. Table 4.1 shows the stock and flow over time of manufacturing FDI to higher-skilled activities (e.g., transportation equipment, industrial machinery, electronics and electrical products, scientific instruments, medical devices, chemicals, rubber, and plastic products) versus lower-skilled, labor-intensive operations (e.g., garments, footwear). Tables 4.2 and 4.3 show the breakdown by sector.

The ratio of flows between higher- and lower-skill-intensive activities was roughly five times larger during 1989–91 but approximately 14 times larger during 2005–07. If the stock of manufacturing FDI is used instead of the flow, the same divergence appears: A ratio of 7 to 1 in 1990 and a ratio of 10 to 1 in 2007 (these ratios are probably understated, moreover, since data on FDI stocks typically do not provide accurate information on reinvested earnings and allowances for accelerated depreciation, which are particularly pronounced in the more capital-intensive, higher-skilled FDI operations).

As shown earlier, both more and less sophisticated FDI operations involve noticeable amounts of subcontracting. But even if one supposes that there is more subcontracting in the less sophisticated activities, the flows and stocks of manufacturing FDI are still heavily weighted toward the more skilled industrial sectors.

The ILO and other agencies do not collect precise data on the number of workers by job classification and level of compensation. But the evidence that

---

32. USAID (2008, 2010). See also comments by Heba F. El-Shazli, Regional Program Director, Middle East, Solidarity Center, on the official labor federations in Egypt and Algeria at the "Labor Forum on the Role of the Labor Sector in Promoting US Foreign Assistance Goals: Lessons Learned to Date," Washington, June 30, 2009.

is available supports the general proposition that as skill levels increase, so do wages. Survey data from industrial sectors such as autos and auto equipment, electronics, chemicals, and industrial equipment—in comparison to garments and footwear—show that foreign investors in higher-skilled activities pay their workers two to three times as much for basic production jobs, and perhaps 10 times as much for technical and supervisory positions, in comparison to what is earned by employees in comparable positions in lower-skilled MNC operations (ILO 2007).

To be precise, these data on types of manufacturing FDI operations do not mean that foreign-investor employment in developing-country manufacturing consists, in aggregate numbers, primarily of higher-skilled workers.[33] One GM high-performance engine export plant in Eastern Europe may employ no more than 800 to 900 workers (paying two times the average national wage and benefit package) (Klein 1995). One Intel semiconductor export plant in Costa Rica may employ only 2,900 workers (paying 150 percent of average manufacturing wages) (Larraín, López-Calva, and Rodríguez-Clare 2001). But one Nike athletic footwear export plant in Vietnam, in contrast, may employ more than 10,000 workers (paying slightly more than the minimum wage) (CESAIS 2002). FDI employment in more sophisticated activities is almost certainly more capital-intensive (hence less labor-intensive) than FDI employment in garments and footwear.

But these data on FDI flows and stocks do mean that the principal thrust of the globalization of industry around the world, via FDI in manufacturing, is to magnify the array of opportunities open to medium- and higher-skilled workers in developing countries.

This helps explain apparent anomalies in previous research. When Feenstra and Hanson (1997), for example, investigated FDI flows into Mexico, they discovered that US affiliates did not tend to employ lowest-skilled labor (Mexico's relatively abundant factor) but rather medium-skilled workers, helping to raise the skill premium in Mexico (as well as, incidentally, in the United States; see chapter 8). The potential of manufacturing FDI to move the host country into novel higher-skilled activities introduces a new realm of transformational qualities—generating "self-discovery" (Hausmann and Rodrik 2003), filling "idea gaps" (Romer 1992, 1994), and supporting the concept of "what you export matters. These transformational qualities are investigated in chapter 7.

The thrust of manufacturing FDI toward middle-skilled activities reinforces the observation that the presence of trained and trainable workers constitutes a strong magnet to attract FDI, especially when the goal is to create a middle- to higher-skilled cluster of foreign firms and their suppliers. Mexico's creation of a "little Silicon Valley" around Guadalajara relies on close linkages with the two dozen well-respected vocational institutions and universities

---

33. Data on what the aggregate employment profile of MNC investors in the developing might look like are insufficient even to make reasonable estimates.

Table 4.2   Manufacturing FDI flows to developing countries
(annual averages in millions of dollars)

Sector	1989–91	1999–2000	2005–07
Lower-skilled			
Food, beverages, and tobacco	2,361	2,600	5,079
Textiles, clothing, and leather	240	200	1,318
Wood and wood products	236	300	1,090
Subtotal	2,837	3,100	7,487
Higher-skilled			
Publishing, printing, and reproduction of printed materials	0	200	145
Coke, petroleum products, and nuclear fuels	309	200	4,976
Chemicals and chemical products	2,047	2,500	7,543
Rubber and plastic products	30	200	557
Nonmetallic mineral products	222	500	1,666
Metals and metal products	1,271	1,300	7,124
Machinery and equipment	2,936	3,600	7,593
Electrical and electronic equipment	844	4,700	5,143
Precision instruments	0	100	66
Motor vehicles and other transportation equipment	328	1,900	2,263
Other manufacturing	838	1,500	932
Unspecified secondary	4,419	36,100	66,357
Subtotal	13,244	52,800	104,365

Notes: Each sector contains some lower- and higher-skilled workers. Wage survey data record higher payments for production-level, technical, and supervisory personnel in the higher-skilled sectors than in the lower-skilled sectors.

Sources: UNCTAD (2009, annex tables A.1.4 and A.1.6) for 1989–91 and 2005–07; UNCTAD (2003) for 1999–2000.

around the city, as has the expansion of the "TI industrial complex" (named for Texas Instruments) at Baguio in the Philippines. Chapter 7 shows that Costa Rica's legendary success in attracting Intel hinged on the president of the country directing the Ministry of Education and the director of Vocational Institutes to design a training program jointly with Intel to provide skilled technicians as needed by the semiconductor industry.

Finally, recognition that most manufacturing FDI takes place in middle-skilled activities magnifies the importance of the observation earlier in this chapter that such investors can become a somewhat unexpected ally in the struggle for better treatment of workers. Producers of semiconductors and industrial equipment have shown themselves simply unwilling to tolerate

Table 4.3   Manufacturing FDI stocks in developing countries
(millions of dollars)

Sector	1990	1999	2006	2007
Lower-skilled				
Food, beverages, and tobacco	10,401	21,917	38,884	46,919
Textiles, clothing, and leather	5,422	11,254	11,399	12,039
Wood and wood products	4,943	13,693	14,851	21,587
Subtotal	20,766	46,864	65,134	80,545
Higher-skilled				
Publishing, printing, and reproduction of printed materials	592	606	274	271
Coke, petroleum products, and nuclear fuels	3,179	14,314	22,736	42,915
Chemicals and chemical products	47,696	46,602	95,776	111,736
Rubber and plastic products	1,915	4,186	7,287	12,285
Nonmetallic mineral products	2,966	9,361	14,268	22,091
Metals and metal products	15,473	28,371	31,408	39,049
Machinery and equipment	10,311	14,453	28,003	32,223
Electrical and electronic equipment	18,231	45,355	78,260	121,960
Precision instruments	498	662	2,214	3,665
Motor vehicles and other transportation equipment	8,226	12,595	40,726	51,088
Other manufacturing	3,079	7,608	10,252	11,193
Unspecified secondary	25,095	321,815	322,073	387,796
Subtotal	137,261	505,928	653,277	836,272

Notes: Each sector contains some higher- and lower-skilled workers. Wage survey data record higher payments for production-level, technical, and supervisory personnel in the higher-skilled sectors than in the lower-skilled sectors.

Sources: UNCTAD (2009, annex tables A.1.4 and A.1.6) for 1990, 2006, and 2007; UNCTAD (2003) for 1999.

the strife and reputational threat posed by labor abuse in low-skill garment plants next door, providing "labor institution externalities" for countries that manage to upgrade the mix of investors (Moran 2002).

Implications for Developing-Country Policy: The Real versus False Debate about Using Manufacturing FDI for Development

The evidence gathered in this chapter identifies the conditions under which a host country may be able to use FDI in manufacturing and assembly to improve efficiency, raise wages, and increase living standards in the domestic economy, while creating backward linkages and capturing horizontal and vertical externalities along the way. Chapter 7 will look more intensely at the potential of manufacturing FDI to upgrade and diversify the host export base, bringing more skill-intensive activities into the domestic economy. Accomplishing these goals involves tough tasks and real dilemmas.

The first requirement is to attract an initial round of manufacturing FDI, which evidence shows is not to be taken for granted. Data from a 2009 benchmark survey show that many low-income-country investment promotion agencies simply fail to answer telephone calls and respond to emails from prospective investors (World Bank Group Advisory Services 2009, chapter 3). Even among investment promotion agencies that are more responsive, most are nonetheless unable to provide information to an investor beyond what already appears on the agency website. The websites themselves often have incorrect or incomplete contact information. In addition, the activities of such agencies need to be backed by genuine economic and regulatory reforms—as well as improvements in indicators from the World Bank's Ease of Doing Business Index—to have any possibility of success.

For countries that manage to improve their business climate, the evidence on investment promotion is not all dismal. Some investment promotion agencies do manage to upgrade their performance dramatically (often with outside help), as was the case with those of Ghana, Botswana, Honduras, Sri Lanka, and Romania (World Bank Group Advisory Services 2009). The first cluster of important tasks includes enhancing the basic business climate, and then figuring out how to establish, fund, and staff an investment promotion agency that can be effective in attracting investors to the host economy.

When FDI does take place, the early round of manufacturing investors typically bring low-skilled operations, often building plants in export processing zones that have few connections to the broader economy. The growth of such zones has been impressive, from 845 zones in 93 countries employing 22.5 million workers in 1997, to 3,000 zones in 116 countries employing 43 million workers in 2002, and to 3,500 zones in 130 countries employing 66 million workers in 2006 (UNIDO 2009, table 6-2). Deriving substantial benefits from export processing zones is highly problematic, however, and history provides many examples of failure (Foreign Investment Advisory Service 2008). Here the key issues are how to provide adequate infrastructure, an appropriate exchange rate, and labor market flexibility without opening the door to worker mistreatment and sweatshop working conditions. There are ample topics for debate. Should export processing zones be distinctive industrial parks (as in the Dominican Republic and the Philippines) or should they have a legal status that allows the foreigner to export from wherever is most favorable (as in Mauritius)? How can the favorable business conditions in export processing zones become the spearhead for broader business-friendly reforms, rather than a substitute for such reforms? Will China's new emphasis on the creation of export processing zones in Africa repeat, or avoid, the problems that have plagued such zones elsewhere (see Brautigam, Farole, and Xiaoyang 2010)?

Will the growing array of multinational investors from emerging markets pose similar or quite distinctive policy challenges for processing zone exports from developing-country hosts (Sauvant, McAllister, and Maschek 2010)?

Next, how can a host country fashion a strategy to move from lowest-skilled FDI to middle- and higher-skilled manufacturing FDI? Later pages will show that using FDI to upgrade and diversify the host-country export base constitutes an arduous task indeed. Chapter 7 reveals complex market imperfections and failures showing that a "reform, reform" formula may often not be enough to attract middle-skill manufacturing FDI. Instead, host-developing-country authorities need to put together packages that combine proactive investment promotion, vocational training programs, and infrastructure improvement to coax risk-averse, first-mover investors into novel sectors like auto parts, electronics, and medical devices. FDI strategy at this stage holds the most promise when integrated with multilateral or regional trade liberalization agreements in which there is steady opening of the host economy to imports of goods and services as well as expanded access to developed- and developing-country markets abroad. Countries that have done well here have climbed several notches up in the ranks of investment promotion agencies to create a well-trained and energetic organization that can market the country with highest-level authority to surround new FDI projects with all that is needed to integrate the local affiliate into the worldwide network of the parent investor. The issues here are how to retain high-quality staff in the investment promotion agencies, avoid turf battles with ministries, and put together packages of infrastructure and labor training programs that attract the participation of first-mover MNCs into untried skill-intensive sectors.

With both lower-skilled FDI and medium-to-higher-skilled FDI, the host will want to broaden backward linkages and enhance the indigenous supplier base. The objective is to combine multinational assemblers and first-tier multinational component producers with growing numbers of local supplier firms. This depends on an investment climate in which local firms can obtain ISO 9000 (quality control) certification, and qualify as original equipment manufacturer producers and contract manufacturers to foreigners, while moving toward becoming fully competitive in international markets along the way. Public-private partnerships between multinationals and local secondary and higher educational institutions to train workers, technicians, and managers have proven crucial for many countries, backed by talent scout programs that can assist new local suppliers with financing equipment recommended by the multinationals. The real issues are how to stimulate foreign investors to search out local suppliers, ensure local suppliers have access to finance, and establish vendor development programs that are free from favoritism and special-interest domination.

These are formidable challenges. Under even the best of circumstances, movement upward in harnessing manufacturing FDI for development is slow and frustrating. Senegal or Tanzania would like to attract new foreign investment, create a supplier base, and enjoy the same level of subcontracting as

Madagascar (Shah 2006). Madagascar would like to use FDI to build a base of foreign and indigenous exporters up to the level of Mauritius (Shah et al. 2005). El Salvador would like to emulate the Dominican Republic's record with specialized middle-skill export processing zones (Hausmann and Rodrik 2005). The Dominican Republic would like to replicate Costa Rica's success in moving up the FDI skill ladder, while expanding backward linkages in the domestic economy. So would Morocco (Khan, forthcoming; UNCTAD 2007a). Costa Rica is disappointed that it lags pre–financial crisis Ireland in FDI-led growth (Larraín, López-Calva, and Rodríguez-Clare 2001). Ireland looks to North Carolina as the model for recovering from the financial crisis and reintegrating the domestic economy into international markets going forward.[34] These expressions of frustration are not simply complaints about the grass always being greener somewhere else. They also point host authorities toward improvements in the local business climate, greater reliability of infrastructure, broader availability of finance, and growing access to imports and export markets.

How to answer these questions and respond to these challenges constitutes the real debate about using manufacturing FDI to assist in host development. Yet the conviction that there must be an easier way to harness manufacturing FDI to host development simply by imposing performance requirements on foreign investors to achieve industrial development and diversification does not disappear easily. At the insistence of developing countries, the 2005 Hong Kong World Trade Organization Ministerial agreed that members be allowed to maintain, for seven years, existing measures that deviate from their obligations under the Agreement on Trade-Related Investment Measures (TRIMs)—in particular, that they be allowed to force domestic-content requirements on foreign investors and to introduce new measures that so deviate on a renewable basis, subject to general phasing out by 2020. Contemporary policy advice from some quarters continues to urge the developing countries in this direction (Gallagher 2010, Cosbey 2009, Gallagher and Chudnovsky 2009, Working Group on Development and Environment in the Americas 2008).

Notwithstanding all the evidence presented earlier in this volume that performance requirements are counterproductive to developing-country economic interests, might there be some new data that could support such policy advice?

At the meetings of the UNCTAD Working Group on Investment Issues each year, representatives have an opportunity to direct the secretariat to further study issues of special interest to developing countries. As a consequence, fresh assessments of the use of performance requirements emerge, and reemerge, on a regular basis. This is a fortuitous exercise, precisely because it shows how bereft is the record of successfully promoting host industrial development via mandatory domestic-content requirements.

---

34. Ian O'Hora, Senior Vice President, Ireland Industrial Development Authority, comments at Harvard Business School, June 18, 2008.

The latest survey by UNCTAD (2007b) of the use of the TRIMs agreement reaffirms results that were found earlier. As has been known for some time, export performance requirements and trade-balancing mandates played a pivotal role in encouraging international auto investors to build world-scale-sized engine and final assembly plants in Mexico and Thailand in the late 1970s. These mandates stimulated international companies to turn away from building subscale plants to produce for protected national markets. Export-performance requirements or trade-balancing mandates that simply use trade rents to cross subsidize a few exports from boutique plants, in contrast, have not laid the foundation for an international competitive industry.

Other than this, the evidence in the UNCTAD (2007b) survey from Argentina, Pakistan, the Philippines, Ethiopia, and Vietnam shows once again what a poor policy tool TRIMs have proved to be. It is particularly difficult to find any support for the imposition of domestic-content requirements on foreign investors. The exception might appear to be found in Vietnam's "localization" policy in the motorcycle industry. But this case turns out to be an exception that proves the rule: Honda, Yamaha, and Suzuki found it profitable to help local suppliers produce large batches of technologically simple components for foreign assemblers in the fast-growing domestic motorcycle industry, thereby reaching local-content levels above 40 percent. The local-content requirements in Vietnam's localization policy had been arbitrarily set at 60 percent; the foreign assemblers never reached this legal mandate. In Vietnam's automotive industry, the evidence casts "doubt on the merit of TRIMs in fostering an indigenous automobile industry." In Vietnam's electronics industry, and wood, milk, cane sugar, and vegetable oil processing industries, "the merits of TRIMs may have been overrated" (UNCTAD 2007b, 133, 141–42).

Korea is sometimes invoked as offering a path to the frontier of world industry that excludes contact with and reliance on MNCs. Some developing-country authorities—including contemporary Chinese government officials—argue that the Korean experience represents an "alternative model" that demonstrates infant industries can grow up to become world-class competitors independent of and parallel to foreigners.

But, while this "model" may describe Korean policies toward the steel and shipbuilding industries with reasonable accuracy, it does not fit with the centerpiece of Korean high-tech success—the electronics industry, where the pace of technological change has been more rapid (Hobday 1995). Instead, all of the Korean electronics firms originated as suppliers to the local affiliates of US, European, and Japanese MNCs. Then, when Korean authorities did close the economy to on-the-ground foreign investment in the 1980s, the Korean electronics firms continued to be contract manufacturers and original equipment manufacturer suppliers to the MNCs, which had by then moved offshore. At the end of the 1980s, 50 to 60 percent of color TVs and VCRs were still shipped from Korea via original equipment manufacturer contracts to MNC purchasers such as RCA, Zenith, Philips, Hitachi, Mitsubishi, Panasonic, and Toshiba (Jun and Kim 1990, 22–23).

The three most successful Korean electronics companies—Samsung, Lucky Goldstar, and Hyundai—all learned the basic skills in the industry in the role of supplying inputs to MNCs in the 1960s. More than 25 years later they still found themselves exporting 60 percent of their electronics output via original equipment manufacturer contracts to MNC purchasers. The original equipment manufacturer contracts allowed them to gradually assume more sophisticated design capabilities, and thereby acquire more competitive skills. In short, as Hobday (1995) points out, the contention that Korea followed a different path than Taiwan, Singapore, and Hong Kong overlooks the most important common industrial trajectory shared by these four countries. They all relied on the guidance and discipline imposed by MNCs to climb the ladder from contract manufacturing to original equipment manufacturing, and then—combining imitation with incremental innovation—to original design manufacturing and occasionally to own-brand manufacture as full-blown international competitors.

As for the contention that China may be the historical exception in using joint-venture performance requirements imposed on foreign investors to force transfer of the most advanced technology to indigenous firms, the data show that, despite the recent rush of foreign investors to enter China, the results are no different from other countries and earlier periods. Long (2005) finds that wholly owned or majority-owned affiliates in China are much more likely to receive the most advanced technology available to the parent than 50-50 or domestic-majority-owned joint ventures. Thirty-two percent of the wholly owned foreign affiliates and 40 percent of the majority-foreign-owned affiliates employed technology as advanced as that used by the parent firm, whereas only 23 percent of the 50-50 share ownership affiliates and 6 percent of the majority Chinese-owned affiliates employed technology as advanced as the parent firm. The imposition of joint ownership requirements, in short, hinders foreign affiliates from reaching the technological frontier in China, as elsewhere.

This observation is reinforced when Blonigen and Ma (2010) investigate whether Chinese domestic firms are keeping up or even catching up with foreign multinational investors in the volume, composition, and quality of their exports. As discussed in chapter 8, Blonigen and Ma show that foreign investors' share of exports by product category and foreign unit values relative to Chinese unit values are increasing over time, not decreasing. Of particular note for the debate about forced technology transfer here, their data show that joint-venture partnerships with foreign firms do not lead to greater catching-up in sophistication of output.

Recurrent Chinese requirements that foreign investors in certain sectors take on Chinese partners and limit equity stakes to 50 percent—backed by other "pillar industry" policies that require "indigenization" and give preference to firms doing R&D within China—are clearly intended to underpin the creation of greater numbers of internationally competitive Chinese multinationals. Complaints from the international business community expose repeated instances of forced technology transfer, if not worse. In some cases—

as in Chinese appropriation of technology to manufacture high-speed railroad networks—Chinese companies clearly achieve mastery of cutting-edge processes. But the aggregate evidence presented in chapter 8 suggests that the preoccupation that China is broadly successful in manipulating foreign investment to force technology transfer to Chinese firms—thus turning itself into an economic superpower—may be overblown (Preeg 2008).

As recounted in chapter 8, foreign investment has indeed laid the basis for China to become a mighty exporter of increasingly sophisticated industrial and electronic products. But the data show that this outcome is largely due to the increased skill content of inputs imported from Taiwan, Japan, Europe, and North America that are then assembled by foreign investors within China for export. Leaving aside the duty-free intermediates that make up the final electronic and machinery products, the evidence does not suggest that either the extent or the skill content of China's own processing activities has increased significantly (Dean, Fung, and Wang 2009; Amiti and Freund 2008).

Despite the appearance of a growing number of indigenous Chinese multinationals, the Chinese economy remains largely a "workbench" assembler of sophisticated components designed and produced outside the country. The important question for both research and policy analysis is why such massive amounts of inward FDI have not produced more horizontal or vertical spillovers into the indigenous Chinese economy (Moran, forthcoming).

The desire to use performance requirements as an easy fix for development reappears in contemporary debate about whether developing countries need more "policy space" in trade and investment agreements to allow them to fashion more effective domestic regulations (Drabek 2010, Gallagher 2010, Cosbey 2009, Rodrik 2009). A strong case can be made that developing countries are too constrained today by the treatment of intellectual property rights—especially in the pharmaceutical industry—in US free trade and bilateral investment agreements (Maskus, forthcoming). An equally defensible case can be made that the definition of expropriation and the requirement for compensation in investor-state dispute settlement must be loosened to allow for the exercise of effective environmental regulation that covers foreign as well as domestic firms (Van Harten 2010). But the evidence simply does not support the contention that a weakened TRIMs agreement or more lenient treatment of performance requirements in the model US bilateral investment agreement will serve developing-country interests, in particular least-developed country interests.

5

A First Look at the Impact of FDI in Services

There is considerable evidence to suggest that trade reform in services—that is, more openness—has a positive influence on long-run growth performance (Mattoo, Rathindran, and Subramanian 2006; Hoekman and Francois 2009; Hufbauer, Schott, and Wong 2010, table 3.1). Research directed specifically at FDI in service industries, however, is only beginning to gain prominence. As suggested from the studies cited in this chapter, the size and importance of FDI in services signal that this is a priority area for next-generation research.

New Investigations

Pioneer researchers in this field, Javorcik and Li (2010), examine how the presence of global retail chains affects firms in supplying industries in Romania. They find that the expansion of global retail investors (Metro and REWE from Germany, Carrefour from France, and Cora from Belgium) leads to a significant increase in total factor productivity in supplier industries. Across all of Romania, the number of direct outlets rose from five in 1999 to 25 in 2001 and 86 in 2005, with total selling space growing tenfold over the period from 43,000 to 463,000 square meters. The presence of outlets in a given region increases the total factor productivity of supplier firms by 15.4 percent. A doubling of the number of chains leads to a 10.8 percent increase in total factor productivity. The impact is particularly pronounced among larger supplier firms (more than 25 employees), with a much smaller impact on small enterprises (fewer than five employees). Data from Javorcik and Li suggest that very small Romanian firms may not have the technology and financial support needed to meet the quality or quantity requirements set by the chains.

The favorable results seen in the expanded penetration of foreign investors in the retail services industry of Romania are mirrored in the examination of foreign investment in banking, telecommunications, electric power, railway transport, road transport, and water distribution in the Czech Republic. Arnold, Javorcik, and Mattoo (2010) find that foreign-owned service providers in these sectors exhibit higher labor productivity than their domestic counterparts and have a higher propensity to invest. When foreigners acquire Czech service firms in these sectors, the new foreign-owned firms enjoy an increase in productivity and investment, and expand their market share.

Arnold, Javorcik, and Mattoo next investigate the relationship between the liberalization of service sectors and the productivity of domestic manufacturing firms. Their indices of "liberalization" include the extent to which foreign investors have entered the Czech service industries (the share of the industry's output produced by foreign-owned companies), the progress of privatization (the share of an industry's output produced by private companies), and the level of competition (the market share of the four largest providers). Controlling for other impacts on domestic firm productivity—including import tariffs—the authors find a strong independent correlation between service-sector reform and the productivity of local firms that rely on services as intermediate inputs. They conclude that opening service sectors to foreign providers is one of the key channels through which reform in services affects productivity in manufacturing.

Similarly, Arnold et al. (2010) show that reform in the service sector in India has been a relatively neglected factor during the post-1991 growth of the country's manufacturing sector. Conventional accounts focus on liberalization of trade in goods and the opening up of industrial licensing policies. Alongside these explanations, reform of services (banking, telecommunications, and transport) had independent significant positive effects on the productivity of domestic manufacturing firms, both foreign-owned and indigenous. A one standard deviation increase in the aggregate index of service liberalization resulted in a 6 percent productivity increase for indigenous firms and a 7.5 percent productivity increase for foreign affiliates (Arnold et al. 2010).

Clearly more research on FDI in services should be a high priority. As in other areas, econometric investigation can benefit from detailed case studies like the investigation of the impact of Wal-Mart in the Mexican retail sector, which is considered in the next chapter.

6

Reconsidering the Debate on FDI "Crowding Out" or "Crowding In" Domestic Investment

The analysis thus far of the impact of manufacturing and services FDI on developing-country host economies has emphasized broader opportunities for middle- and higher-skilled jobs and for internationally competitive host-country operations, with the potential for horizontal and vertical spillovers. This perspective tracks the contemporary shift in thinking about the nature of FDI itself as a force to enhance the quality of activities in the host economy by introducing global industry best practices and cutting-edge technology. FDI is thus much more than a mere provider of additional capital or a means of simply raising the level of internal investment.

However, there persists a rather primitive preoccupation with FDI as a mechanism to augment or diminish the level of gross investment in the host economy. Nowhere is this more evident than in the debate about whether foreign investment "crowds in" or "crowds out" domestic investment.

Aggregate Analysis

What should be the expected relationship between inward flows of FDI and levels of host-country investment, and why? What should researchers anticipate that they will find when a given country undertakes "FDI liberalization"? What outcomes should be considered either favorable or unfavorable for host-country development?

Agosin (2008, 8) has argued, "The promise of FDI liberalization is that it will attract new foreign investment and that new FDI will lead to increases in overall investment rates and translate into economic growth. This is termed the 'crowding in' of domestic investment. In the case of Latin America during the period 1971 through 2000, FDI actually 'crowded out' domestic investment—displacing domestic producers. In contrast, East Asia's FDI crowds in domestic investment. These findings partly explain why Latin America has experienced fairly lackluster growth whereas East Asia has been growing rapidly." The raw results from trying to establish a correlation between FDI and levels of domestic investment are quite mixed. Agosin and Mayer (2000) report that in 1970-96, Asian developing countries experienced a neutral or crowding-in effect from FDI and Latin American developing countries experienced neutral or crowding out—as stated by Agosin (2008) above—while African developing countries experienced no pattern at all. Agrawal (2000) finds a complementary relationship between FDI and domestic investment in India, Pakistan, Bangladesh, Sri Lanka, and Nepal during 1965-96. Blonigen and Wang (2005) find that FDI is much less likely to crowd out domestic investment in developing countries than in developed ones. Looking at developing countries alone, Wang (2010) compares the contemporaneous effect of FDI with the lagged effect and finds that the contemporaneous effect is neutral, the lagged effect is positive, and the cumulative impact (the sum of contemporaneous and lagged effects) provides a net addition to the developing-country capital base.

What kinds of dynamics might explain these diverse results?

At one extreme, suggests Wang (2010), might be Intel's decision to build a semiconductor plant in Costa Rica (considered in more detail in chapter 7). There were no other firms in the industry, and over time the Intel plant attracted new input suppliers from the ranks of local businesses, augmenting overall investment opportunities and almost certainly adding to the host-country stock of capital. At the other extreme might be a hypothetical French acquisition of an indigenous pineapple processor in West Africa, after which both capital gains obtained by the previous owners of the acquired company and profits from the new owner are shipped abroad, suggesting a loss of capital for the host economy. Most country experiences, Wang suggests, are likely to be somewhere in between, combining crowding-out *and* crowding-in effects.

Three Prominent Case Studies

Three of the most detailed examinations of the impact of new waves of FDI on the preexisting industry base in the host country can be found in the McKinsey Global Institute (2006) study of liberalization of the Indian auto sector after 1993; the Javorcik, Keller, and Tybout (2008) study of Wal-Mart's entry into Mexico after the passage of the North American Free Trade Agreement (NAFTA); and the Gallagher and Zarsky (2007) study of the growth and shake-out of the "little Silicon Valley" around Guadalajara, Mexico. All three suggest that Schumpeterian cycles of "creative destruction" are going to be more important—for better or for worse—than simple additions to, or subtractions from, the capital base at any given point in time.

Auto Sector Liberalization in India

In India, the McKinsey Global Institute (2006) shows that lowering trade protection and first-time permission for foreign multinationals to set up wholly owned affiliates in the early 1990s sent a shock wave across the host auto industry. In the horizontal direction, competitive pressures drove one of the largest indigenous auto firms (PAL) into bankruptcy while two others (HM and the Maruti-Suzuki joint venture) struggled as their capacity utilization dropped. The host-country capital base in this initial period almost surely contracted. Over the next five years, however, foreign firms moved into India with world-scale-sized plants: Daimler Chrysler ($54 million in 1994), General Motors ($223 million in 1994), Honda ($120 million in 1995), Hyundai ($456 million in 1996), Fiat ($455 million in 1997), and Ford ($433 million in 1999).

In the vertical direction, participants in the previously protected Indian auto parts sector experienced severe competitive pressures, and many, if not most, did not survive (McKinsey does not provide precise data). But initial consolidation among indigenous firms was followed by extraordinary expansion by both Indian and foreign investors. The internal auto parts industry tripled in size, including both local Indian firms and international component suppliers. Toyota set up a "Toyota Village" around its assembly plant to house its suppliers; Hyundai created an industrial park for providers of automotive inputs; Ford brought in Ford AGC (Auto Component Group); and GM induced Delphi to come to India.

Precise figures on the capital base are not available, but it is almost certain that the Indian experience would ultimately qualify as a crowding-in episode for both assemblers and suppliers. Vehicle production more than doubled during the first decade after liberalization (from 2.3 million to 5.3 million vehicles annually). Labor productivity climbed on the order of 20 percent per year, although total employment in the industry declined slightly. From the point of view of Indian consumers, prices dropped at an average rate of 4 to 6 percent per year.

Wal-Mart in Mexico

Unsettling winds of creative destruction are similarly present in the analysis by Javorcik, Keller, and Tybout (2008) of Wal-Mart's penetration of the Mexican market. After passage of NAFTA, the Wal-Mart parent bought a controlling interest in its joint venture with the Mexican partner firm Aurrera in 1997. The new majority-owned affiliate, named Walmex, climbed rapidly over the ensuing decade to take a 46 percent share of the country's consumer goods market (sales of $10.1 billion by 2002), forcing many smaller retailers out of business along the way. In the horizontal direction, the major Mexican supermarkets sought reinforcements via joint ventures with outsiders (Comercial Mexicana with Price-Costco, Gigante with Carrefour and Office Depot), while the indigenous Mexican firm Soriana continued to compete as a standalone Mexican firm.

In the vertical direction, Walmex revolutionized warehousing, distribution, and inventory management, requiring drivers with certified credentials to set up appointments at centralized warehouses and make deliveries on standardized palettes (rentable from Walmex) with contents shrink-wrapped and cushioned by corner protectors. Suppliers were required to reduce prices and provide product innovations on an annual basis. The result was heavy competitive pressure within what had been—as the Mexican participants themselves described the sector—a protected, "clubby," and somewhat corrupt industry (Javorcik, Keller, and Tybout 2008, 1565). Many Mexican suppliers were driven out of the market, but the scale of opportunities for those that remained was much larger: Roughly 25 domestically owned small and medium-sized producers of store-brand (*marca blanca*) detergents and cleaners, for example, proved able to hold their own against national and international competitors.

While aggregate numbers for the capital base in the retail sector (supermarkets and suppliers) are once again not available, it is possible that this period of consolidation would fit into the crowding-out category: Between 1996 and 2004, the number of jobs shrank by 20 percent while the wages of workers in the remaining jobs decreased by 18 percent in real terms (Durand 2007). Total value added in the detergents, surfactants, and cosmetics industries rose by 50 percent over the same period, representing a climb in real value added per worker of nearly 90 percent. The famous Wal-Mart "price squeeze" effect showed up in benefits to consumers—after netting out effects of material-input cost changes, prices came down relatively faster all across the country for detergents, surfactants, and cosmetics than for other chemical products or for manufactured products in general.

The Walmex study does not look at the impact on the incomes of suppliers such as farmers, but a study by Michelson (2010) on Wal-Mart's entry into Nicaragua does. Here the Wal-Mart presence reduced the sales of traditional retailers (a crowding-out effect), but at the same time raised supplier-farmer incomes significantly. Michelson uncovers evidence of three overlapping mechanisms that might drive this positive impact on local farmers: A contract with the supermarket loosens farmers' liquidity constraints, appears to increase farmers' productivity, and spurs farmers' investment. However, problems of endogeneity and selection bias prevent Michelson from nailing the causal relationship down.

Little Silicon Valley around Guadalajara

The liberalization of informatics policy in Mexico after 1985 opened the floodgates not just for IBM but for Hewlett-Packard, Intel, Lucent Technologies, and NEC to build world-class plants near Guadalajara. According to Gallagher and Zarsky (2007), foreign investment in the information technology (IT) sector tripled between 1995 and 1998, leading IT exports to quadruple by 2002. IT exports surpassed the value of Mexico's entire crude oil production when they reached $9.3 billion in 1999. Mexico became the 11th largest exporter of IT products in the world economy, with only Malaysia and China ahead among developing countries. At its height in 2002, FDI in electronics accounted for nearly 6 percent of all Mexican manufacturing output, 27 percent of all exports, and 9 percent of employment (second to the FDI-led auto sector in share of manufacturing output and employment).

Backward linkages during the earlier import-substitution phase of Mexican informatics policy had consisted of indigenous firms supplying largely passive components to meet the domestic-content requirement of the highly protected boutique foreign plants, resulting in a pool of Mexican suppliers that—as Cline (1987) reports—typically had to operate with subscale plants using production techniques and quality control processes well back of the industry frontier. When the major US and Japanese computer firms built their wholly owned export facilities in the 1990s, they simultaneously recruited their international supplier base to join them near Guadalajara, including Jabil Circuit, Sanmina-SCI, Flextronics, Solectron, and NatSteel—an outcome of consternation to Zarsky and Gallagher, since this coincided with a 71 percent decline in the number of indigenous supplier firms between1985 and 1997 (a crowding-out effect).

But is such consternation warranted? When multinational investors bring their own suppliers with them to set up plants nearby, should this be considered destruction of the national supplier base and creation of an "enclave economy," or might this better be characterized as "cluster building" of an internationally competitive industry? Previous evidence from the Indian and Thai auto sectors and from the Thai hard-disk-drive sector showed that the largest and most powerful initial set of backward linkages is formed when international suppliers to the prime multinationals follow the latter into the domestic market.

The bursting of the IT bubble in 2001 hit the Guadalajara electronics complex hard. Lucent, NEC, and Motorola shut down their operations. The international contract manufacturers cut back. By 2003, two major IT firms remained: IBM and Hewlett-Packard, backed by a handful of international component firms like Sanmina-SCI, Plantronics, Jabil Circuit, and Flextronics, and some 12 indigenous Mexican suppliers. Subsequent to this, however, there were signs of resurgence through what Zarsky and Gallagher (2008, 41) characterize as "impressive industrial upgrading." Plantronics' strategy was to rely on superior quality control (1,129 defective units per million in Mexico compared with 11,680 defective units per million in China) to make up for the difference in wages ($2.20 per hour in Mexico versus $0.60 per hour in China).[1] Jabil Circuit concentrated on built-to-order and configure-to-order businesses, training Mexican workers for these more complex production processes, while

---

1. David Luhnow, "Up the Food Chain: As Jobs Move East, Plants in Mexico Retool to Compete," *Wall Street Journal*, March 5, 2004, A-1.

relocating long-production-run commodity products in Asia. As in the liberalization of the auto sector in India and the retail sector in Mexico, measurement of expansion or contraction of the capital base in the IT industry around Guadalajara would have to aggregate substantial movements in both directions, and a measurement of investment levels prior to the international financial crisis of 2008 would almost certainly be lower than the height during previous periods, continuing to dip through 2009 while beginning to recover in 2010.[2]

Conclusions

What do these three cases have to say about FDI and the evolution of the host-country capital base in the industry? At a minimum, they suggest that researchers should look for lagged effects. But the larger message may be more important. All three reinforce the doubt expressed by Lipsey and Sjöholm (2005) as to whether preoccupation with the absolute amount of capital invested should be a central focus of host-country attention. Much more important for host authorities, they argue, is whether FDI raises the productivity of the capital in use, creates more long-term competitive and higher-skilled jobs, and generates backward linkages with spillovers and externalities for the domestic economy.

Even more heretical, however, the dynamics of Schumpeterian creative destruction witnessed here suggest that crowding out is not always "bad" for the host economy, and may sometimes bring long-term benefits, for local firms and workers as well as for local consumers.

2. See the website of El Bosque Industrial Park at www.elbosqueindustrialpark.com (accessed on February 1, 2011).

7

FDI, Host-Country Growth, and Structural Transformation

The preceding chapters have examined how manufacturing and service-sector FDI can improve the efficiency with which factors of production are used in the host economy, raising domestic economic welfare. They have introduced the search for increases in total factor productivity in the horizontal and vertical direction (externalities benefiting rivals and/or suppliers), as well as the possibility of discovering export, labor market, and labor institution externalities. Chapters 2 and 3 investigated the potential benefits from FDI in natural resources and infrastructure.

This chapter takes a more comprehensive look at how all these potential contributions might affect the host developmental track. It begins with the "simple" albeit controversial question of whether FDI augments the host-economy growth rate. It then introduces detailed investigation of the possibility that foreign investment can help bring about structural transformation in the host economy, assisting with "self-discovery" (Hausmann and Rodrik 2003), overcoming "idea gaps" (Romer 1992, 1994), and helping to upgrade and diversify exports (drawing on the "what you export matters" literature). The chapter examines what kinds of market failures impede the recasting of the host production frontier via FDI from taking place naturally.

All in all, the analysis here completes the investigation of the 12 principal channels through which FDI can have an impact on host-country development (box 1.1). The chapter poses a number of critical questions. How large are the potential gains from these different kinds of impacts? What is the magnitude of the potential gains when FDI helps the host expand along lines of comparative advantage? Or when FDI helps the economy do more of what it already does more efficiently? Or when FDI introduces new and more sophisticated economic activities into the host economy, allowing the host to upgrade and diversify exports?

Are these potential gains from FDI adequately measured in contemporary trade-and-investment models? How might these potential gains from FDI be represented and their size estimated in a new generation of trade-and-investment models? What is the relationship between estimates of the potential gains from FDI and the vexing question of whether host authorities should provide subsidies and incentives to attract foreign investment?

This chapter shows how contemporary attempts to add FDI to traditional models of trade liberalization, and estimate the results, are insufficient and incomplete. It suggests improvements in the way the contribution from trade and FDI might be calculated. It points out some obvious—but consistently ignored—weaknesses in how economists typically assess whether host authorities should provide subsidies and incentives to attract FDI.

Fundamentals in the Debate

The observation of the differential impact of manufacturing FDI in protected domestic markets versus internationally open markets, as noted in chapter 4, turns out to be important—indeed crucial—for resolving the debate about whether FDI leads to faster host-country growth. This debate pits path-breaking work by Blonigen and Wang (2005) against equally fundamental critical analysis by Carkovic and Levine (2005).[1]

Blonigen and Wang (2005) argue that the widespread practice of using databases that combine observations about the impact of FDI on developed economies with observations about its impact on developing economies is likely to lead to incorrect results because the motivations for FDI differ (Moran, Graham, and Blomström 2005). When datasets are kept separated, they show that vertical FDI is more likely to account for FDI flows from rich to poor countries, whereas horizontal FDI predominates among developed economies.

Focusing specifically on the relationship between FDI and host-country growth, Blonigen and Wang show that the commingling of data from developed and developing countries is responsible for the apparent discovery of insignificant effects of FDI on per capital growth. They examine the relationship between decade averages of total FDI inflows (from the 1970s and 1980s) and per capita GDP growth in recipient developing countries. When the rich and poor country datasets over this period are not mixed, Blonigen and Wang find that FDI does have a significant positive effect on per capita growth in developing countries, once a threshold in host educational levels has been crossed. Since the authors use aggregate FDI inflows—without differentiating between extractive, infrastructure, manufacturing, and services FDI—their analysis is exposed to the flaw identified earlier in trying to combine effects of widely different varieties of FDI. Indeed, their failure to find a correlation among states

---

1. See Cline (2010) for a review of the literature on the relationship between FDI and developing-country growth. Cline also focuses on Blonigen-Wang versus Carkovic-Levine as a centerpiece of this debate.

with lower education levels may, like the analysis of Borensztein, de Gregorio, and Lee (1998), be due to the fact that extractive industry FDI associated with the "resource curse" dominates in the poorer human resource states.

Carkovic and Levine (2005) come to fundamentally different conclusions. They investigate the FDI-growth relationship during a longer period (35 years, from 1960–95, averaged over five-year intervals). Their research combines panel techniques with cross-country growth regressions in order to avoid weaknesses they find in studies that attempt only the latter. Their analysis indicates that FDI fails to produce a significant independent positive impact on the rate of host-country growth. Their investigation commingles data from developed and developing countries in the manner that Blonigen and Wang criticize, but Carkovic and Levine report that they cannot find a positive effect even with the data groups kept separate.

These two sets of results thus appear to be in conflict. But upon closer examination, argues Melitz (2003), they point in a common direction. Melitz notes that when Carkovic and Levine investigate the relationship between FDI and host-country growth with controls for initial per capita GDP, level of skilled labor, inflation, and size of government, their results actually confirm the Blonigen-Wang finding that above-historical-average FDI flows are significantly correlated with above-historical-average host-country growth rates. This positive relationship disappears only when Carkovic and Levine add controls for trade openness and the availability of host-country credit. The independent effect of FDI on host-country growth is no longer significant only if the degree of trade openness is ignored.

However, as Blonigen and Wang showed—and as Melitz (2003) reminds us—FDI flows to developing countries are largely driven by vertical production relationships that are highly dependent on lower trade barriers. Greater openness to trade is a requirement for FDI aimed at processing imported intermediate inputs and exporting final products. Vertical FDI and trade are necessary complements, and what is striking in Carkovic and Levine's results, Melitz points out, is that joint changes in both trade and FDI flows are significantly correlated with growth. The policy implication is clear: Trade and FDI liberalization must go together to allow FDI to increase host-country growth.

But what about the finding that increases in FDI alone (in the absence of increases in trade) do not necessarily lead to higher developing-country growth rates? Here Melitz draws directly on evidence of the kind presented in these pages that FDI attracted into a protected market distorts the host economy. To the extent that such FDI replaces imports, by definition such FDI restricts trade. Melitz concludes that developing-country policies that use FDI as part of an import-substitution policy break the link between FDI and host-country growth. In this way the findings of Blonigen-Wang and Carkovic-Levine ultimately support and reinforce each other. In fact, Carkovic and Levine provide new underpinning to the FDI-trade-growth relationship, suggests Melitz, by showing that this correlation is not driven by unobserved country characteristics.

Discovery that "What You Export Matters"

Contemporary attempts to link trade performance with higher standards of living as well as higher rates of growth argue that these both come about not simply by producing and exporting more goods and services, but by upgrading and diversifying the production and export base of the country. Certainly the amount of exports matters, but the composition of exports matters more. Schott (2004, table V) finds that the quality of exports (proxied by unit values) is positively correlated with the exporting country's level of development. Hummels and Klenow (2005, 718) offer evidence that richer countries tend to export not just more goods but a wider set of higher-quality goods. Hausmann, Hwang, and Rodrik (2009) show that countries that manage to export higher-productivity goods enjoy both a faster rate of growth and a higher standard of living. Conversely, the inability of a country to export more diverse and sophisticated goods extracts a large growth penalty.

In short, what you export matters.

As for the concern that more openness exposes a domestic economy to greater volatility transmitted through international markets, the evidence shows that countries that diversify exports experience less volatility than those that do not (Haddad, Lim, and Saborowski 2010).

Having said all that, structural transformation in a less-developed economy—that is, the production and export of new and more sophisticated goods and services—does not come about easily or naturally. There are important market failures and impediments inhibiting the process. Identifying the nature of these market constraints, and figuring out an effective way to overcome them, is crucial to climbing up the development ladder. Here FDI can play a central role by generating "self discovery" and transmitting "new ideas."

But what exactly is "self discovery" and how can FDI help bring this about? To illustrate the meaning and importance of this term, Hausmann and Rodrik (2005) investigate what they portray as a paradox: How can a country be a star reformer but not be a star performer? The country they examine is El Salvador. Following the civil war of the 1980s, the country imposed fiscal discipline, liberalized trade and investment, improved business and financial regulations, modernized the tax system, and privatized state-owned energy and telecommunications companies. These reforms led to an initial period of recovery, including one significant new nontraditional industry—export-processing maquila zones (involving both foreign and indigenous investors) that produced low-skill-intensive garments and footwear. Maquila exports rose from small levels in the early 1990s to almost $500 million in 2000 (3.5 percent of GDP). But the economy overall began to stagnate in the late 1990s, not moving beyond levels of per capita income comparable to what El Salvador had achieved in the late 1970s.

Why, Hausmann and Rodrik ask, did economic, institutional, and regulatory reform not result in steadily growing levels of national income? The proximate cause they identify is low investment (a rate of national investment a full 5 percentage points lower during 1996–2000 than in the earlier pre–civil war period, 1974–78). But they find that this cannot be attributed to the high cost or lack of availability of investable funds, nor to a poor investment climate. Rather, the bottleneck is an inability of indigenous and foreign entrepreneurs to identify new nontraditional activities that might be based in El Salvador, a bottleneck all the more severe for the country in this period with the demise of the Multi-Fiber Arrangement governing international trade in textiles.

In the face of great uncertainty about where new profitable activities might be found, markets left to their own devices are not very good at facilitating the kind of structural transformation that a country like El Salvador needs, argue Hausmann and Rodrik. They suggest two kinds of market failures that might be responsible.

First, they conceive of entrepreneurs engaging in "cost discovery" in developing countries with an undiversified production structure. As entrepreneurs explore the cost structure of new activities in the economy, they unwittingly provide positive externalities for other entrepreneurs. For projects that turn out successful, other investors learn that the goods or services involved can be profitably produced and follow the entrepreneurial "first mover" into the new sector. For projects that turn out to be failures, the entrepreneur bears the losses alone. In short, new activities generate valuable information that might—if successful—be imitated by others, leading to an informational externality and appropriation problem.

Second, new activities often require interlocking complementary investments (a coordination externality). Host-country public policy, conclude Hausmann and Rodrik, must be directed toward identifying the binding constraints on international and domestic investment and overcoming the associated market failures. Micro, macro, and institutional reform may be a necessary condition for improving economic performance, but it is not a sufficient condition. The authors' bottom line is that mere "reform" is not enough. Nor is simply "letting markets work."

To address problems of the sort bedeviling Hausmann and Rodrik, a key insight comes from the work of Paul Romer. When a country needs to break out of some given mold and undergo a process of structural transformation, Romer argues that FDI has a special role to play (Romer 1992, 1994).[2] FDI can be the transmission mechanism for what endogenous growth theory calls "ideas" about new and more sophisticated economic activities. After all, notes Romer—who is a founder of endogenous growth theory—developing countries do not have to *produce* ideas in order to *use* ideas. Developed countries have a large stock and a continuous flow of ideas that could yield large increases in standards of living if they were deployed around the world. Multinational investors are the means for such deployment.

---

2. For the earlier beginnings of exogenous growth theory, see Romer (1990).

Romer examines a country, Mauritius, that found itself upon independence in the 1960s (as noted earlier) one of the poorest agriculture-dependent nations in the world, with sugar accounting for 99 percent of exports. In 1960–88, however, the country achieved an average per capita growth rate of nearly 3 percent per year, far above regional counterparts such as Sri Lanka. The explanation, according to Romer, lies in the island's strategy of encouraging foreign investors to set up operations with the status of export processing zones. What did the foreigners bring that was not otherwise available? Oddly enough, Romer points out, foreigners did not represent a significant source of the savings needed to finance export processing zone investment; domestic savings ultimately accounted for a large fraction of that investment. Nor did they provide unique access to technology, strictly speaking, since sewing machines were widely available in Mauritius and other machinery could be openly purchased on international markets. Rather, what the foreign companies had to offer was an integrated package of "ideas" about how to run a modern garment factory, how to ensure quality, how to manage relations with textile importers in developed countries, and how to maneuver through the web of trade quotas.

How valuable was the contribution that the foreign investors brought to the host economy? Here Romer reinforces the insight from Hausmann and Rodrik. The importance of what the foreign investors introduced lay not in simply introducing additional resources, nor in merely increasing the efficiency with which the economy of Mauritius used factors of production. Rather, their package of ideas placed Mauritius along the frontier in a hitherto unknown sector. The result from FDI was not simply to allow Mauritius to do what it already did more productively, but to introduce the country to an entirely new realm of productive activity. In this process, FDI provided a direct channel to the best practices in an international industry.

This observation would be rather commonplace, argues Romer (1994), except that it turns out to be quite at odds with how conventional economic analysis measures the cost of restrictions on trade and investment or the benefits from attracting new flows of such trade and investment. The typical trade liberalization framework, Romer points out, implicitly assumes that the set of activities undertaken within an economy never changes. As a result, the predicted efficiency loss from restrictions on trade and investment is small, on the order of the square of the tariff rate (for trade analysis). Once this assumption is loosened, however, opening the possibility that trade and investment can introduce new activities (new segments of industry, new production techniques, new capital goods, and intermediate inputs) into a given economy, the fraction of national income that is lost when there are restrictions (or gained when new flows are attracted) is likely to be much larger—that is, *seven to 20 times larger* (Romer 1994, 34). The difference in estimating the welfare losses or gains when holding the set of activities constant versus allowing them to vary might surely be an order of magnitude, and more if there are important complementarities among aspects of the new activities. In the case of Mauritius, FDI propelled the country to achieve seventh place among the 15 top-performing exporters of manufactured products over almost three decades (1970–96), below Singapore and Hong Kong but ahead of well-known stars like Thailand, Portugal, and Israel (Radelet 1999, table 3).

The use of "new ideas" and "self discovery" in conceptualizing how FDI might contribute to a host country merits special attention because these concepts emphasize discontinuities in the development process. In other words, above and beyond the impact when foreign investors bring capital, management, and technology that allow the host to do what it already does more efficiently, there is the potential that foreign investors may provide the wherewithal for the host country to undertake entirely new kinds of activities that set the domestic economy on a new growth trajectory.

The characterization of a host economy expanding activities on the extensive margin as opposed to the intensive margin—important though this insight is—does not acknowledge the market failures or address the gaps, jumps, and other nonmarginal changes involved when a country moves from producing garments to producing semiconductors, or from producing garden tools to producing high-performance auto engines (the respective cases of Costa Rica and Slovakia, considered next). Nor does the extensive-margin/intensive-margin dichotomy provide an opportunity to consider the likelihood of externalities associated with one kind of activity as opposed to another. The mere observation that engaging in exports may involve fixed costs has revolutionized traditional trade theory; how much more important might it be to incorporate new technologies, production processes, quality control standards, and marketing strategies?

Are Romer-like magnitudes from foreign investors' "new ideas" on host-country welfare far-fetched when compared to the contemporary real world? If such estimates are not unrealistic—that is, if gains from FDI are indeed large and not all captured by the foreigners—should host authorities offer subsidies to inward FDI in order to secure the benefits?

Magnitude of Benefits from FDI and the Question of Incentives for Foreign Manufacturing Investors: Observations from Costa Rica

Costa Rica provides perhaps the most thoroughly researched exemplar for accomplishing—in slightly more than a decade, 1996–2007—what Hausmann and Rodrik (2003) wish might be possible for El Salvador.

How valuable would it be for El Salvador—or another country on the cusp of trying to move from lower-skilled FDI to more sophisticated higher-skilled FDI—to replicate what Costa Rica has achieved? To bring about structural transformation via FDI, what is the role of subsidies and incentives for foreign investors?

The standard policy prescription to answer these questions is to calculate the value of the externalities FDI brings to the host economy, and provide subsidies to foreign investors equal to that value. However valuable it would be to have such a calculation, this approach is almost entirely useless to developing-country policymakers. The campaign to attract Intel to Costa Rica shows why.

The Hausmann-Rodrik diagnostic offers a subtle but important reformulation of how to proceed—namely, to identify the binding constraints and market failures that hinder FDI from flowing into untried and uncertain activities, and devote resources and effort to undoing the constraints and overcoming the market failures, recognizing all the while that host policymakers will have to make sizable upfront expenditures of resources long before they can discover what the ultimate payoffs will be.

Costa Rica began with the logical first step, what today would qualify as fortifying the country's business climate or basic "doing business" indicators. Building on a well-recognized tradition of democratic stability unique in Central America, Costa Rica used a first round of economic reforms to attract FDI in labor-intensive export operations in the 1980s. But the Costa Rican case illustrates precisely what Hausmann-Rodrik uncovered, that the simple recipe "reform, reform" may not be enough to induce FDI of a kind that can bring about structural transformation.

As labor costs rose and competition in garment and footwear sectors increased, Costa Rican President José Figueres restructured the country's investment promotion agency (Coalición Costarricense de Iniciativas de Desarrollo [CINDE]) in 1992 with a mandate to seek out more advanced international investment, as epitomized by targeting the semiconductor producer Intel (Spar 1998, 2006; Nelson 2009). CINDE discovered that reducing imperfections in information markets means not simply supplying data in a form that facilitates comparison among countries on the part of investors but committing to actions that will allow the host to break into the ranks of credible alternative sites that the parent is willing to investigate.

Attracting FDI into novel activities in novel locations is considerably more arduous than conventional investment-decision models suggest (Pindyck 2009, Dixit and Pindyck 1994). The usual approach focuses exclusively on assessing the net present value of revenue streams from the investment adjusted for the risk of the project. This implicitly assumes total reversibility of making the investment and ignores the value of waiting to gain more information (and thus reduce uncertainty). The more sophisticated contemporary models of the investment decision, as pioneered by Dixit and Pindyck (1994), introduce the irreversibility and positive value to the firm of waiting to gain more information. The existence of some sunk costs that cannot be recouped if the firm regrets having made the investment weighs upon the investment decision, as does the value of waiting, since such delay may allow the firm to learn more about the uncertain operating conditions and reduce the likelihood of such regret. The opportunity to invest can be evaluated as a call option. To invest is to exercise the option and should be done only when the payoff is large enough to offset the value of waiting for more information.[3] As a result, the calculus of whether to move ahead on an investment has to surmount more stringent hurdles than the naïve net-present-value criterion would indicate. Attracting a foreign firm to invest is all the more tricky when the would-be host has no previous entrants in a particular industry and faces competition from other hosts whose business environment might be better known.

Intel's short list for its next semiconductor fabrication plant included Indonesia, Thailand, Brazil, Chile, and Mexico, and for two years Intel headquarters would not even grant CINDE an appointment to make Costa Rica's case for consideration. Here was the hurdle: Intel had to be convinced to make an irreversible investment under uncertainty when the kind of information that would provide genuine comfort to headquarters could only be acquired by "trying out" or, to mix metaphors, "test driving" the facility. In short, the imperfection in FDI information markets replicates George Akerlof's well-known challenge of how to convince a buyer to make a large capital investment (purchase a used car) when that buyer is afraid of being stuck with a lemon (Akerlof 1970).[4]

Following the Hausmann-Rodrik algorithm, to address this challenge requires identifying the binding constraints on the investor and taking concrete steps to eliminate uncertainties. In the case of Intel in Costa Rica, the binding constraints were fear of interruptions in production, slow time to market, and shortages of trained manpower. What was needed were concrete steps to reduce uncertainties, including providing a substation on the public power grid dedicated to the prospective Intel plant, renovating the national airport to facilitate rapid shipments, and directing the Ministry of Education to codesign a vocational training program for IT workers with Intel's human resource executives.[5] By offering this package of expensive commitments to Intel, Costa Rica crossed the threshold onto the semiconductor producer's short list of prospective sites.

---

3. For application of this framework to the FDI decision, the seminal article is Brennan and Schwartz (1985).

4. Here the "quality uncertainty" market imperfection was not one of asymmetric information, strictly speaking, as if CINDE knew that Costa Rica was a feasible site for semiconductor assembly whereas Intel did not. In the absence of much relevant evidence, neither side could estimate very accurately the likelihood that the project would prove to be a success. To a certain extent, a host country can provide "an extended warranty" (promise to fix), as in Akerloff's model, by signing bilateral investment treaties or agreements with multilateral financial guarantors (like the MIGA of the World Bank Group) that specify binding international arbitration of investment disputes. But this provides a buffer only against political risk, not against commercial uncertainties.

5. The Figueres administration argued that the rate charged for electricity at the new substation dedicated to meet Intel's needs was a competitive market rate, although this has been subject to debate in Costa Rica. Intel agreed to contribute to the cost of the substation in return for a special rate.

Only at the very end of the negotiations in 1996 did the words "incentive" or "subsidy" explicitly enter the dialogue, when Intel executives insisted that Costa Rica match the package of tax breaks and locational supports the other alternative host governments had approved, or else lose the deal.[6] Costa Rica acquiesced. Nelson (2009, 58–59) points out that Costa Rica's minister of foreign trade did no more than promise to lobby the legislature for a change in the tax law, and that the new formula did not pass until 1998, well after Intel had made its decision to invest.

Was securing the Intel investment "worth" these host-country expenditures? The building of the Intel plant in Costa Rica generated a moderate amount of backward linkages and explicit externalities. In 2000, a survey of 80 Intel suppliers indicated that 37 percent of service providers and 17 percent of goods providers received direct training from Intel (Larraín, López-Calva, and Rodríguez-Clare 2001). By 2008, Intel had purchased $43 million in goods and services from 300 local suppliers. Perhaps more importantly, however, the attraction of Intel provided an important demonstration effect for investors in electronics and other nontraditional middle-skilled sectors.

Within three years of Intel's arrival, the country tripled its stock of FDI to $1.3 billion. Of 61 multinationals with operations in Costa Rica, 72 percent reported that the Intel decision to build a plant played an important signaling role in their own decision to invest (36 in electronics, 13 in medical devices, three in business services, and nine in other sectors) (Larraín, López-Calva, and Rodríguez-Clare 2001). Western Union chose Costa Rica to be its technical support center; Proctor & Gamble did the same for back-office services. Before the financial crisis hit in 2008, the country's exports of FDI-based goods and services exceeded $5 billion.[7]

Over the course of 2008, Intel joined with these foreign companies and domestic counterparts to reform Costa Rica's Free Trade Zone Law covering worker treatment and environmental practices in line with World Trade Organization standards—evidence of a "labor institution externality" as identified earlier.[8]

So does Costa Rica fit into the economist's paradigm of first calculating the externalities and then subsidizing FDI by a comparable amount?

---

6. Business school case study literature shows that MNC headquarters do not base international investment decisions simply on the relative size of subsidies and tax breaks; rather, they typically instruct field negotiators to identify an array of sites with comparable basic operating conditions for any given prospective FDI project, and then induce incentive competition between them as a "tie breaker."

7. Costa Rican GDP per capita in 1995 was $3,376 and in 2007 it was $10,303 (Economist Intelligence Unit purchasing power parity, $5,905), according to the IMF's World Economic Outlook database (US dollars in current prices), www.imf.org (accessed on February 1, 2011).

8. US Secretary of State's Award for Corporate Excellence 2009, background materials, US Embassy, San José, Costa Rica, June 2009.

The takeaway for developing-country policymakers from Costa Rica is just the reverse. Refusing to make the expenditures until the presence of externalities can be demonstrated, and gauging the level of expenditures as a function of the value of the externalities, simply do not a represent a plausible strategy for host governments that want to use FDI for structural transformation of their economies. Quite the contrary, host authorities have to make costly upfront expenditures to improve the business climate, reform institutions, renovate investment promotion agencies, put expensive infrastructure and vocational training packages in place, and, alas, probably approve tax breaks and locational incentives—and all this while spillovers and externalities are no more than a gleam in the eyes of even the most optimistic public officials. The best those officials may be able to manage is to structure as many expenditures as possible to benefit the economy as a whole, not just the foreign investors.

The Costa Rican case may illustrate one of the more favorable outcomes from attracting new foreign investors, but it is not unique. Leaving aside demonstration effects and the possible generation of externalities, the social returns of investment promotion agency expenditures to marketing a country appear to be on the order of four times the direct costs involved (Morriset and Andrews-Johnson 2003, Wells and Wint 2000). Active investment promotion agencies, according to Harding and Javorcik (2007), increase FDI flows to developing countries. Comparing data from 109 countries with an investment promotion agency and 31 without one, they find that the presence of such an agency is correlated with higher FDI inflows. More specifically, investment promotion agency activities attract more FDI into those sectors explicitly targeted by the agency in the post-targeting period relative to the pre-targeting period and nontargeted sectors. Particularly potent are investment promotion agencies that have some semiautonomous status—either as an autonomous public body, a joint public-private or private entity, or a semi-autonomous agency reporting to a ministry—rather than merely being the subunit of a ministry. However—and this is a key point—investment promotion agency efforts to market the country are effective only if the would-be host has a good product to sell. Harding and Javorcik (2007, table 21) show that there is a strong positive and significant interaction between investment promotion agency outcomes and business climate indicators for government effectiveness, regulatory quality, control of corruption, and voice and accountability.[9]

Targeted efforts by host authorities to correct possible market imperfections and capture economic externalities are not the same, however, as wholesale giveaways, such as tax holidays, submarket rate loans, and across-the-board subsidies. The data reveal wasteful competition in locational incentives among alternative investment sites. This competition now pits developed- and developing-country sites against each other, particularly when, according to Mutti and Grubert (2004) and Mutti (2003), companies are setting up plants

---

9. Somewhat surprisingly, the influence of proxies for political stability and the rule of law are not statistically significant.

to produce internationally traded goods. Along the same lines, Harding and Javorcik (2007, 29–30) find that incentive competition diverts FDI flows among countries within a given geographical region, although they do not find FDI diversion among less-developed-country income groups.

The international economic crisis of 2008–10 appears to have done no more than initiate a pause in the awarding of investment incentives. Among developed countries, ThyssenKrupp's complex to smelt Brazilian iron ore in Mt. Vernon, Alabama received an investment incentive package of $811 million in 2007 (Thomas 2010). Among developing countries, Tata Motors secured a soft loan of about $2 billion in 2008 for a new facility in the state of Gujarat in India with an interest rate of one-tenth of 1 percent for 20 years, a net-present-value subsidy of about $1 billion (Thomas 2010, chapter 7). Toyota's decision in June 2009 to go ahead despite the economic crisis with a new assembly plant in Sorocaba, Brazil with a capacity of 150,000 vehicles per year came after a bidding war that involved alternative sites in China, India, and elsewhere in Brazil.

Under prisoner-dilemma pressures, no single would-be host can "just say no" to foreign MNCs demanding incentives. The appropriate public policy response should be an international agreement to cap and roll back locational incentives, a task all the more daunting because subnational states, provinces, and even municipalities must be brought under regional or multilateral discipline.

Contribution of Trade and FDI Liberalization

Is the case of Costa Rica an extreme outlier? When FDI plays the transformative role that Paul Romer (1992, 1994) celebrates, is the magnitude of the impact much larger, as he argues, than what results from mere trade liberalization?

Practical examples today suggest that Romer-like estimates of the benefits from liberalizing trade and FDI simultaneously are not implausible. As the world recovers from the international financial crisis, how valuable would it be for Romania to harness FDI for development the way Slovakia has done? Looking toward 2014, how appropriate would it be for Morocco to spend to upgrade its FDI base from lower- to higher-skilled export operations, as Costa Rica did? In both cases, business climate reform, vocational training initiatives, and infrastructure improvements would have to accompany the targeting of more sophisticated foreign investors.

The hypothetical comparison of the contribution of FDI to Slovakia today with the potential contribution of FDI to Romania 10 years hence is in fact quite apt, as Romania follows Slovakia as a new entrant into the European Union. Once Slovakia turned away from the populist policies of Vladimír Mečiar in 1998, the two successive administrations of Prime Minister Mikuláš Dzurinda undertook major structural reforms and macroeconomic stabilization. After initial shocks, economic growth climbed steadily to make the country one of the top performers in the European Union, reaching 8 to 9 percent growth per year before the downturn in 2008. FDI provided a main engine of growth, rising from small numbers to a stock of some $20 billion in 2008, and helping Slovakia attain the second-highest foreign investment stock per capita among the new members of the European Union ($8,600 FDI per capita in 2007), with only Estonia achieving more (Vienna Institute for International Economic Studies 2008). Benefiting from a well-educated workforce, foreign firms moved rapidly beyond lower-skilled activities, concentrating in the automotive sector. FDI in auto parts and assembly became the main driver of the Slovak economy, accounting for 35 percent of total industrial production prior to the 2008 economic crisis, with exports of $27 billion in 2007. The principal market players (Volkswagen, PSA Peugeot-Citroen, and Kia) all built world-scale plants that are integrated on both import and export sides with their EU and global supply chains and produced 571,000 units annually going into 2008. When the PSA Peugeot-Citroen and Kia plants reach full capacity as the international economy recovers in 2010 with concurrent expansion of auto parts production, Slovakia is projected to become the largest automotive producer per capita in the world. The per capita GDP in Slovakia rose from $4,155 in 1998 to $13,857 before the crisis hit in 2008.[10]

Romania, meanwhile, joined the European Union on January 1, 2007. Its geographic location and relatively low wage rates ($6,000 per year for skilled workers in comparison to $39,000 in the EU-15) show some of the same promise for FDI-led growth as Slovakia, and aggregate levels of FDI have risen substantially. But most FDI has remained at the low end of the value chain (Italian companies producing footwear and garments), with only the beginnings of automotive, electronics, or other more sophisticated industrial goods and services (Kalotay 2008). There is no question that Romania's economic interests would be served by improving the country's business climate, including undertaking institutional reforms and reducing corruption. If Romania can make credible progress on such reforms, the question is how much should Romanian authorities be willing to spend of their own scarce resources—and how much should international donors be ready to underwrite—to provide specific infrastructure improvements, design vocational training programs, and build industrial parks that can be used to replicate the Slovak experience attracting middle-skilled FDI in manufacturing (and services) as international economic growth recovers in 2011. The answer would appear to be that Romania should spend a very sizable amount.

Similarly, in analytical terms, how valuable would it be for Morocco to use FDI to diversify and upgrade its domestic economic base the way Costa Rica has done? The prospects for broad-based economic and social development in Morocco are favorable across many fronts (Khan, forthcoming). The country has enjoyed political and economic stability, with widely noted prog-

---

10. International Monetary Fund, *World Economic Outlook* database, US dollars in current prices, www.imf.org (accessed on February 1, 2011).

ress in deepening its democratic institutions. The economic fundamentals are strong: The macroeconomic environment has shown considerable stability, with low rates of inflation, a modest buildup of international reserves, and a moderate public-debt-to-GDP ratio (especially external debt). Morocco finds itself in close geographic proximity to the large EU economy with which it has a beneficial market-access agreement. In 2006, the country completed a bilateral free trade agreement with the United States.

Yet Morocco exhibits the same difficulties with structural transformation that Hausmann and Rodrik (2005) uncovered in El Salvador. With promulgation of the economy-opening FDI code in 1995, foreign investment in Morocco began to grow at a fast pace, with by far the largest proportion in garments and footwear (the textile sector remains the country's biggest employer). But FDI exports in Morocco remain largely clustered at the lower-skill end. Its export basket contains fewer skill-intensive goods than comparison countries at a similar income level, such as Egypt, the Philippines, China, India, Indonesia, Thailand, and even El Salvador.

What are the binding constraints on diversifying and upgrading the export base in Morocco? The supply of indigenous skilled workers and managers remains low, secondary and higher education institutions remain weak (enrollment rates are below those of Egypt, Tunisia, and Jordan, and management and organizational skills are not widely taught at universities). The business climate appears incapable of supporting large numbers of small and medium-sized enterprises. Labor market "protections" make it hard for local or foreign firms to adjust the size of the workforce as international conditions change, and create disincentives to the hiring of skilled labor. Tax rates have a high marginal impact on workers and managers as they begin to move up the income scale, inducing many who acquire skills to migrate to Europe rather than staying at home in Morocco. The exchange rate has an anti-export bias.

Oddly enough, the "binding constraints" analytics of the World Bank, IMF, and other multilateral institutions stop with the above, with scant mention of improving efforts at attracting FDI. Morocco's national investment promotion agency (Investir au Maroc) scores in the lowest "very weak" ranking of the World Bank Group Advisory Services' (2009) benchmarking report, well below Jordan and Tunisia, and in the same category as Syria and Yemen. However, the World Bank's economic memorandum for Morocco in 2006 and subsequent progress reports and consultations from 2008-10, as well as reports of IMF visits, fail to address how the country can use FDI and multinational corporate partnerships to upgrade and diversify its industrial base (World Bank 2006; IMF 2008, 2009).[11]

Morocco's basic economic strategy plan—*Le Plan Emergence*—identifies textiles, handicrafts, agribusiness, seafood processing, offshoring and near-

---

11. The binding constraints analysis of Hausmann and Rodrik is frequently used—including by the originators themselves—with great enthusiasm for domestic industrial policies to promote local entrepreneurship, but with little attention to the potential of foreign investment.

shoring, and industrial activities (automotive, aeronautics, and high-performance electronics) as the pathway for future export growth. What Morocco needs is to turn its newly reconstituted investment promotion agency (Agence Marocaine de Développement des Investissements [AMDI]) into a powerful national vehicle for turning industrial parks around Tangiers (TangierMed), Casablanca, and elsewhere into magnets for more sophisticated foreign investors. Labor market reforms can then be combined with new vocational and technical training initiatives to serve all firms entering *Le Pan Emergence* sectors.

The Morocco case also shows that the "what you export matters" argument is not limited to manufacturing FDI. Morocco has for decades been the world's largest exporter of phosphate rock and acid. In the past decade, the national phosphate company (OCP) has begun a dedicated campaign to move the country along the path of dynamic comparative advantage into fertilizers and other agrochemicals (Khan, forthcoming). Productivity gains and economies of scale—plus joint ventures and investments by international agrochemical companies—offer the promise of much higher domestic value added in the phosphate sector along with more extensive spillovers and backward linkages to indigenous firms. The development of Jorf Lasfar, a chemical port hub, stands alongside the Tangiers industrial complex as a center for upgrading and diversifying exports from Morocco.

Rather than dwelling on the Costa Rica story, CzechInvest in the Czech Republic and InvestPenang in Malaysia might be instructive models for Morocco (Khan, forthcoming). CzechInvest shows how a national investment promotion agency such as Morocco's new agency could use a favorable location on the periphery of Europe to attract relatively sophisticated investors for cross-border operations. InvestPenang shows how a regional investment promotion agency like TangierInvest could use FDI to build a world-class industrial and science park export cluster.

How much of their own scarce resources should Moroccan authorities be willing to expend—and how much should international donors be ready to provide—to try to generate the demonstration effect and capture the externalities that the Czech Republic, Malaysia, or Costa Rica have secured through their FDI attraction efforts? Once again, the answer can hardly be of small magnitude.

Trade-and-FDI Modeling: Dynamic Effects, Extensive plus Intensive Margins, New Varieties of Intermediates, and Continuous Real-Time Technology Upgrades

What is needed are models that provide guidance to developing-country authorities about what to realistically expect from simultaneous trade and investment liberalization when accompanied by complementary improvements in the business climate, infrastructure, and access to skilled labor. The most recent models of trade liberalization point in the direction of large gains derived when foreign investment is added to the mix, but trade modelers have not yet attempted the tricky task of explicitly incorporating FDI into the modeling exercise.[12]

The opening of an economy to greater trade provides static welfare gains through increased specialization along the lines of each country's comparative advantage, and greater exploitation of economies of scale, which leads to more efficient use of resources. These lead to a first kind of "dynamic" effect, namely, new opportunity for investment. But the welfare benefit from this deepening of capital has to be carefully circumscribed because the process of adding to the capital stock does not come for free, but requires squeezing additional resources out of the domestic economy (Rodrik 1992). In all, as Rutherford and Tarr (2002) point out (echoing Romer), the results from traditional modeling exercises exhibit what they label "a troubling problem"—trade liberalization appears to increase the welfare of a country by only about .5 to 1 percent of GDP, a rather small outcome.

The second and larger kind of dynamic effect is the contribution that trade liberalization makes to total factor productivity, separate from increases in output per worker due to increased capital per worker. Here the estimates of the long-term elasticity of output per capita with respect to trade relative to GDP (over a 10- to 20-year horizon) vary rather widely from 0.14 to 0.96, as found in a review by Cline (2004, chapter 5) of the eight major studies in this field.[13] But while FDI is occasionally mentioned discursively as a possible contributor to total factor productivity, not one of these eight studies incorporates an FDI channel explicitly into the model or estimates the magnitude of the impact.

At the lower end of the estimations, for example, Choudhri and Kakura (2000) use Krugman's (1986) model of the technology gap to identify three channels through which an increase in trade might facilitate the transfer of technology: Greater exposure to foreign products may make imitation easier; increased contact with foreign agents could lead to more rapid transmission of foreign technological knowledge; and larger imports of foreign components could expand access to foreign technological improvements embodied in such goods and facilitate production of final goods. Choudhri and Kakura find that increased import competition in medium-growth (but not in low- or high-growth) manufacturing sectors enhances overall productivity growth. Here the long-term elasticity of output per capita with respect to trade is 0.14.

At the upper end of the estimations, the World Bank (2002) uses a computable general equilibrium model to project the influence of trade liberalization on productivity growth. The World Bank's estimate of the long-term elasticity of output per capita is 0.80. Its model incorporates a fixed capital

---

12. The author is particularly grateful to comments on this section from Kamal Saggi.

13. See Hufbauer, Schott, and Wong (2010, appendix A) for a more extensive summary of trade growth, GDP growth, and openness ratio comparisons from regression and computable general equilibrium models, albeit still without explicit FDI contributions.

account balance, however, that (as stated in the study itself) "forecloses" FDI as a channel for growth (World Bank 2002, 179).

These studies are nonetheless useful for suggesting that any contribution that FDI might make to total factor productivity would have sizable welfare effects. Cline (2004) points out that the simple average of the estimates in the eight studies is a long-term elasticity of output with respect to trade of 0.5, and suggests that the contribution from an increase in total factor productivity is eight times larger than from induced capital investment (0.4 of the 0.5 long-term elasticity).

Another major conceptual advance comes from the Rutherford and Tarr (2002) exercise cited earlier. Picking up on Romer's analytics, they argue that proper modeling of the impact of trade liberalization requires quantifying the welfare effects of increasing the number and variety of intermediate inputs (p. 249). Following Dixit-Stiglitz (1977), their model allows additional types of inputs to reduce the costs of producing final goods within the economy; that is, a larger variety of intermediate inputs enhances total factor productivity in the economy by allowing producers to select inputs that more closely match their production requirements. This magnifies the welfare gains dramatically: Large numbers of simulations indicate that there is virtually no chance of a welfare gain of less than 3 percent, whereas there is a 7 percent chance of a welfare gain larger than 18 percent. Moreover, when their model is modified to allow the participants in the domestic economy to borrow abroad (even with all loans fully repaid within the model horizon), the gains are roughly tripled. What would their results look like if they incorporated foreign investor intrafirm imports and exports of intermediate inputs, injections of technology for wholly owned domestic plants and for suppliers, and use of capital that only had to be repaid to the extent the entire operational package was successful?

Turning to the newest micro models of trade, when Arkolakis, Costinot, and Rodríguez-Clare (2009) ask how much larger are the gains from trade than previous estimates, their answer is: not much.[14] But when Ramondo and Rodríguez-Clare (2009) include multinational production as well as trade, their results indicate that the gains from "openness" (multinational production plus trade) are five times as large as the gains from trade alone. Even here, however, their concept of multinational production does not include the spread of "ideas" (new technologies, quality control procedures, marketing techniques) through multinational production networks, let alone vertical or horizontal spillovers—a point they acknowledge (Ramondo and Rodríguez-Clare 2009, 30).

The evidence reviewed in earlier pages helps identify how contemporary trade models have to be expanded and reconfigured to capture the benefits

---

14. The micro trade models they review include Anderson and Van Wincoop (2003), Chaney (2008), Eaton, Kortum, and Kramarz (2008), Melitz (2003), and Melitz and Ottaviano (2008).

from trade and FDI liberalization simultaneously. A new generation of models is needed that identify the contribution of FDI

- to total factor productivity in both the horizontal and vertical directions,
- in providing export externalities,
- in providing labor market externalities,
- in upgrading and diversifying exports,
- in expanding the variety of intermediate inputs,
- in building up supplier networks (including externalities in teaching and support), and
- in providing capital that only has to be repaid to the extent the projects are successful.

These models will have to move beyond marginal changes in a given set of activities to nonmarginal changes and novel activities. The result will provide estimates of genuine "dynamic comparative advantage" in which multinational investment allows the host economy to shift from one production frontier to other more advanced production frontiers (Markusen 2002, 2005; Grossman and Helpman 1991, chapter 7; Aghion and Howitt 1998).

Large as these new estimates may become, however, the evidence introduced in this volume shows that even the bigger numbers are likely to understate the benefits that might be derived from linking a host developing economy to multinational supply chains. When an international investor builds a disk drive plant in Malaysia or a high-performance auto engine plant in Mexico as part of the parent's strategy to compete in international markets, the host is not simply placed at the frontier of the international industry in some novel sector but is also linked into an upgrading process that takes place constantly on a real-time basis. A model that accurately depicts the contribution of such FDI to development will have to incorporate each one-year, two-year, and 10-year improvement in disk drive or auto engine technological changes, production process improvements, and quality control enhancements (Grossman and Helpman, appendix to chapter 4).

8

Globalization of Industry via FDI: Consequences for Developed-Country Home Economies

What are the consequences of outward FDI for the developed-country home economy? FDI in the extractive sector increases the supply and lowers the price—ceteris paribus—of imported oil, natural gas, and minerals for the home country of the outward investors. But if there is little transparency about revenue streams and weak accountability on the part of host authorities, FDI in the extractive sector may undermine—or even ruin, at least in the medium term and quite probably over the longer term—host-country prospects for broad economic and social development. This has economic, foreign policy, and national security consequences for home countries, in particular (but not limited to) the United States.

FDI in infrastructure improves the functioning of power, telecommunications, water, sewage, and transport systems around the world, which is not likely to detract in any way from home-country welfare unless, as a condition of the foreign investment, host authorities are made to bear all foreign exchange risk—and all supply-and-demand risk via take-or-pay contracts—within a multinational dispute settlement regime that considers inability to pay as unwillingness to pay. This also has economic, foreign policy, and national security consequences for home countries, once again in particular (but not limited to) the United States.

But what about FDI in manufacturing?

There has been growing concern across developed countries about the consequences for the home economy as multinational corporations (MNCs) spread technology and reposition production around the globe. Nowhere has this been more apparent that in the United States, where President Obama has pledged that his administration will "end tax breaks for corporations that ship jobs overseas."[1] Nobel laureate Paul Samuelson's 2004 critique of whether trade liberalization always confers net positive benefits to all partners and Lawrence Summers' suggestion in 2008 that the economic success of developing countries (particularly China) might be damaging to US interests (and particularly the interests of American workers) have added sophisticated new dimensions to the debate.[2]

"Historically, US workers used to have kind of a de facto monopoly access to the US's superlative capital and know-how (scientific, engineering and managerial). All of us Yankees, so to speak, were born with silver spoons in our mouths," declares Samuelson (2004). Are US multinationals, as well as multinationals of other nations, taking those "silver spoons" and delivering them to "non-Yankees" in a manner that leaves workers, firms, and communities at home less well off? Does the globalization of industry via FDI come at the expense of home-country economic interests, or does it complement and strengthen the home economy?

Rekindling an Old Debate about US MNCs and US Economic Interests

Preoccupation with outward manufacturing investment—be it about "runaway plants" or a "hollowing out" of the industrial base—have long been a subject of intense controversy in the United States and abroad. The questions of Paul Samuelson and Lawrence Summers about the role of multinationals in shifting technology across borders in ways that might harm workers and communities in the home economy require fresh examination in terms of how the globalization of industry via FDI takes place.

Economic history, asserts Samuelson (2004), is replete with examples where a nation or a region suffers permanent measurable loss in per capita real income from the "adverse headwind" generated from low-wage competitors and technical imitators. A prime example, cites Samuelson, was the movement of textile, shoe, and other manufacturers from New England to the low-wage South early in the last century.

The Samuelson concern that the United States might start to suffer lower permanent per capita real income as a result of the globalization of trade and investment rests on two formal assessments of how the outcome might be detrimental: first, an assessment of whether the United States continues to enjoy positive gains from trade; and second, an assessment of whether the United States has begun to suffer unfavorable terms of trade (Edwards and Lawrence, forthcoming). These assessments require examining whether

---

1. President Barack Obama, State of the Union Address, January 27, 2010, available at www.whitehouse.gov (accessed on February 1, 2011).

2. Samuelson (2004); Lawrence Summers, "America Needs to Make a New Case for Trade," *Financial Times*, April 27, 2008; and "A Strategy to Promote Healthy Globalization," *Financial Times*, May 4, 2008.

consumers and producers continue to reap benefits from specialization, division of labor, and economies of scale as globalization proceeds; and investigating the relative prices of US exports versus US imports along the way (does the evidence show the United States having to generate higher levels of exports to pay for a given level of imports?).

These formal models draw on traditional trade theory in which the location of production is determined by relative costs that are a function of the natural endowments of countries around the world. Exogenous changes in technology add a dynamic dimension to how the global structure of production might evolve. But, as noted in chapter 7, traditional trade theory does not adequately encompass the phenomenon of multinational corporate investment: International companies operate according to a centralized strategy in imperfectly competitive markets, creating technology (including management, quality control, and marketing procedures) that headquarters can then deploy at home or abroad with some margin of choice about where to locate specific activities and how to integrate the stages of production.

Standing apart from the formal assessment of trade effects—and the tests of whether the United States continues to enjoy gains from trade and favorable terms of trade—is a separate and distinctive concern about the consequences of the current behavior of MNCs. Preoccupation with multinational corporate transfer of technology and placement of production pervades the Samuelson critique and reappears in the Summers commentary. The concerns take three forms: (1) that US-based MNCs may follow a strategy that leads them to abandon the home economy, leaving workers and communities to cope on their own with few appealing alternatives after the multinationals have left; (2) worse, that US-based MNCs may not just abandon home sites but drain off capital, substitute production abroad for exports, and "hollow out" the domestic economy in a zero-sum process that damages those left behind; and (3) worst, that US-based MNCs may deploy a rent-gathering apparatus that switches from sharing supranormal profits and externalities with US workers and communities to extracting rents from the United States.

These concerns cannot be ignored. The globalization of economic activities is no longer simply a function of impersonally evolving trade flows. MNCs are a major force in creating technology, establishing the international structure of production, determining the location of high-valued jobs and activities, and dictating the consequent pattern of trade. Indeed, for the United States, some 38 percent of all goods exports and 26 percent all service exports are intrafirm transactions within the confines of MNCs themselves.

But do multinational investors deploy their operations according to their own self-interested and profit-driven strategies in ways that are disadvantageous or harmful to the economic interests of the home country, which for Samuelson/Summers means the United States? Each of the three concerns above contains a hypothetical outcome that can be compared with contemporary evidence from the United States and other home countries.

Outward FDI and Abandonment of the Home Economy?

The first proposition that underlies the "new critique" of the globalization of industry is that developed-country MNCs—in the Samuelson/Summers analysis, US-based MNCs—take self-interested actions without regard to their country of origin that lead them to abandon their former sites, leaving workers and communities in the home economy bereft of productive activities and well-paying alternatives.

This proposition has its origin in an analogy. When confronted with the opportunity to use cheap Southern labor, observes Samuelson, the owners of textile, shoe, and other manufacturing firms in New England left early in the 20th century to set up alternative facilities in South Carolina or Alabama. Lowell, Massachusetts, and other New England locations were left to struggle with finding some other industry; of the few options they had, almost all involved lower-paying and less desirable jobs than before the textile and shoe companies departed. It took many decades for appealing alternatives to emerge—IT companies along Route 128, biotech firms along the Charles River, financial management and insurance firms in Boston and Hartford—all of which owed nothing to the original textile, shoe, and other manufacturing firms that had departed.

How closely does this analogy—textiles, shoes, and manufacturers abandoning New England and moving to the low-wage South early in the last century—match evidence about outward manufacturing FDI during the contemporary period?

To be sure, the globalization of industry via trade and investment does include US companies relocating operations abroad, as examined next. It includes dislocating workers and forcing communities to search for new industries. However, contrary to the "abandonment" portrait, the globalization of economic activities via the actions of US multinationals features an ongoing presence in the home economy on the part of the parent corporations that undermines the essence of the analogy.

A US multinational is defined as a business enterprise headquartered in the United States that has a 10 percent or more ownership stake in at least one affiliate in another country (Barefoot and Mataloni 2009).[3] In absolute numbers, the ranks of US MNCs are rather small, including less than 1 percent of all US firms (2,278 US MNCs with 25,796 foreign affiliates in 2007). But US MNCs continue to have a disproportionately large economic impact on the US home economy: They generate 19 percent of total US employment and 24 percent of total US output. Also important to note, however, is that their operations remain overwhelmingly concentrated in the home economy. In 2007 (latest data available), US MNCs generated total value added of $3.706 trillion, with more than 70 percent located in the United States, and 30 percent abroad. They employed 22 million workers in the United States, and 10 million abroad.

---

3. The latest Bureau of Economic Analysis (BEA) data are from 2007.

Table 8.1 Employment in US multinational corporations, 2000–2007
(thousands of employees)

Year	Total	United States	Non-US
2000	32,057	23,885	8,171
2001	30,929	22,735	8,194
2002	30,373	22,118	8,255
2003	29,347	21,105	8,242
2004	29,843	21,177	8,667
2005	30,573	21,472	9,101
2006	31,245	21,748	9,497
2007	33,741	22,003	10,017

Notes: *Business Week* cites Bureau of Economic Analysis data to the effect that from 2000–05, US multinationals cut more than 2 million jobs at home. But this is true only in the sense that by 2006, US multinationals' domestic employment rolls had not yet returned to the all-time high reached in 2000. Michael Mandel, "Multinationals: Are They Good for America?" *Business Week*, March 10, 2008, 41–46.

Over time, US MNCs have increased employment and output in an absolute sense, with a slightly rising share of total US output and a slightly declining share of total US employment. In 1982 (the first year for which annual MNC employment data were collected), US MNCs employed 18.7 million American workers (25 percent of the total civilian workforce); in 2007, they employed 22 million workers (19 percent of the total civilian workforce). In 1994 (the first year for which annual output data were collected), the value of domestic output by US MNCs was $1.3 trillion or 24 percent of total private US output; in 2007, the value of domestic output was $2.6 trillion, also 24 percent of total private US output. In cyclical terms, US MNCs' output and employment both peaked in 2000, started to decline, then saw output rebound in 2003 and employment in 2004–06.

Between 1984 and 2004, US MNCs expanded employment at their foreign affiliates by 3.8 million and at their home operations by 3.2 million. From 1990 to 2000, this ratio was particularly beneficial for the United States, as US MNCs created almost two jobs at home for each job created abroad. Between 2000 and 2003, however, US MNCs continued to expand employment abroad but decreased the number of jobs at home (during the downturn in the US business cycle after the dotcom bubble burst). Then, between 2004 and 2007, US MNCs returned to expanding payrolls both at home and abroad, adding 826,000 jobs in the United States and 1.4 million jobs overseas (table 8.1) (Barefoot and Mataloni 2009).

Under the umbrella of complementary job creation, it is logical to expect that US multinationals will create jobs in line with relative growth rates in the countries where they have operations, with the United States sometimes growing more slowly than various other markets. The types of operations in the home country are likely to be more capital-intensive, R&D-intensive, and skill-intensive—and hence fewer in number—than more labor-intensive production and assembly activities in the developing world. Borga and Lipsey (2009) show that US parent firms are more capital-intensive than their foreign affiliates, and that affiliates located in developed countries are more capital-intensive than those located in developing countries. An assessment of the strength of the contribution home-country multinationals make to the home-country economy should not depend therefore on whether the number of jobs created or the rate of growth of job creation by US MNCs at home and abroad happen to be equal or not.

The principal contribution that US MNCs should be expected to make to the home economy is to reallocate economic activity in ways that raise US living standards. Here, benefits emerge in the form of the new, better, cheaper, and more reliable goods and services that US MNCs produce at home and import from abroad, and from the competition they generate in the economy more broadly. But another key measurement is the specific kinds of jobs and activities that these multinationals generate at home. The plants of US MNCs are the most productive plants in the United States in terms of both total factor productivity and labor productivity. They are also the most technology-intensive and pay the highest wages. US multinational parents accounted for 29 percent of all US private-sector investment in 2007 and 74 percent of all US private-sector R&D. The plants of US MNCs show labor productivity 16.6 percent higher than large domestic firms, and 44.6 percent higher than small US firms (Doms and Jensen 1998; Bernard, Jensen, and Schott 2009). Their total factor productivity is 4.2 percent higher than that of large domestic firms and 11.1 percent higher than that of small domestic firms. The plants of US MNCs use more technologies from the US Census Bureau's Manufacturing Technology Survey's list of 17 advanced technologies than do large or small domestic firms.[4] Finally, US MNCs pay wages that are 7 to 15 percent higher than wages at comparable domestic plants (Richardson 2005a, 113).

In addition to the high productivity, value added, and wages directly associated with US multinational parents in the United States, these multinational firms also purchase large amounts of goods and services from US suppliers and account for a sizable amount of US exports. In 2007, US MNC purchases from US home-country firms amounted to $6 trillion, some 89 percent of all their purchases. In the same year, US MNCs exported goods from the United States valued at $559 billion, nearly half (49 percent) of all US goods exports in 2007 and more than half (51 percent) in 2006. Of these, $215 billion (38 percent) were shipped directly from US plants to sister affiliates abroad.

---

4. US Census Bureau, www.census.gov (accessed February 1, 2011).

In short, far from supporting the Samuelson "abandonment" hypothesis, US MNCs continue to make a large and growing contribution to the home economy even as they move outward from the United States. The home-country focus of MNCs is not limited to US corporations. Rugman (2005, 3) finds that for the 500 largest MNCs from the United States, Europe, and Asia, 320 average 80 percent of their sales in their own home region of the triad.[5]

The globalization of industry brings inward investment into the home economy at the same time outward investment is taking place, a phenom-enon that is not present in the model in which manufacturers abandoned New England. In 2006 (the latest data available), US affiliates of foreign multi-nationals owned $5.5 trillion in assets, produced $515 billion of goods and services in the United States, and accounted for 6.1 percent of total US private output, up from 3.8 percent in 1988 (Anderson 2008). US affiliates of foreign multinationals employed 5.3 million workers, equal to 4.6 percent of the US workforce, up from 3.5 percent in 1988. They accounted for a disproportion-ately large share of US exports (19 percent), physical capital expenditures (10 percent), and R&D expenditures (14 percent) (Bernard, Jensen, and Schott 2005). So the globalization of industry involves vast flows of technology, production, and job creation *into* the United States at the same time that outflows to offshore locations take place.

In terms of raising US living standards by improving access to quality jobs, foreign-owned plants in the United States are more capital-intensive, more productive, use a higher proportion of nonproduction workers, and pay higher wages than the average US-owned plant (Doms and Jensen 1998). Controlling for industry, size, age, and state (location), foreign-owned plants in the United States still show superior operating characteristics compared to domestically owned plants. The performance of foreign affiliates is second only to the performance of the US plants of US MNCs multinationals. Foreign-owned plants in the United States pay wages 2.5 to 7 percent higher than do compa-rable domestic plants (Richardson 2005a). Figlio and Blonigen (2000) find that foreign-investor firms raise local real wages more than domestic firms do.

Similarly, foreign investors in the United States spend more on R&D in the country than other similar firms, only slightly behind the rate of R&D expenditures of US parents of US MNCs (the most R&D-intensive of all firms in the United States) (Graham and Marchick 2006, chapter 3).[6] In some subsec-tors—such as computer manufacturing and communications equipment (which includes telecommunications equipment)—the affiliates of foreign firms spend a greater portion of value added on R&D than do US parents of multinationals in the same subsector. Whether because of these R&D expendi-tures or because of imports of external R&D, it turns out that these inflows of

---

5. Rugman reports that these 500 largest MNCs account for more than 90 percent of the world's stock of FDI, but he does not provide more detail on their stocks or flows.

6. The comparison is for majority-owned affiliates of foreign investors in the United States.

foreign investment into the United States constitute an important channel for technology spillovers to domestic companies, especially in high-tech sectors. Keller and Yeaple (2009) calculate that between 8 and 19 percent of all productivity growth among US firms between 1987 and 1996 was derived from the growing presence of non-US investors in the US economy. The disproportionately large positive impact on the US high-tech industry includes such sectors as chemicals, computers and office equipment, electronic components, scientific instruments, and medical instruments.

One illustration of the contribution of foreign affiliates to the US economy (along with the potential for technology spillovers) is that a key to the success of General Motors' potential turnaround is the Chevrolet plug-in hybrid Volt, and one of the keys to the success of the Volt, in turn, is the lithium-ion polymer battery. GM awarded the contract for the battery to the winner of GM's 2009 Supplier Recognition Award, LC Chemicals of Korea. LC Chemicals ships the battery cells from Korea to GM's Global Battery Systems Lab outside Detroit, where battery packs are assembled and tested. GM conducts joint R&D with LC Chemicals in both Korea and the United States, and has joined with the University of Michigan to create a battery-specific engineering curriculum and battery lab. In April 2010, GM began an $8 million expansion of the Global Battery Systems Lab in Warren, Michigan, nearly doubling the size of what is already the largest automotive battery lab in the United States. In July 2010, President Obama drove the Volt with the lithium-ion polymer battery at the Detroit-Hamtramck assembly plant.

Turning to the home-country export base, a majority of US goods exports are generated within multinational corporate networks: In 2006 (latest data available for combined analysis), the export of goods by US parent companies, by US affiliates of foreign companies, and by unaffiliated companies in the United States via purchases from US-owned affiliates abroad amounted to $727 billion, 70 percent of all US goods exports. Of this total, US multinational parents exported $532 billion (51 percent of total US exports in 2006), while US affiliates of foreign multinationals exported $195 billion (19 percent of total US exports). Almost half of these exports consisted of intrafirm trade within multinational networks; that is, goods exports from US parent companies to their foreign affiliates and US-based affiliates to their foreign parent companies constitute approximately 35 percent of all US goods exports.

Looking at US trade in goods overall (imports as well as exports), Bernard, Jensen, and Schott (2009) find that the "most globally engaged" firms in the United States—US-headquartered multinationals and US affiliates of foreign multinationals—account for approximately 80 percent of all US trade flows into and out of the country, and employ 18 percent of the entire US civilian workforce. These most globally engaged firms have a higher probability of survival than other firms, and if they engage in some form of related-party transfers with affiliates outside the United States they have even lower failure rates than firms that trade at arm's length. Despite fears that the import behavior of these most globally engaged firms might swamp domestic production plus exports—and thereby destroy US jobs on a net basis—new entrants that joined this grouping between 1993 and 2000 experienced employment growth of close to 100 percent.

Multinationals also play a large and growing role in the export of services. Service exports from US parents to their foreign affiliates and from US affiliates to their foreign parent companies totaled $103 billion in 2006, representing 26 percent of all US private service exports (and accounting for almost one-third of all growth in US private service exports) over the previous decade (Jensen and Kletzer 2008). The United States shows a strong comparative advantage in the export of high-wage, high-skill services; US MNCs and US affiliates of foreign MNCs are likely to remain an important channel for exploiting this comparative advantage (Jensen, 2011 forthcoming).

Thus, in the contemporary period, the globalization of industry leaves the home economy with a high-performance, high-productivity, and high value-added core—exceptionally R&D-intensive and dynamic—that exploits the evolving comparative advantages in the country. To be sure, these industries may be located in sites different from eras gone by—in Raleigh-Durham, Austin, Palo Alto, and Seattle rather than Detroit, Gary, and Toledo—and the costs of churning and displacement are no less real in the contemporary period than they were a century ago. But the focus of public concern and public policy should be on dealing with these genuine burdens of dislocation without being burdened by a New England analogy that is inaccurate, misleading, and outdated.

Outward FDI, Runaway Plants, Lost Capital?

The second testable proposition in the Samuelson/Summers critique of globalization envisions a fate worse than abandonment, namely that outward investment by home-based MNCs (US-based MNCs) substitutes external production for exports, drains off capital, and "hollows out" the home economy in a zero-sum process that damages those left behind.

This proposition contains two distinct assertions: first, that outward investment by US-based MNCs replaces exports that might be sent from multinational plants at home with external production; and second, that outward investment by US-based MNCs siphons away capital, replacing investment that might be made at home. The common theme is that outward investment by US-based MNCs is a win-lose phenomenon that harms the economy where the FDI originates.

The concern that US MNCs set up production abroad to substitute for exports that otherwise could be made from the home economy has a long and venerable history, beginning with the Burke-Hartke legislation (sponsored by the AFL-CIO) in the 1970s and culminating—at least rhetorically—with Ross Perot's "great sucking sound" characterization of the North American Free Trade Agreement (NAFTA).

But does the evidence from the United States (and other developed countries) show that MNC production abroad actually substitutes for exports that otherwise could be produced in the home economy?

To determine the answer, one must look closely at the counterfactual—what would happen in the home economy if the MNC did *not* make the outward investment? This is crucial both to evaluate the substitution hypothesis and to appraise the oft-suggested policy proposal to make it more expensive and difficult for home-country MNCs to build plants abroad.

A pioneer in the testing of the substitution hypothesis was Thomas Horst (Bergsten, Horst, and Moran 1978, chapter 6). Subsequent analysis, summarized next, has grown increasingly sophisticated. But reviewing the Horst approach is particularly useful because his method shows clearly what the counterfactual would be if the outward investments undertaken by MNCs did not take place.

To conduct a fair test, it is not enough to acknowledge simply that MNCs invest more at home and export more from home plants than the typical or average home-country firm. As Horst noted, MNCs are not "typical" or "average"—they are larger, do more R&D, engage in more advertising, and have other characteristics that set them apart. This is a methodological insight that continues to be neglected in contemporary analysis. Both the McKinsey Global Institute (2010) and Slaughter (2010), for example, report that US MNCs make a disproportionate contribution to the US economy in comparison to other firms along a number of metrics.[7] But US MNCs should be expected to perform better than other companies because they are different from other companies and found in nonaverage sectors. Perhaps they should be expected to do even more investment at home or engage in even more exporting from home plants.

To discover whether US MNCs substitute production abroad for exports from the US home economy, what is needed is to compare the export behavior of "likes with likes" while varying only the extent of outward investment. In other words, one must compare the export behavior of large firms that undertake outward investment with those that do not, and compare the export behavior of firms with high R&D or extensive advertising that undertake outward investment with those that do not.

Table 8.2, which is constructed from Horst's arrangement of the data, does even better than this. The table compares the export behavior (exports as a percentage of domestic shipments) of likes with likes by measuring the exports of group types of firms: those firms that essentially stay at home in the United States (first column), that have begun to engage in just a bit of outward investment (second column), that have expanded their outward investment substantially (third column), and those that have thoroughly globalized their production (fourth column).

---

7. McKinsey and Slaughter examine the same latest BEA data as does this volume.

Table 8.2 Export performance of particular types of industries by foreign investment levels (exports as percent of domestic shipments)

Industry	Low or none	Low to middle	Middle to high	High
High technology	2.3	7.8	9.7	7.6
Low technology	1.3	3.0	2.5	3.5
High level of advertising	1.0	2.8	2.4	4.6
Low level of advertising	1.4	4.8	7.5	7.7
High level of unionization	1.9	5.5	4.4	3.8
Low level of unionization	1.3	3.2	7.0	7.8

Notes: These figures are introduced to illustrate the methodology and the counterfactual. More recent data are cited in the text.

Source: Adapted from Bergsten, Horst, and Moran (1978, table 3.3).

This set of like-with-like comparisons demonstrates that US firms that undertake outward investment actually achieve higher levels of exports as a percentage of domestic shipments than firms that stay at home in the United States, and that this superior export performance—and demonstration of superior competitiveness in the face of global pressures—increases as they globalize their operations. The percentage of domestic shipments that leaves the home market destined for external markets rises as the MNC engages in larger amounts of international investment (the exact relationship in the fourth column is somewhat murky in this set of comparisons, but subsequent statistical analyses below show a persistent positive correlation). This demonstrates that outward investment by US MNCs enhances the competitiveness of their home-country operations, measured in comparison to similar kinds of firms that do not undertake, or do not undertake as much, outward investment. Outward investment is in fact a *complement* to greater production at home, not a *substitute* for it.

Most important, this set of like-with-like comparisons provides a clear picture of the counterfactual—what would the situation in the home market look like if MNCs did not engage in outward investment at all, or did not engage in outward investment so extensively? The performance of firms shown in columns 2, 3, and 4 of table 8.2 would resemble the performance of their look-alike peers in column 1. This shows that the stay-at-home option does not strengthen the home industrial base or lead to more exports from home. On the contrary, the stay-at-home option leads to a less competitive industrial base in the United States and fewer exports from the United States. If US MNCs were prevented from moving abroad, or if obstacles and disincentives were put in their path, the United States would be weaker and the labor market less filled with export-related jobs; that is, the good job/bad job ratio in the US labor market would be *worse*, not better.

Somewhat surprisingly, this positive relationship between outward investment and exports holds for US low-tech (low-R&D) industries just as for high-tech industries, and for heavily unionized industries just as for nonunionized ones. That is, outward investment creates more export-related jobs in the US economy for low-tech workers and unionized workers, just as it does for US workers overall, in comparison to US firms with similar workers that do not engage in outward investment.

Subsequent studies, relying on more sophisticated statistical techniques, have consistently demonstrated the complementarity between MNC outward investment and exports from a more competitive industrial base at home. Lipsey and Weiss (1981) found a positive correlation (after controlling for firm characteristics) between outward investment and exports for all levels of investment. They discovered moreover that the level of manufacturing activity in a given country by US firms was positively associated with US exports from the same industries to that country and negatively associated with exports by producers of rival nationalities. Along the same lines, they noted that the presence of firms from foreign countries in a given country was negatively related to US exports and positively related to foreign countries' exports. In a somewhat mercantilist vein, they concluded that direct investment by US MNCs in any one country tended to increase US exports and market shares in that country and reduce those of producers of rival nationalities, and that non-US MNCs' operations tended to raise their countries' exports and market shares, and reduce those of US firms. A smaller US MNC presence outside the United States would reduce MNC exports to, and market share in, other countries. Lipsey and Weiss' counterfactual outcome was the same as Horst's: Making home-country MNCs cut back on outward investment hurts the access of home-country workers to export-related jobs.

A later study by Lipsey and Weiss (1984) showed that the complementarity between outward investment and domestic exports was strong not only for intermediate goods sent abroad for further processing but also for exports of finished products shipped by the parent US firms. This study found that a higher proportion of foreign operations by US firms was associated with higher average compensation at home.

Nor is this complementarity an idiosyncratic finding about US MNCs. As Swedish MNCs were subjected to criticisms from domestic labor, Blomström, Lipsey, and Kulchyck (1988) found a similar complementary relationship between outward investment by Swedish multinationals and home-country exports and employment. Outward investment by Japanese MNCs shows the same kinds of effects at home (Lipsey, Ramsterrer, and Blomström 2000). The complementarity is almost as great for manufacturing as for distribution— Head and Ries (2001) calculate that a 10 percent rise in FDI abroad in manufacturing and distribution would increase exports from home plants in Japan by 1.2 and 1.5 percent, respectively.

More recent studies confirm that the relationship between outward investment and home-country exports is predominantly complementary (Markusen and Maskus 2003). When labor substitution does show up in the data, it is almost entirely limited to competition between alternative low-wage locations in the developing world, rather than vertically between parent and affiliates in less-developed regions (Brainard and Riker 1997).

Further evidence about whether outward investment might be transferring production abroad that otherwise would remain competitive at home can be found in a comparison of unit values at home and at overseas plants in the developing world. Edwards and Lawrence (forthcoming) argue that if outward investment by multinationals simply relocated production from the home economy to developing countries, one would expect a rise in unit values for production and exports of goods in the sector involved in the latter location. But they find within-sector unit values to be much lower in the new developing-country plants in comparison to the home market—between 15 and 30 percent of medium- and high-technology products in the same category exported by the United States in the case of China—with no change in these relative unit values over the entire period from 1990 to 2006. Edwards and Lawrence conclude that what is taking place is production-fragmentation via FDI—the transfer of low-skill-intensive, low-unit-value operations abroad—rather than production relocation of higher-skill-intensive, higher-unit-value operations in which the home market continues to have a comparative advantage.

Turning to the contention that outward investment by US MNCs "drains off" capital that otherwise would be invested at home, the evidence also suggests complementarity rather than zero-sum dynamics in parent MNC strategy. Desai, Foley, and Hines (2005a) discover that years in which US multinational firms make greater capital expenditures abroad coincide with greater capital spending by the same firms at home. But the correlation between the domestic and foreign growth rates of multinational firms might occur for reasons other than an interaction between operations in both locales—a pharmaceutical company may discover a new drug or a software company may develop a new process that leads to simultaneous increases in activity at home and abroad. Desai, Foley, and Hines (2005b) use an instrumental variable that predicts foreign investment but does not directly affect domestic operations. Their instrumental variable is a firm-specific weighted average of foreign GDP growth that can be used to forecast growth rates of foreign investment in that country by the MNC. These predicted growth rates in turn can be traced back to explain possibly related changes in home-country activity by the MNC. Using this procedure, they find that 10 percent greater foreign investment by the MNC triggers 2.2 percent additional domestic investment. They show that there are similar positive relationships between foreign investment and home-country exports, R&D spending, numbers of employees, and employee compensation.

Looking specifically at one of the most sensitive target locations for outward investment, Branstetter and Foley (2010) find that US firms that invest in China simultaneously invest more in the US home market as well.

The evidence thus paints a picture in which outward investment is an integral part of MNC strategy to maximize the competitive position of the whole corporation, a goal for which headquarters raises the needed amount of capital from sources all around the globe. In determining where to deploy capital and where to locate production, relative costs—including relative wages and benefits (as well as relative skills and relative productivity)—play a definite role. But in the end, operations at home and abroad complement each other as the MNC parent tries to make the deployment of tangible and intangible assets most productive and profitable. As pointed out earlier, in 2007 US MNC plants accounted for 49 percent of all US goods exports, of which 38 percent were shipped directly to overseas affiliates of the US parent (Barefoot and Mataloni 2009). US MNC capital investment in the domestic economy in 2007 was $483 billion in comparison to $169 billion outside the United States. Thus, for every $1 invested abroad, US MNCs invested $2.85 at home.

The finding that home-country firms that engage in outward FDI export more from home than similar firms that do not engage in outward investment bears directly on the composition of good jobs/bad jobs in the home-country market, since export-related jobs across all developed countries offer a wage and benefit premium in comparison to other jobs in comparable firms. In the United States, export jobs pay wages 10 to 11 percent higher than non-export-related jobs (Richardson 2005a). Thus, outward investment by US MNCs results in a higher proportion of good jobs (relatively high wages and benefits) compared with bad jobs (relatively lower wages and benefits) at home.

The benefits that accrue to US companies that engage in outward investment are not limited to their superior export performance. US MNCs that invest abroad use frontier production processes more frequently in their home-country plants, have higher levels of worker productivity, and enjoy more rapid growth rates of overall productivity than others (Bernard, Jensen, and Schott 2005). Taken together, American-owned firms that engage in outward investment pay their blue-collar production workers 7 to 15 percent more than comparable nonoutward investors (7 percent more in large US MNC plants, 15 percent more in small US MNC plants) (Richardson 2005b). Given their higher productivity, US firms that invest abroad enjoy lower levels of bankruptcy and are less likely to suffer job loss than similar firms that do not engage in outward investment. This outcome makes intuitive sense, but as it contrasts strongly with conventional wisdom, it is worth restating: Contrary to popular perception, outward investment by US MNCs leads to a more stable job base at home.

EU multinationals that establish affiliates abroad are larger, more profitable, and more productive than firms that do not. Using large-firm-level data from 12 countries of the euro area for 2003 and 2006, Geishecker, Görg, and Taglioni (2009) find that EU firms that engage in outward investment enjoy a higher rate of productivity growth and a higher survival rate. Their higher performance is associated with a larger number of affiliates and more numerous locations.

To be sure, these findings do not imply that the home-industry sector where the outward investment originates is always expanding on a net basis. What is striking, however, is that US firms that engage in outward investment offer better prospects for their workers than firms that do not in both expanding and contracting industries. That is, home-country companies in contracting sectors that are "globally engaged," to use Richardson's characterization—importing, exporting, engaging in outward investment, or connected to inward investors—show themselves to be the most successful participants in those sectors. Across sectors, whether expanding or declining, the superior benefits associated with "globally engaged" firms accrue to average-skilled as well as high-skilled workers, to union members as well as nonunion workers, to minorities, and to those who live in small towns as well as large urban areas.

To illustrate this result in a declining sector, it is useful to revisit the family history ("Pam's family") that Lewis and Richardson (2001) trace through five generations. Pam's great-grandmother, grandmother, and mother worked as seamstresses in Cumberland, Maryland for the minimum wage. Pam herself worked her way up from sewing to customer service at the Schwab garment company, responsible for the Ralph Lauren line of children's clothes, via computer courses at a local community college. Over the course of the 1990s, the total number of jobs at Schwab remained remarkably constant (unusual for the sector), but their composition changed as sewing and cutting moved offshore, replaced by marketing, distribution, and business-service occupations. As of 2001, Pam supervised five managers and 18 contract supervisors with the task of ensuring that correct bar codes, labels, and prices arrived at correct destinations around the globe on time. Pam's son, meanwhile, became manager at Schwab's distribution center in Martinsburg, West Virginia. Both Pam and her son enjoyed wages and benefits—and profit sharing—that placed the family more squarely in the middle class than the grandmother and great-grandmother could have ever achieved.

The more frequent story for declining industries may involve net job losses. Between 2002 and 2006, North Carolina lost some 72,000 manufacturing jobs concentrated in textiles and furniture fabrication (Kletzer, Levinsohn, and Richardson 2007). To attempt to replace these jobs, North Carolina partnered with newly arriving businesses to design courses in the state's community college network to provide the skills their workforce would need.[8] A state recruitment director singled out Regina Whitaker as a model for their effort. In 1996, just out of high school, Regina took a job at the same yarn texturing plant where her mother had worked for three decades. As that company relocated labor-intensive production operations to China and Brazil, workers in the Piedmont region were laid off. In 2003, Regina enrolled in biotechnology

---

8. Peter S. Goodman, "In North Carolina, a Second Industrial Revolution," *Washington Post*, September 3, 2007.

classes at Forsyth Technical Community College, and when she graduated was hired as a lab technician at Targacept, a biotech firm in Winston-Salem, with a salary that she reported was "significantly more" than she had earned at the yarn factory. Over this period the number of workers in biosciences increased from 20,000 to 47,000.

Looking at companies that remained in the North Carolina textile sector finds support for the Richardson "global engagement" rule that even in declining industries there may be international opportunities for US firms, workers, and communities. As Glen Raven lost out in the struggle to sell nylon pantyhose from its Piedmont plant, the US parent shifted to producing and weaving high-grade industrial yarn, as used in upholstery.[9] These more capital-intensive operations downsized from 225 to 156 employees, while compensation rose, with wages rising from $10.50 to $22 per hour. The largest destination for Glen Raven's exports from North Carolina became China, increasing fivefold between 2003 and 2006, to $52 million per year. Although Glen Raven has not yet invested abroad as other successful high-end US textile firms have, the company's story illustrates the more general finding that US firms can exploit the changing international dimensions of industries that are in decline at home.

Turning to middle-skill industrial sectors in which the United States has historically had worldwide comparative advantage but which are now increasingly beset by international competition, it may be more useful to ask not whether aggregate employment has expanded or contracted but what would have happened if US companies were hindered or restricted in their ability to invest abroad. One of the best-selling and most successful trucks in the world historically has been Ford's F150 series. In 2004–05, Ford fundamentally redesigned the F150 line, making the Ford Essex Engine Plant in Windsor, Canada the exclusive source of the 5.4 liter, 32-valve, high-performance Triton V-8 engine and choosing Ford's contract manufacturer, IMMSA of Monterey, as the sole supplier of the M450 chassis, using inexpensive but reliable Mexican steel alloy. Ford's prospects for holding its share of the truck market vis-à-vis the Toyota Tacoma and the Isuzu D-Max, as well as the Chrysler Dodge Ram, depend on this NAFTA-integrated supply chain. Despite the United Auto Workers' visceral condemnation of NAFTA, the fate of UAW workers at Ford's US assembly facilities depends on that agreement.

Finally, the disk drive industry represents a sector where US MNCs demonstrate ongoing prowess along the international frontier. Seagate is the world's leading provider of hard disk drives, whether computed on the basis of revenue or units shipped, with approximately 45 percent of the global market (McKendrick, Donner, and Haggard 2000; Seagate Technology 2008). Seagate products are found in computers (servers, desktops, laptops, and notebooks), digital video recorders, video game consoles, portable media players, and auto-

---

9. Ibid.

motive navigation systems. For fiscal years 2006–08, approximately 30 percent of Seagate disk drive revenue came from customers in North America, 27 percent from customers in Europe, and 43 percent from customers in the Far East. Hewlett-Packard and Dell each account for approximately 10 percent of Seagate revenue, Lenovo less. Sony PlayStation 3 and Microsoft Xbox are the largest buyers for video game consoles.

Seagate has management, R&D, and design facilities in California (Sunnyvale and Scotts Valley), Massachusetts (Shrewsbury), Minnesota (Minneapolis), Colorado (Longmont), Pennsylvania (Pittsburgh), Oklahoma (Oklahoma City), and Singapore. The company's principal wholly owned manufacturing facilities are located in China, Malaysia, Northern Ireland, Singapore, Thailand, and, in the United States, in California and Minnesota. Seagate's worldwide employment was 45,000 in 2008—8,000 managers, engineers, and other staff in the United States, and 37,000 abroad, mostly production line personnel. Providing a clear illustration of the discussion in chapter 4 of the *Parental Supervision* (Moran 2001) paradigm, Seagate's competitive position in world markets depends—as do 8,000 relatively high-compensation employees in the United States—on tight integration between home-country and overseas facilities. Seagate's principal competitors are Fujitsu, Hitachi, Toshiba, Samsung, GS Magicstor (Japan), and Western Digital (United States).

Overall, as some sectors where there is outward investment expand and other sectors contract, there will surely be job losses and dislocations for some workers while others gain new opportunities. Indeed, Bernard and Jensen (2007) show that once favorable plant characteristics that enable the plants to survive (size, age, employment of skilled labor) are controlled for, US MNC-owned plants are more likely to close, justifying anxiety on the part of their better-treated workers. Multinational firms simply have more readily available margins to adjust than do nonmultinationals—that is, they can make changes in the mix of technology, marketing, and supplier inputs more easily than nonmultinationals and they can respond to changes in market conditions more rapidly. They embody attributes extraordinarily valuable to the home economy (frontier practices, large-scale operations, superior jobs) that are less frequently possessed by nonmultinationals, and these attributes are accompanied by more speedy mechanisms for modification.

Changing patterns of MNC investment, like changing patterns of technology deployment more generally, contribute to job losses and dislocations for some workers as well as to new opportunities for others. The appropriate response by home-country authorities is to design adjustment and retraining programs to cushion the impact on those adversely affected, not to impede capital flows and engage in a futile effort to preserve jobs in uncompetitive home-country economic activities.

Outward FDI, Strategic Trade Theory, and the Capture of Rents Abroad?

The third testable proposition in the Samuelson/Summers critique of globalization embodies the most nightmarish scenario of all, that US-based MNCs may deploy a rent-gathering apparatus that switches from sharing supranormal profits and externalities with US workers and communities to extracting rents from the United States.

The theory behind FDI is that companies take the trouble to build plants and coordinate activities across borders—rather than simply sell products or license technology—because they possess "intangible assets" that afford them higher profits when they maintain control over all operations. FDI takes place only in industries where markets are not perfectly competitive. The presumption is that MNCs, when successful, can collect rents from their activities, some of which may be shared with their workers, and generate externalities that benefit countries where their operations are located.

Summers argues that the United States may not "necessarily benefit from the economic success of its trading partners" if the economies of those trading partners become powered by MNCs, thereby shifting rent collection to the new host states. "Stateless elites whose allegiance is to global economic success and their own prosperity rather than the interests of the nation where they are headquartered" may share rents and externalities that used to be captured by US workers and communities with external workers and communities in new MNC locations.[10]

To quote Paul Samuelson again, "Historically, US workers used to have kind of a de facto monopoly access to the US's superlative capital and know-how (scientific, engineering and managerial). All of us Yankees, so to speak, were born with silver spoons in our mouths." Perhaps multinational corporate investment is offering monopoly access—and silver spoons—to "non-Yankees."

A first look at the evidence supports apprehension about possible rent shifting. Popular outrage about sweatshops and the possible abuse of workers often leaves the impression that multinational manufacturing and assembly investors predominantly engage in labor-intensive operations and that the work consists primarily of low-skilled, low-wage jobs. But the data presented earlier in table 4.1 reveal a different thrust by manufacturing multinationals. As shown there, by far the majority of manufacturing FDI flows to higher-skilled industrial sectors in developing countries, and the relatively higher growth of more skill-intensive investor operations is speeding up over time. These data show that the globalization of industry around the world via FDI in manufacturing expands opportunities available to medium- and higher-skilled workers in developing countries. It might be quite plausible to argue therefore

---

10. Lawrence Summers, "American Needs to Make a New Case for Trade," *Financial Times*, April 27, 2008.

that auto workers and managers at MNC plants in Mexico and Brazil or electronics workers and managers at MNC plants in Malaysia and Thailand—or for that matter workers at Intel's semiconductor plant in Costa Rica who earn 150 percent of the average national manufacturing wage—partake of the rents associated with their employers in ways only US workers and managers were able to do 30 years ago.

But other evidence tempers this conclusion. From 1978 through 1990, Lawrence (1996)—extending work first done by Katz and Summers—shows that average rents earned by production workers and managers in US manufacturing did not change much. Moreover, Lawrence reminds us, most trade in high-rent sectors takes place among developed countries; trade involving developing countries typically involves low-rent sectors.

Might this be changing? The evidence that FDI takes place predominantly in higher- rather than lower-skilled activities offers the possibility that the answer might be affirmative. But this evolution probably fits better with Vernon's (1971) product-cycle model of gradual dispersion of middle- to higher-skilled assembly operations than with Brander and Spencer's (1981) strategic trade model of one highest-rent, highest-externality location abruptly replacing another. These FDI activities are not the "commanding heights" of highest-rent strategic trade industries and do not appear to be heading in that direction very rapidly (Krugman 1986).

As for the possibility of extracting rents from US consumers or generating adverse terms of trade for the United States, the evidence from one of the most controversial cases—exports from China—shows just the opposite: Average prices of goods exported from China to the United States fell by an average of 1.5 percent annually between 1997 and 2005 (Amiti and Freund 2008). Schott (2004) finds that while China exports more products in common with OECD countries than would be expected given the country's level of development (thanks largely to FDI), Chinese exports sell for a substantial discount relative to OECD varieties of the same product. The reason would seem to be that quality upgrading in each product category takes place more rapidly in OECD countries than in China.

At the end of the day, the data show no more than that US-based workers and managers may be less unique in their ability to extract rents from outsiders, rather than revealing that multinational investment has allowed non-US-based workers and managers to capture some new powerful ability to extract rents from Americans.

Moreover, the answers to the question of what it means when multinational investors transfer technology into the country that is generating the most contemporary anxiety—China—show some surprising results.

How Is FDI Transforming the Chinese Economy?

In 2003, China overtook the United States as the largest destination for foreign investment in the world, and then settled into second place.[11] FDI inflows reached $168 billion in 2008, declining slightly to $143 billion in 2009 (UNCTAD 2010c, annex table 1). As shown below, these FDI flows have transformed China's industrial base, shifting the composition of Chinese exports from low-skill-intensive to high-skill-intensive goods and services.

This transformation of China that is being carried out by multinational manufacturing investors raises important questions and generates profound anxieties. Is FDI helping propel China to become an export superpower, "displacing Japan as the predominant economic power in East Asia," as Preeg (2008, 130) declares, making the country the "economic hegemon" in the region?

The evidence shows clearly that MNCs in manufacturing have been the force that has carried China's exports from low-skill-intensive to high skill-intensive products. In 1992, the low-skill-intensive sectors in China accounted for 55 percent of its exports (Amiti and Freund 2010). By 2005, these same low-skill-intensive sectors' share had fallen to 33 percent. The composition of exports had shifted from a predominance of agriculture, apparel, textiles, footwear, and toys to machinery and transport products. Here the strongest export growth has been machinery, and within this broad classification telecom equipment, electrical machinery, and office machines constitute the largest shares. These more sophisticated sectors are dominated by processing trade, an arrangement in which imports are allowed into the country duty-free and are then assembled for export. Processing trade exports of machinery and electrical products grew from $9 billion in 1992 to $323 billion in 2006, that is, from 22 to 63 percent of all exports. Processing trade, in turn, is dominated by foreign multinationals (called foreign-invested firms, including both joint venture and wholly owned affiliates of foreign multinationals), especially for more sophisticated products. The buildup of the foreign presence has been nothing short of remarkable (Feenstra and Wei 2010). In 1992, foreign multinationals accounted for 5 percent of exports in ordinary trade and 45 percent of processing exports; by 2006, those figures had risen to 28 and 84 percent, respectively.

The share of processing trade—and the foreign firm share of exports—climbs rapidly as the skill intensity of the products increases (Koopman, Wang, and Wei 2008). For apparel, processing exports as a share of industry exports in 2002 was 45.1 percent, with foreign firms accounting for 39.2 percent of industry exports. For household electrical appliances, those figures were 79.1 and 56.9 percent, respectively; for electronic devices, 89.7 and 87.5 percent; for telecommunications equipment, 91.2 and 88.4 percent; and for computers,

---

11. This section draws on Moran (forthcoming).

99.1 and 99.4 percent. In short, FDI flows have revolutionized China's industrial base and shifted the composition of Chinese exports from low-skill-intensive to high-skill-intensive goods and services.

The rapid growth in Chinese exports of what are classified as advanced technology products (ATPs) to developed countries, and a Chinese surplus in ATP goods in China-US bilateral trade, leads to speculation that China is "leapfrogging" ahead technologically (Ferrantino et al. 2010). But foreign investors have been responsible for more than 92 percent of all Chinese ATP exports since 1996 and 96 percent since 2002. Within this 96 percent foreign-investor-dominated channel, there has been a shift to wholly owned MNC exporters from joint venture companies. State-owned enterprises have an ATP trade deficit with the United States, while private Chinese firms and collective enterprises contribute very little to ATP trade. There is a sizable technological gap between Chinese ATP imports and exports. Chinese ATP imports from the United States consist of large-scale, sophisticated, high-valued equipment and devices, whereas ATP exports to the United States are small-scale products or components in the low end of the ATP value-added chain. Some 40 percent of the unit-value ratios between US-exported and Chinese-exported ATPs are between 1 and 10 times greater for the US ATP exports to China, one-third are between 10 and 100 times greater, and more than 13 percent are at least 100 times greater. In some categories, China both imports and exports the same product (e.g., microscopes), but the types imported from the United States cost 10 to 20 times more than the types exported to the United States, suggesting a sizable difference in features and capabilities.

Separate measurements by Edwards and Lawrence (2010) and Edwards and Lawrence (forthcoming) show similar results: The unit values of US imports of medium- and high-technology goods from China lie between 15 and 30 percent of the same-category products exported by the United States. Remarkably, Edwards and Lawrence find that there has been no significant change in these relative prices over the entire period 1990–2006. They conclude that US imports of so-called high-technology products from China are not close substitutes for US high-technology exports to China.

So, despite the emergence of a handful of Chinese national champions (perhaps seven to nine), foreign MNCs dominate the commanding heights of China's high-tech export sector. The Columbia University Vale Center–Fudan University ranking in 2010 of the largest 18 Chinese multinationals lists just four firms in the manufacturing sector: Lenovo, Shanghai Automotive Industry Group, ZTE, and Haier.[12] UNCTAD's list of the top 100 nonfinancial transnational corporations from developing and transition economies lists four Chinese manufacturing firms: ZTE, Lenovo, China Minmetals, and TVP

---

12. Report by the Vale Columbia Center on Sustainable International Development and the Fudan (China) University School of Management, "Chinese Multinationals Gain Further Momentum," December 9, 2010, www.vcc.columbia.edu (accessed on February 1, 2011).

Technology (UNCTAD 2010c, annex table 27). To this rather small roster, one might want to add Huawei, TCL, and Gree.

In the processing trade, there is some debate about how the import share of Chinese processing trade has evolved. Nicholas Lardy (2002) has gathered data that indicate the import share of Chinese processed exports has declined from approximately 85 percent in 1989 to about 55 percent in 2009. Koopman, Wang, and Wei (2008) estimate that Chinese domestic value added in processed exports was 18 percent in 1997, 26 percent in 2002, and 18 percent in 2006, suggesting that the import share of Chinese processed imports has remained roughly constant during the period they survey. They show that the percentage of the value of the final product that derives from imported components rises as the sophistication of that final product increases and as the predominance of foreign investors rises. As of 2002, for wearing apparel, the percentage of the value of the final product that derives from imported components was 62.4 percent; for household electrical appliances, 76.3 percent; for electronic devices, 85.2 percent; for telecommunications equipment, 91.6 percent; and for computers, 96.1 percent.

Linden, Kraemer, and Dedrick (2007) provide a fascinating look at who captures value in advanced electronics products exported from China, and where those who capture value are located. "Value capture" means the margin for the firm after paying for inputs and labor. The authors' target is Apple's iPod, assembled in China with a retail price of $299 in 2005. In their estimation, by far most costly input in the iPod is the 30GB hard drive from Toshiba, which costs $73, or more than 50 percent of the total input cost, with a margin for Toshiba of about $20, which the authors assign to Japan. The second most valuable input is the display, with a factory price of $20, plus a margin of $6 for Toshiba-Matsushita, which they again assign to Japan. Next are two microchips from US companies, Broadcom and PortalPlayer, leading to a $7 margin assigned to the United States. The SDRAM Memory comes from Samsung, with $0.67 assigned to Korea. There are more than 400 additional inputs, with values ranging from $4 to fractions of a penny. Apple's gross profit meanwhile is $80, or $155 if distributed through Apple's own retail outlet. The margins for the companies involved in the creation of the iPod (above costs of materials and labor) total $190. Of that total, if the iPod is sold in the United States, $163 accrues to the United States, $26 to Japan, and $1 to Korea. Some portion of $75 allocated to retail and distribution would go to other players if the iPod were sold outside the United States.

Linden, Kraemer, and Dedrick (2007, 10) conclude that "the value added to the product through assembly in China is probably a few dollars at most" (the popularly accepted figure is $4). They argue that while Apple's margins are high within the electronics sector, the "geography" of value capture for the iPod is fairly representative for the industry. Koopman, Wang, and Wei (2009) support this contention with their finding that Japan, the United States, and Europe (EU-15) are the main sources of foreign content for computers and electronics in China, accounting for about 60 percent of imported components.

At the end of the day, China's high-tech export explosion represents MNCs bringing high-skill-content and high-value-added inputs into China, assembling them into final products (or semi-assembled intermediates), and exporting them to world markets. The increase in skill content of Chinese exports since 1992 is largely due to the increased skill content of imported inputs that are then assembled for export. At the same time, FDI payments for Chinese materials and labor used in the operations of the foreign plants have remained low because domestic value added has remained low, especially for more sophisticated skill-intensive products. From a comparative perspective, the share of domestic value-added in FDI operations in China in high-skill-intensive sectors such as computers and telecommunications ranges from less than one-half to slightly more than one-half of what is found in other developing countries where comparable measurements can be made, such as Mexico.

The evidence comes from de la Cruz et al. (2009; 2010, tables 7 and 8), who are able to compare the outcome of manufacturing FDI in China rigorously to other developing countries where there are similar processing-trade regimes. The most accurate comparison can be made with Mexico, where the maquiladora firms and the government's Program for Temporary Imports to Produce Export Goods resemble China's processing trade system.

In low-skill-intensive industries, such as apparel, the FDI-dominated processing industries show a relatively large share of domestic value added in both countries: a 35.4 percent share for Mexico and a 37.6 percent share for China.

In the middle-skill-intensive automotive sector, the FDI-dominated processing industries show what de la Cruz et al. characterize as "medium" domestic value-added in both countries: a 35.2 percent share in motor vehicles and 23.9 percent share in auto parts for Mexico, and a 33.8 percent share in motor vehicles and 28.7 percent share in auto parts for China. Mexico, however, scores a much higher 43.8 percent domestic value-added share in "other transportation equipment" (for which there is no comparable category in the authors' data for China). For China, Lardy (2002) notes that for some vehicle lines the domestic content has been climbing over time: The popular Santana, produced by a joint venture between Volkswagen and Shanghai Automotive, was launched in 1985 with a domestic content of 2 percent but recorded domestic content well over 90 percent by the late 1990s. Other large volume production vehicles, such as the Buicks produced by GM and Shanghai Automotive, followed a similar track.

For high-skill-intensive sectors, such as computers and telecommunications equipment, both countries have a much lower share of domestic value-added in the FDI-dominated processing sectors. What is interesting to note is that Mexico's small domestic value-added share (8.5 percent share in computers, 14.9 percent share in telecommunications) is nonetheless nearly twice as large as that for China for computers (3.4 percent) and even larger for telecommunications (8.4 percent).

Moreover, leaving aside the duty-free intermediates that make up the final electronic and machinery products, it is not clear that there has been significant change either in the extent or in the skill content of China's own processing activities (Dean, Fung, and Wang 2009; Amiti and Freund 2008).

Turning from measurement of domestic content in foreign-owned factories to measurement of impact from FDI on surrounding firms in China, assessments of horizontal and vertical spillovers from multinational investors to indigenous Chinese firms (private or state-owned) appear to be relatively weak in comparison to other countries in Asia, as do export externalities (Moran, forthcoming). The reasons include lower pay at Chinese companies and brain drain from them to foreign MNCs, gaps in technology and quality control standards, adaptability limitations, and intercultural communication problems.

Blonigen and Ma (2010) investigate the extent to which Chinese domestic firms are keeping up or even catching up with foreign exporters. They do not try to measure spillovers directly. Instead, they compare the volume, composition, and quality of exports of the two groups. They find that the general pattern over 1997–2005 runs exactly counter to what one would expect if Chinese firms were catching up—foreign firms' share of exports by product category and foreign unit values relative to Chinese unit values are increasing over time, not decreasing. In other words, Chinese exporters are not even catching up, let alone keeping up, with foreign multinational investors in China.

Deepening the impact of foreign investment on the indigenous economic base in China—expanding the linkages from international investors and deriving more spillovers from their presence—will require improving the business climate for domestic firms, upgrading worker skills, creating engineering and managerial talent, reforming financial institutions, and improving infrastructure. All these reforms are under way, to a greater or lesser extent.

Thus far, however, the aggregate data simply do not show FDI to be a powerful source for indigenous-controlled industrial transformation.[13] The result is that China has remained a low-value-added assembler of more sophisticated inputs imported from abroad—a "workbench" economy largely bereft of the magnified benefits and externalities from FDI enjoyed by other developing countries. Despite the appearance of a small number (seven to nine) of increasingly well-known Chinese national champions in manufacturing in the domestic market and abroad, most of the burgeoning new activities taking place in China have been remarkably well constrained to and contained within the plants owned and controlled by foreign multinationals and their international suppliers.

---

13. Branstetter and Foley (2010) note that US MNCs actually do relatively little R&D in China (three-tenths of 1 percent of their worldwide R&D and less than 13 percent of their R&D in the Asia-Pacific region), and most R&D activity in China appears to consist of customizing innovations discovered elsewhere for the Chinese market.

In their dissection of the "value capture" flows for Apple's iPod, described earlier, Linden, Kraemer, and Dedrick (2007) suggest that the value added attributed to the parent company that contributes a component or performs an integrative function to a product in China flows directly back to MNC headquarters. This is almost surely too simplistic—especially for US MNCs—given the American territorial tax system with the foreign tax credit and deferral that encourage US MNCs to use transfer pricing to keep accumulations of earnings offshore. Rather than try to track down capital flows and hiding places in integrated MNC networks, the more sensible approach is to ask a slightly different kind of question: If MNC headquarters use earnings from China, like earnings from elsewhere, to fortify their corporate position in world markets, what kinds of activities will those earnings help maintain or expand, and where will they be located?

In coming to an answer to this question, it is striking to note even in today's globalized world how remarkably home-based MNCs from developed countries have remained. For the United States, the most recent data show that US-headquartered MNCs have 70 percent of their operations, make 89 percent of their purchases, spend 87 percent of their R&D dollars, and locate more than half of their workforce within the US economy (Barefoot and Mataloni 2009). This predominant focus on the home economy has persisted over time and changes only very slowly at the margin.

The home-market-centered orientation for MNCs across the developed world is not dissimilar (Rugman 2005). Thus, while manufacturing MNCs may build plants in China, shift production to Vietnam, outsource to Mexico, take a chance in Costa Rica or the Czech Republic, or develop a new application in Israel, the largest impact from deployment of worldwide earnings is to bolster their operations in their home markets.

Maintaining the Home Economy as a Competitive Base for MNC Investment

The analysis presented here shows that the globalization of industry and services via FDI may well be, in Lori Wallach's famous phrase, "trade on steroids." But the pejorative connotations associated with this phrase are almost entirely inaccurate empirically. To be sure, FDI generates losers as well as winners. But MNCs do not spread technology and capital in ways that harm the aggregate interests of workers in the developed countries. MNCs do not locate their operations in a zero-sum manner that favors host economies at the expense of the home economy. The two-way flow of inward and outward investment does not create an outcome that can be reasonably characterized in any way as "hollowing out" the home economy.

Outward FDI from the United States or from other home countries is understandably the most controversial phenomenon. MNCs do close plants at home and build plants abroad, and they demonstrably threaten workers in labor negotiations that they will ship jobs overseas if the workers ask for wages or benefits that the MNC considers excessive. But the evidence consistently shows that the expansion of MNC operations abroad and the strengthening of MNC operations in the home country are complementary. The answer to the counterfactual—would the home country be better off, or would workers in the home country be better off, if home-country MNCs were prevented from engaging in outward investment?—is negative time and time again.

Of particular note is the empirical support for Richardson's (2005b) observation that outward FDI takes place in home-country industries in decline as well as in home-country industries in ascent, but that in both cases, firms that are "globally engaged," including involved in FDI, perform better than counterpart firms that are not.

Looking more specifically at possible policy changes for the United States, President Obama has pledged that his administration will "end tax breaks for corporations that ship jobs overseas."[14] This is widely interpreted to mean that the Obama administration will end deferral for US MNCs. At first glance, the analysis presented here would appear to support such a position—the "classical" conclusion is that home countries should pursue the objective of equalizing the tax burden on foreign and domestic income so that multinationals make investment decisions based entirely on commercial considerations, not tax concerns (capital-export neutrality).[15]

Capital export neutrality ostensibly justifies the elimination of deferral. The latest assessments by Hufbauer and Kim (2009) suggest, however, that this would be counterproductive: US tax policy already places US multinational operations at home at a competitive disadvantage vis-à-vis rival multinationals. Hufbauer and Kim recommend that the US tax regime be shifted toward a territorial system, coupled with favorable expense allocation rules (the United States would tax all income earned at home, but would not tax active business income earned abroad). A shift of US policy that instead places obstacles in the way of US MNCs using the home economy as the hub of their global operations would penalize them in comparison to their rivals, and leave their US suppliers, workers, and local communities less competitive and worse off.

Evidence about outward investment and home economy competitiveness from other developed countries parallels what is found for the United States. However, notwithstanding concerns about the leakage of technology to Eastern Europe, the export of jobs from Sweden, or the "hollowing out" of Japanese manufacturing, the data show a complementary relationship between investment at home and investment abroad across the developed world, not a zero-sum threat to home-country welfare.

---

14. President Barack Obama, State of the Union Address, January 27, 2010, available at www.whitehouse.gov (accessed on February 1, 2011).

15. Bergsten, Horst, and Moran (1978, chapter 6) calculated that US tax policy was closer to capital export neutrality than commonly supposed. Deferral gave outward investment only a small advantage, which was offset by the denial of the US investment tax credit and acceleration of depreciation.

9

Policy Implications

This volume lays out the underpinnings for a "second generation" of research on the relationship between foreign direct investment and development. The policy message that emerges is far more complex and nuanced than the much criticized prescription of the "Washington consensus" that foreign investment flows are good, and the more FDI the better.

For example, FDI in natural resources can generate revenues for public services, economic diversification, and social development; or it can produce corrupt rule, political upheaval, economic stagnation, and ongoing poverty. FDI in infrastructure can bring electricity, water, and other services to ever larger numbers of businesses and households, including poorer households; or it can impose lopsided economic and foreign exchange burdens on beleaguered public authorities at the national and subnational level. FDI in manufacturing (and services) can bring low-skill jobs and exports, and more importantly, it can provide a path for the host economy to move from lower- to higher-skilled economic activities, with thickening backward linkages and valuable spillovers; or it can lock the host economy in inefficient and noncompetitive economic activities.

In each area, the key to determining the positive or negative FDI outcome is the policy environment established by developing-country host governments and reinforced by developed-country authorities and aid agencies, multilateral financial institutions, labor organizations, NGOs and civil society groups, and the corporate social responsibility community (including, in particular, the investors themselves).

The data presented in this volume also add nuance to the grand pronouncements about what is or is not known in terms of how to stimulate growth or enhance development.[1] On the one hand, it is not accurate to say that "we know nothing" about how FDI can help host countries raise living standards. Nor is it accurate to say that the effect of FDI is "random," or that FDI can bring no positive impact to the poorest countries. On the other hand, it is not sensible to expect to find a simple answer to a question such as "will more FDI make Pakistan grow faster?" Or "will more FDI solve problems of poverty in Africa?" Or "can FDI bring sustainable development to Mali or Cambodia?" Particular types of FDI can—depending on the host-country policy framework—contribute to augmenting real income through the 12 principal channels identified in box 1.1. But the gigantic task of raising growth rates that endure, and generating broad increases in economic and social welfare, is likely to be slow and arduous even under the best of circumstances.

Developing Countries

For FDI in the extractive and infrastructure sectors, transparency of payments and revenue streams, backed by comprehensive and effective new laws against corrupt payments, will determine whether exploitation of natural resources and provision of infrastructure services constitute a major advance—or setback—for host development. As described in chapters 2 and 3, progress here requires overlapping efforts among developed- and developing-country authorities to:

- reform the Organization for Economic Cooperation and Development (OECD) Convention on Combating Bribery of Foreign Public Officials in International Business Transactions as well as the home-country laws based on it (including the US Foreign Corrupt Practices Act [FCPA]),
- strengthen and expand the Extractive Industries Transparency Initiative (EITI and EITI++), and
- ensure that all international investors (including those from non-OECD states) are governed by the same regulations.

Host developing countries will have to establish credible timetables to implement EITI auditing procedures and ensure that such procedures apply uniformly to each and every investor, with company-by-company publication of results. Within a robust regulatory environment, it should not prove insurmountable to address more technical issues involving fiscal measures to manage Dutch disease, tax measures to share revenues in boom and bust conditions, and arrangements to share foreign exchange risks or design workouts when unexpected shocks occur.

---

1. See the Barcelona Development Agenda, www.bcn.es (accessed on August 26, 2010). See also Easterly (2001), Sachs (2005), and Collier (2007).

Turning to FDI in manufacturing, the evidence presented here forces reconsideration of two widely held views: first, that there is no evidence that FDI generates externalities for recipient economies; and second, that the benefits of FDI can be had if policymakers just let markets work. The data show that manufacturing FDI has a particularly powerful role to play in shifting a host country from a traditional economic base to low-skilled, labor-intensive, export-led growth, and then again in moving the host up the path into the supplier networks of higher-skilled manufactured products. Along the way, there are possibilities for many kinds of spillovers and externalities, especially in the vertical direction with an expansion of backward linkages.

But the data examined here also show that while the mantra of "reform, reform" is a necessary condition for host countries to harness manufacturing FDI for development, it may well not be a sufficient condition. Both poorer and less poor developing countries face imperfections in information markets (broadly speaking) for attracting manufacturing FDI. They need proactive investment promotion agencies and strategies to market their economies as sites for new FDI. Investment promotion agencies in turn must be backed by what can be fairly costly infrastructure and manpower training programs that provide the credibility that host-country commercial potential exists, thereby propelling their countries onto the short list of realistic sites for international investors. Packages of assistance to help developing countries attract and launch ever more sophisticated FDI activities, particularly in the context of regional or bilateral trade agreements, will be discussed later in this chapter as key ingredients through which developed countries and multilateral financial institutions can help catalyze manufacturing FDI.

But strong manufacturing FDI flows themselves are no panacea for development. The health and vitality of indigenous firms will always be the key to domestic job creation and economic growth. Steady improvement in the local business climate, under increasingly competitive conditions, will play a major role in the important task of helping indigenous firms become more productive all across the domestic economic landscape. Success in improving the local business climate will, at the same time, enhance prospects for local companies to become suppliers to multinational investors. To accomplish this, hosts may experiment with imaginative supplier-identification and vendor-promotion programs. But the indispensable prerequisite remains a domestic setting in which local firms enjoy business-friendly regulations, infrastructure services, financing, and duty-free imports just as the foreigners do.

A complete wish list of host-country policies to take advantage of FDI would include regional or global constraints on investment subsidies and incentives fully coordinated with national and state entities in the developed world. Of course, the political economy of accomplishing this in the real world might render this outcome fanciful.

Absent from the list is greater leeway for developing countries (including the poorest developing countries) to impose domestic-content and joint-venture mandates on multinationals. The evidence examined here repeatedly shows that the imposition on multinational investors of performance requirements—particularly domestic-content requirements—runs counter to host-country development interests throughout the world, including in Korea, India, and China.

Developed Countries

The first implication for developed countries is simple and straightforward, but nonetheless defies much contemporary rhetoric that asserts the contrary: The globalization of industry (and services) via FDI is not a zero-sum process in which the success of the developing world comes at the expense of the developed countries.[2]

Outward FDI in manufacturing and assembly enhances the distribution of good jobs/bad jobs in the home country and strengthens the competitiveness of firms, workers, and communities at home. Outward FDI initiates a win-win process that benefits workers as well as companies on both sides of developed- and developing-country borders. Accompanying these favorable outcomes, outward investment also leads to various forms of job dislocation, creating losers (as well as winners) whose needs must be forthrightly acknowledged and addressed. But the home economy is stronger and more resilient with outward FDI than it would be if home authorities adopted measures to limit or retard companies from setting up operations abroad. Developed-country authorities can justifiably endorse the flow of FDI to the developing world, even while designing domestic training and adjustment programs for those hurt by globalization.

Looking at the United States more specifically, the data introduced here show that it would be unwise in the extreme to make the US home economy a less favorable setting from which to conduct international business activities. Today, US multinational corporations (MNCs) concentrate more than 70 percent of their operations at home, constituting the most technology-intensive and productive segment of the US economy and offering higher wages and benefits than other companies as a result. They now conduct three-quarters of all US private-sector R&D. Using the US economy as the base for integrating their global operations—which includes engaging in outward investment—strengthens the domestic operations of US MNCs and allows them to generate more exports (and higher-paying export-related jobs) than firms that do not engage in outward investment. Making it more difficult to engage in outward investment would not strengthen the home economy in the United States. Quite the contrary, placing obstacles in the way of US MNCs using the United States as the center for conducting global operations would leave them and the suppliers, workers, and communities where they are located worse off and less competitive in the world economy.

---

2. For the trade counterpart of this argument, see Edwards and Lawrence (forthcoming).

Most developed countries recognize that they serve their own interests as well as the interests of the developing world by helping home-country companies identify investment and export opportunities abroad. Sixteen of the 22 major developed countries help home-based multinationals both export to and invest in developing economies; one of those that do not is the United States.[3]

The US Foreign Commercial Service, for example, assists US firms in bidding on foreign contracts and developing export markets, but it is not trained or allowed to assist US companies in setting up supply chains abroad.

The constraints on the Overseas Private Investment Corporation (OPIC) are even more severe. Whereas 14 of 19 official political-risk insurance agencies in the developed world provide crucial coverage for projects with powerful development impact—including labor-intensive FDI export projects from least-developed countries and middle-skill-intensive FDI export projects from more advanced developing countries—OPIC is prohibited from offering coverage to what US labor organizations consider "sensitive sector" investments (including textiles, auto parts, or electronics) or to agricultural processing projects if the crops grown are "in surplus" in the United States.[4] Concern about congressional reaction also effectively prevents OPIC from offering support to investors that wish to establish or manage export processing zones.

What is needed is to rededicate OPIC to its original mission to promote development by providing political-risk insurance to those projects that most benefit poorer countries. Alongside OPIC, meanwhile, the Millennium Challenge Corporation should work with recipient countries to design compacts that overcome constraints to investment, tying local entrepreneurs to global markets and helping authorities implement compacts that facilitate both local and multinational private-sector activity.

While the analysis in this volume has shown that outward FDI generally strengthens the competitiveness of home-country industries, developed countries may rightly be skeptical that this will be the outcome in all cases without exception. Developed-country authorities may therefore require that their political-risk insurance agencies provide a "net benefits" test to projects receiving official support. But OPIC is not permitted to perform any such test. It is instead required to report to Congress if any single job might be lost in the United States as a result of an outward investment (even if the net outcome is positive), effectively denying coverage to all such cases, rather than following the more appropriate procedure of determining whether the home economy is better or worse off overall if the investment takes place.

The evidence presented here does show, however, that developed countries should not support all manufacturing FDI flows to the developing world,

---

3. See the investment component of the Center for Global Development's Commitment to Development Index 2010, www.cgdev.org (accessed on February 1, 2011).

4. Ibid., footnote 3; see also Moran (2003).

especially not highly protected manufacturing projects that subtract from host economic welfare. It is disheartening therefore to discover that 16 of 19 national political-risk guarantee agencies—plus their counterparts in the regional development banks and the World Bank Group—fail to screen out FDI projects that require high trade barriers to survive.[5] For example, the political-risk insurance agencies of the United States, United Kingdom, Canada, Japan, Germany, France, and Italy, as well as the World Bank's Multilateral Investment Guarantee Agency (MIGA), assess only the likelihood that applicants can earn a profit, not whether the applicants' operations will make a positive contribution to host development. Since highly protected, foreign-owned plants are often quite lucrative, these projects pass this profitability test and qualify for coverage. Worse, some agencies, such as OPIC, provide insurance against the "threat" that the host might break a promise to protect a US investor against international competition, and pay the claim if the host lowers barriers to imports (O'Sullivan 2005). The cost-benefit demonstrations that FDI undertaken for import substitution subtracts from host welfare and retards domestic development should lead national insurers to refuse to provide official support to such projects.

Complementing this, developed-country governments should take steps to reaffirm multilateral commitment to the Agreement on Trade Related Investment Measures (TRIMs)—which prohibits the imposition of domestic-content and trade-balance requirements on multinational investors—in the World Trade Organization. In the same vein, the argument for greater "policy space" to impose performance requirements in bilateral investment treaties—particularly the US model bilateral investment treaty (BIT)—runs contrary to the interests of the developing world. This empirical observation bears repeating. Rodrik (2009, 2010), for example, correctly identifies ongoing structural transformation as being the most rewarding path for developing-country growth as the current international economic crisis winds down. But instead of following the promising strands in his own analysis in Hausmann and Rodrik (2003, 2005)—which suggest that FDI can help overcome entrepreneurship gaps, with trade and investment liberalization fostering the expansion of indigenous supply chains in the host economy—Rodrik reverts to 1950s-style industrial policy, trade restrictions, and imposition of performance requirements (especially domestic-content mandates) on foreign investors.[6]

In extractive industries and infrastructure, developed countries will want to support FDI in a manner that strengthens, rather than undermines, host-country institutions and good governance mechanisms. This will require changing the interpretation of what qualifies as corruption under the OECD

---

5. See the Center for Global Development's Commitment to Development Index 2010, www. cgdev.org (accessed on February 1, 2011).

6. For example, Rodrik consistently misreads Korea's development path in high-performance electronics, which, as noted here, was largely a phenomenon involving original equipment manufacturers, accompanied by learning from multinational buyers as well as "learning by doing" more generally.

convention, as spelled out in chapter 2, and ensuring that subsequent OECD peer reviews of home-country antibribery legislation (including the US FCPA) promote conformity with the new definition. To enhance transparency of payment streams, developed countries can ensure that their own investors participate in the EITI and EITI++, urge developing countries where they have influence to join the EITI, support the development of specific work plans (covering international investors of all nationalities) to adhere to EITI principles, and endorse company-by-company reporting of revenue streams. To assist in making EITI and EITI++ programs more credible, developed countries should help fund the training of local parliamentarians and civil society participants to monitor transactions between international investors and public authorities.

Alongside efforts to ensure that EITI principles apply to all investors in any given country, developed countries should endorse the refusal of international investor-state arbitral panels to enforce contracts obtained by corrupt means, including contracts of Chinese, Russian, and other non-OECD investors. The goal is to ensure that exemplary investors in natural resources and infrastructure enjoy a level playing field where their best practices do not set them at a disadvantage to their less exemplary counterparts.

Finally, developed as well as developing countries would benefit from a multilateral effort to limit locational incentives, subsidies, and other giveaway programs as alternative sites compete to attract international investment.

Multilateral Financial Institutions

The analysis advanced here bears directly on two of the most fundamental questions faced by the World Bank, as well as by regional banks such as the IDB, ADB, AfDB, and EBRD. First, given the vast expansion of international private capital flows over recent decades, do these multilateral financial institutions continue to have a robust role to play in any capacity except as funders of poverty-related social projects? Second, should these institutions pull back from involvement in middle-income countries and devote their efforts exclusively to the poorest developing economies?

With regard to the first question, the preceding pages lay out a broad array of evidence to demonstrate that international markets alone will not maximize or optimize the contribution of private investment to development. Public-sector interventions may be needed to:

- compensate for information asymmetries: MNCs are not all-knowing, it is costly to search for investment opportunities, and would-be hosts have to capture the attention and interest of potential investors.

- address coordination externalities: infrastructure services, vocational training, and worker health have to be meshed with the needs of investors in overlapping fashion.

- deal with problems in making credible commitments: contract enforcement and regulatory stability may need outside support.
- attend to appropriability problems and first-mover disadvantages: pioneer investors in new types of economic activity, or in chaotic and dangerous situations, may need external guarantees.
- ensure that international standards are set and enforced as a worldwide public good: public-sector intervention here may in fact be the *only* way to achieve this objective.

Across all of these fronts, carefully designed multilateral financial agency involvement can help break down the barriers that prevent markets from functioning efficiently and help shape the behavior of private actors to comply with important social, economic, and environmental norms. More specifically, multilateral financial agency programs such as political-risk insurance, guarantees, equity positions, loans, and policy advice can make a difference beyond what private markets supply in such areas as:

- improving and providing impartial monitoring of the business climate as a public good, accompanied by capacity building for judicial and regulatory institutions;
- designing, staffing, and funding investment promotion agencies and overcoming information deficits;
- overcoming failures in making credible commitments to honor contracts and helping to design investment agreements;
- improving governance and transparency, and combating corrupt payments in extractive and infrastructure investments;
- ensuring observance of recognized standards for socially and environmentally responsible private-sector development; and
- promoting investment in postconflict and humanitarian crisis states.

This list of undertakings does not duplicate what private actors are likely to provide on their own and is not at all confined to the poorest countries or the lowest levels of development. Indeed, some of the biggest payoffs to carefully configured multilateral interventions, as identified in previous pages here, can accrue to countries trying to climb into the higher ranks of the developing world.

Thus, as the world emerges from the financial crisis and FDI begins to flow again in robust fashion, the World Bank Group (including the International Financial Corporation [IFC] and MIGA) and regional development banks will continue to have vital functions in helping developing countries—including middle-income developing countries—harness foreign investment for development. But important recalibration is needed.

With regard to natural-resource FDI, the EITI++ agenda must now be transformed into concrete work plans with monitored results and shaped to extend the umbrella of transparency and noncorruption to investors from all countries via company-by-company reporting of revenues. The most significant expansion of the EITI++ approach, as recommended in chapter 2, is to provide support for developing-country authorities in the actual negotiation of oil and mining investment agreements. This expansion of EITI++ has a parallel in helping structure FDI in infrastructure so as to ensure appropriate distribution of risks of fluctuation in supply and demand and foreign exchange exposure, backed by work-out mediation when forecasts go awry, as recommended in chapter 3.

With regard to FDI in manufacturing and assembly, the market failures associated with upgrading the host production and export base and expanding backward linkages to local suppliers highlight a crucial function for external assistance. The World Bank Group (especially the IFC and MIGA) and regional development banks can play a catalytic role in overcoming coordination externalities by providing help for customized investment promotion, FDI-associated infrastructure, and vocational training for workers and technicians. There is a growing body of evidence—particularly internal IFC assessments—showing that policy advice and financial support for development are most effective when offered together. Past practices of simply providing World Bank consultant reports on policy reform, supplemented by training seminars for middle-level host bureaucrats, have proven to be of very limited utility. What is needed are multilateral lending institution packages of operational recommendations, on-the-ground technical support, and concrete resources linked to and backed by host policy champions and local monitors.

In fact, high-payoff assistance to developing economies to use FDI as part of a strategy to upgrade and diversify exports has not been a priority for multilateral lending institutions. Instead, the focus of their rapidly growing efforts to support the private sector in developing countries has been directed almost exclusively to removing liquidity constraints for small and medium-sized firms—an extraordinarily tricky undertaking, often with low payoff even when successful (Perry 2010). Multilateral development bank lending to private firms reached 35 percent of total operations in 2008, three times larger than in 2003. Of this total, nearly 40 percent of the loans and 60 percent of equity investments went to financial intermediaries in the hopes of reducing liquidity constraints on small and medium-sized firms.

Finally, the World Bank and regional development banks must screen out support for FDI projects that rely on trade protection to survive, as recommended previously for national aid agencies and political-risk insurers.

Other Organizations and Groups

The analysis presented here addresses policies that host and home countries might adopt to optimize the benefits from FDI and from the external support that might be provided by multilateral lending institutions and national assistance agencies. But it also highlights important roles for the other players involved.

International Labor Organizations and Civil Society Groups and Nongovernmental Organizations

As recently as a decade ago, it was not difficult to find numerous critiques of the intervention of self-appointed, nonrepresentative NGOs in the affairs of international investors. Today it has become clear that Transparency International, Global Witness, Publish What Your Pay, Revenue Watch Institute, and other international civil society groups and NGOs—as well as their local counterparts—provide a public good and help with setting and monitoring international standards in a way that today's most rigorous public policy analytics would support. This is well recognized already in the activities associated with supporting the EITI and related anticorruption efforts, but the evidence introduced here shows that the need for external pressures extends deep into the operations of manufacturing MNCs as well.

However, positioning civil society groups and NGOs to optimize the contribution of FDI to broad-based sustainable social and economic development requires some shaking up of the conventional wisdom among these groups.

Popular calls to demand higher minimum wages or living wages for workers are likely to be counterproductive for reasons explained in this volume (e.g., because such moves render plants uncompetitive and discriminate against younger, older, and single workers). The same goes for attempts to prevent employers from altering the level of employment in response to fluctuations in external markets.[7] The challenge is to incorporate productivity-based wages and labor market flexibility into the agenda for reasonable treatment of low-skilled workers. For a particular segment of low-wage operations, employees supplying inputs to highly branded retailers (including collegiate retailers) should receive a premium, delivered directly from oligopoly profits and consumer pockets, as described in chapter 4.

In order to upgrade the production base and diversify exports, international labor organizations and civil society groups will want to recognize the negative consequences of imposing performance requirements (such as joint-venture and domestic-content requirements) on multinationals. They should abandon antagonism toward the TRIMs agreement and turn away from the misdirected effort to rewrite this portion of the US model BIT. International labor and civil society groups will want to become supporters, not opponents, of limits on performance requirements.[8]

---

7. The demand that international investors pay wages high enough to support a family has become ubiquitous. The adverse consequences for younger, single, and entry-level workers are often simply left unaddressed. See ILO (2008) and OECD Watch, "Key Issues for a Review of the OECD Guidelines," December 2009, http://oecdwatch.org (accessed on February 1, 2011).

8. Comments on the US Model Bilateral Investment Treaty submitted by the Center for Environmental Law, EarthJustice, Friends of the Earth US, Oxfam America, and Sierra Club, July 31, 2009. Also see Cosbey (2009).

Topping this off, international labor and civil society groups will want to endorse business-friendly treatment of local firms to allow indigenous supply chain development.

In terms of combating the denial of worker rights and the abusive treatment of labor, the evidence shows that international labor and civil society groups have mutually supportive and complementary roles to play. This means that any effort by one group to monopolize the international effort to support workers and deny legitimacy to others does a disservice to production laborers around the world.

Corporate Social Responsibility Advocates

It is commonplace to open discussion of corporate social responsibility by acknowledging that there is no common definition of what is encompassed in the concept.[9] With regard to socially responsible multinational corporate investment, the most fundamental requirement is for companies to acknowledge and observe the 10 fundamental standards in the UN Global Compact that span four critical areas:[10]

Human Rights

- Principle 1: Businesses should support and respect the protection of internationally proclaimed human rights
- Principle 2: Make sure that they are not complicit in human rights abuses

Labor Standards

- Principle 3: Businesses should uphold freedom of association and the effective recognition of the right to collective bargaining
- Principle 4: Elimination of all forms of forced and compulsory labor
- Principle 5: Effective abolition of child labor
- Principle 6: Elimination of discrimination with respect to employment and occupation

---

9. The Monitor Institute (2009, 13) identifies corporate social responsibility as socially responsible investing, social investing, mission-driven investing, sustainable and responsible investing, blended value, values-based investing, mission-related investing, ethical investing, responsible investing, impact investing, program-related investing, triple-bottom-line investing, and environmental, social, and governance investing.

10. See the website of UN Global Compact, www.unglobalcompact.org (accessed on February 1, 2011).

Environment

- Principle 7: Businesses should support a precautionary approach to environmental challenges
- Principle 8: Undertake initiatives to promote greater environmental responsibility
- Principle 9: Encourage the development and diffusion of environmentally friendly technologies

Anticorruption

- Principle 10: Businesses should work against corruption in all its forms, including extortion and bribery

Next, socially responsible international companies should set up internal systems—and provide internal training to employees and managers—to ensure compliance and then report results. Perhaps the most widely recognized reporting system is that of the Global Reporting Initiative.[11]

The recommendations above notwithstanding, the analysis provided here moves markedly beyond "complying" and "reporting" to a much more proactive role for investors with regard to their mainline operations. In order to handle "resource curse" issues, for example, the Global Reporting Initiative pronounces that international investors should "report the percentage of total number of management and nonmanagement employees who have received anticorruption training" and "provide a description of significant impacts of activities, products, and services on biodiversity in protected areas and areas of high biodiversity value outside protected areas."[12]

The recommendations here are much more specific and assertive. Socially responsible international resource investors should:

- use their influence on the ground in individual resource-rich countries to bring new governments into the EITI and EITI++ fold;
- develop industrywide model practices to preserve the environment, address the needs of indigenous peoples, and incorporate full-life-cycle community planning into their projects, while simultaneously providing capacity building for monitoring on a national and local level; and
- in their own self-interest, use their influence on the ground in individual resource-rich countries to bring about transparency of revenue streams on a company-by-company basis (thus exposing non-OECD investors to the same scrutiny as OECD investors), rather than insisting on aggregate-

---

11. Global Reporting Initiative, G3 Guidelines, www.globalreporting.org (accessed on February 1, 2011).

12. Ibid.

only reporting of revenue streams (thus allowing non-OECD investors to avoid close scrutiny).

In order to promote backward linkages, the Global Reporting Initiative tells its adherents to report on "how much do you buy locally." But the analysis presented here proposes much more targeted queries:

- Has the socially responsible investor designated a manager to be a "talent scout" to identify and pursue possible indigenous suppliers (or work with local vendor development agencies)?

- Does the socially responsible investor have a program to provide production advice, managerial advice, and advance purchase orders to potential indigenous suppliers (a teaching externality)?

- Does the socially responsible investor have a system to "qualify" and "certify" potential indigenous suppliers (a labeling externality)?

- Does the socially responsible investor have a plan whereby indigenous suppliers are introduced to sister affiliates in the region (an export externality)?

With regard to influencing the environment for business, the Global Reporting Initiative protocol asks international corporations to report on their public policy positions and on their participation in public policy development and lobbying (as recommended in OECD guidelines). Corporate social responsibility pressure of the kind recommended here would want to push international corporations in the direction of support for labor institution externalities, such as ensuring that all members of the business associations with which they are connected (no matter what skill level their operations) operate with common and mutually acceptable human resource standards, albeit not with identical wage levels.

One could go down the long list of reporting protocols in the Global Reporting Initiative or other industrywide or industry-specific company codes of conduct to try to translate the findings about optimizing the contribution of FDI to development into specific practical recommendations for action. The thrust of such an endeavor would, in each case, spring from the conviction that the strongest contribution FDI can make to the growth and welfare of the host country comes from well-structured, well-run, and environmentally sound mainline operations of MNCs.

At the end of the day, the findings presented in this volume should not detract from the efforts of many in the pro-poor sustainable development community who simply want to pressure international corporations to "give back" more to the communities where they operate. The most frequent objective of these demands is for international corporations to be more involved in community-based social projects or in aiding local organizations and initiatives. But the evidence presented here shows that the principal benefits from foreign investors come from the direct effects their core operations can have on the host economy, not from the philanthropy that might accompany their on-the-ground activities. Advocating large-scale, corporate-sponsored social programs or poverty reduction initiatives should not substitute for insistence that mainline multinational investor operations be run in an open, competitive, and well-structured manner. Corporate charity surely has its place, but the pro-poor sustainable development policy community will want to begin to shift its focus more directly to supporting the 12 channels identified in this volume through which FDI can help raise living standards.

10

Lessons and Conclusions: The Second-Generation Research Agenda

The preceding pages are filled with suggestions about which areas in the interaction between foreign investors and developing host economies need further investigation. This final chapter provides an opportunity to pull together lessons and conclusions about how such research can be carried out to achieve the most useful and accurate results.

Three lessons stand out.

First, it is important to reiterate—since almost all first-generation research ignored this point—that investigations that use aggregate FDI data for statistical analysis of the "impact" of FDI on the host economy are almost certainly going to lead to unreliable results. FDI in natural resources, infrastructure, manufacturing, and services leads to such different activities, diverse impacts, and distinctive policy challenges that the idea of combining them all into a single FDI "flow" that might produce some single "result" does not make sense.

Across countries, investigations simply will not produce intelligible results if they derive a correlation using data from predominantly extractive industry FDI in some countries and from predominantly export-oriented manufacturing FDI in others in order to come to conclusions about the FDI-and-host-welfare relationship. Within a single country, the adventures or misadventures of FDI in infrastructure take place on a different plane from the positive or negative impacts of FDI in industrial manufacturing. Empirical analysis must deal with the two separately.

Second, second-generation investigations of the impact of FDI on host economies will be much more revealing and useful to the extent that they combine firm survey data and case studies with increasingly sophisticated econometric analysis. In identifying horizontal and vertical externalities from foreign investors to domestic firms, multimethodology research added to econometric analysis can add confidence about causality and identify channels through which spillovers occur. In the area of FDI and export externalities, the finding that the probability of doing more-than-expected exporting is positively correlated with close-by presence of foreign investors, but uncorrelated with close-by concentration of export activity more generally, is a tantalizing discovery. But how much richer and more useful will it be to know whether the host exporters are part of FDI supply chains that benefit from spillovers in a vertical direction, or are instead independent of those supply chains and operating in parallel with them as the beneficiaries of spillovers in a horizontal direction? If what is being observed is a vertical phenomenon, have the host exporters received direct "export coaching" from foreign firms? Or have they gained new export expertise indirectly? A modest effort at survey research or case study analysis, carried out in parallel with econometric tests, can provide the answers.

Does the presence of foreign firms generate labor market externalities that benefit local workers in the host economy more broadly? As shown earlier, the econometric answer often appears to be yes, controlling for labor force characteristics, sector characteristics, and regional characteristics. But why *is* this? And what host policies might enhance this effect? Under what circumstances do some kinds of foreign investors (those with higher-skill-intensive operations) lead the movement for voluntary or mandatory enforcement of better treatment of workers (including those who work in lower-skill-intensive operations) at the zone, regional, or national level—a labor institution externality? Once again there is a rich opportunity to combine direct observation with econometric analysis.

So if the potential payoffs from combining survey research, industry studies, and project case studies with econometrics are so significant for analysts and policymakers alike, does this mean that the evolution toward multimethodology research techniques will come about naturally or easily? Unfortunately, the answer is most definitely not. There are significant market imperfections and perverse incentive structures that prevent socially optimal outcomes from today's economics profession.

What are these imperfections and structures? The Brookings Trade Forum grappled with this question in 2007 (Collins 2008). Participants almost unanimously agreed that multiple methodological approaches to investigating the impact of FDI on host economies would improve research results and make them more relevant for policymakers. With equal virtual unanimity, they identified the roadblock to this outcome as the editors and editorial boards of the leading economics journals who discourage or refuse to accept manuscripts that stray beyond strict econometric techniques, even as a complement to those techniques. To be fair, few of the academics who joined in the criticism of the economics journals reported that they actually encouraged their own graduate students to engage in survey research or case study investigations (one or two indicated that they did). So progress might require some broadening, upgrading, and retooling of the skill set of the economics professoriate, as well as broadening the perspectives of editors, editorial boards, and reviewers of the leading economics journals.

A further market imperfection in achieving broader and deeper investigative undertakings is found in the "guild" (monopoly) problem embodied in the National Bureau of Economic Research (NBER). Like any monopolist, the NBER is skilled at coopting occasional individuals who do not use the conventional research techniques favored within the guild. But the NBER assiduously defends its self-referential monopoly. The budding young second-generation professor or graduate student eager to investigate the interactions between FDI and development might think that the "Research Summary" of the NBER International Trade and Investment Program might be a summary of research in the field. In truth, it is a summary of nothing but the NBER's research in the field. This second generation professor or graduate student would never come across 90 percent of the sources cited in the bibliography of this volume. The same young professor or graduate student fortunate enough to get into any one of the NBER Summer Institutes devoted to international trade and investment would be introduced to the work of many fine scholars, but would have no occasion to meet up—either in person or as a footnote— with scholars such as David G. McKendrick, Richard F. Donner, Stephan Haggard, Greg Linden, Kenneth L. Kraemer, or Jason Dedrick.

A final obstacle to the deployment of multiple investigative methodologies originates in an epistemological misunderstanding that pervades conventional economics literature. As noted earlier in this volume, the term "anecdotal evidence" carries a pejorative connotation if it signifies that such evidence is confined to a single (or small number of) observation(s) and that there is a high probability that a few additional observations will show different results. In fact, however, case studies, industry studies, and small-number samples can be structured across regions, time periods, and economic sectors in ways that minimize selection bias and render quite small the likelihood that the next observation will overturn the previously observed relationship among variables (King, Keohane, and Verba 1994). So second-generation researchers will want to take care not to dismiss all such observations as simply "anecdotal" when in fact that research might rigorously support or critique what is observed in large correlations.

Third, this volume reveals the need for more, better, and deeper investigation of the political economy of multinational investors, multilateral lending institutions, and host-country policymaking. The interplay between the indigenous policy process and external actors has come up in many contexts in this volume. Foreign investors in natural resources can choose to acquiesce in (or even fuel) corruption and the preservation of autarchic government. Or those same investors can choose to help strengthen the Extractive Industries Transparency Initiative (EITI) and create a level playing field for all investors by supporting company-by-company reporting of revenues. Foreign investors in manufacturing and assembly can choose to avoid (or even hinder) independent monitoring of factory conditions. Or those same investors can choose to lead industry associations that promote better treatment of workers and discipline those in the industry that fail to comply. Multinational investors can choose to adhere to corporate social responsibility codes that simply report the amount of inputs purchased from the host economy. Or those same investors can choose to devise corporate social responsibility codes that designate "talent scouts" to find potential suppliers in host economies, set up vendor development and certification programs, and introduce successful indigenous participants to international markets. The World Bank and the regional development banks can choose to write advisory reports and fund projects associated with those reports. Or they can choose to fund on-the-ground advisory missions, identify indigenous "reform champions" among host-government agencies, launch strong capacity-building initiatives as part of program packages, and fund processes as well as projects.

These few examples reveal that highly delicate questions about external intervention by international investors and multilateral lending institutions are certain to emerge. Second-generation research about the relationship between FDI and development cannot simply ignore the real-world political economy of host-country policy formation.

References

Acemoglu, Daron, Simon Johnson, and James A. Robinson. 2003. An African Success Story: Botswana. In *In Search of Prosperity: Analytic Narratives on Economic Growth,* ed. Dani Rodrik. Princeton, NJ: Princeton University Press.

Aghion, Philippe, and Peter Howitt. 1998. *Endogenous Growth Theory.* Cambridge, MA: MIT Press.

Agosin, Manuel. 2008. Does Foreign Investment Lay a Foundation for Economic Growth? In *Foreign Investment and Sustainable Development: Lessons from the Americas,* Working Group on Development and the Environment in the Americas. Washington: Heinrich Boll Foundation North America.

Agosin, Manuel, and R. Mayer. 2000. *Foreign Investment in Developing Countries: Does It Crowd-In Domestic Investment?* UNCTAD Discussion Paper 46. Geneva: United Nations.

Agrawal, Pradeep. 2000. *Economic Impact of Foreign Direct Investment in South Asia.* Washington: World Bank.

Aitken, Brian J., and Ann E. Harrison. 1999. Do Domestic Firms Benefit from Direct Foreign Investment? Evidence from Venezuela. *American Economic Review* 89, no. 3 (June): 605-18.

Aitken, Brian, Gordon H. Hanson, and Ann E. Harrison. 1997. Spillovers, Foreign Investment, and Export Behavior. *Journal of International Economics* 43, no. 1-2 (August): 103-32.

Aitken, Brian, Ann Harrison, and Robert E. Lipsey. 1996. Wages and Foreign Ownership: A Comparative Study of Mexico, Venezuela, and the United States. *Journal of International Economics* 40, no. 3-4: 345-71.

Akerloff, George. 1970. The Market for "Lemons": Quality Uncertainty and the Market Mechanism. *Quarterly Journal of Economics* 84, no. 3 (August): 488-500.

Alfaro, Laura, and Andrés Rodríguez-Clare. 2004. Multinationals and Linkages: An Empirical Investigation. *Economia* 4, no. 2: 113-69.

Alfaro, Laura, Sebnem Kalemli-Ozcan, and Selin Sayek. 2009. FDI, Productivity and Financial Development. *World Economy* 32, no. 1 (January): 111-36.

Alfaro, Laura, A. Chanda, Sebnem Kalemli-Ozcan, and Selin Sayek. 2006. *How Does Foreign Direct Investment Promote Economic Growth?* NBER Working Paper 12522. Cambridge, MA: National Bureau of Economic Research.

Amiti, Mary, and Caroline Freund. 2008. *The Anatomy of China's Export Growth*. World Bank Working Paper 4628 (May). Washington: World Bank Development Research Group, Trade Team, Policy Research.

Amiti, Mary, and Caroline Freund. 2010. What Accounts for the Rising Sophistication of Chinese Exports? In *China's Growing Role in World Trade*, ed. Robert C. Feenstra and Shang-Jin Wei. Chicago: University of Chicago Press for the National Bureau of Economic Research.

Anderson, Thomas. 2008. US Affiliates of Foreign Companies: Operations in 2006. *Survey of Current Business* (August): 186–203.

Anderson, James E., and Eric Van Wincoop. 2003. Gravity with Gravitas: A Solution to the Border Puzzle. *American Economic Review* 93, no. 1: 170–92.

Andres, Luis A., J. Luis Guasch, Thomas Haven, and Vivien Foster. 2008. *The Impact of Private Sector Participation in Infrastructure: Lights, Shadows, and the Road Ahead*. Washington: World Bank.

Arkolakis, Costas, Arnaud Costinot, and Andrés Rodríguez-Clare. 2009. *New Trade Models, Same Old Gains?* NBER Working Paper 15628. Cambridge, MA: National Bureau of Economic Research.

Arnold, Jens, Beata S. Javorcik, and Aaditya Mattoo. 2010. *Does Services Liberalization Benefit Manufacturing Firms? Evidence from the Czech Republic*. Policy Research Working Paper 4109. Washington: World Bank.

Arnold, Jens, Beata Javorcik, Molly Lipscomb, and Aaditya Mattoo. 2010. *Services Reform and Manufacturing Performance: Evidence from India*. Discussion Paper 8011. London: Centre for Economic Policy Research.

Asiedu, Elisabeth, and Hadi Salehi Esfanhani. 2001. Ownership Structure in Foreign Direct Investment Projects. *Review of Economics and Statistics* 83, no. 4: 647–66.

Austin, James E. 1990. Mexico and the Microcomputers (A) (Abridged). Harvard Business School Case 390-093. Cambridge, MA: Harvard Business School Publishing.

Auty, Richard M. 1994. *Patterns of Development: Resources, Policy and Economic Growth*. London: Edward Arnold.

Balasubramanyam, V.N., M. Salisu, and David Sapsford. 1996. Foreign Direct Investment and Growth in EP and IS Countries. *Economic Journal* 106, no. 434 (January): 92–105.

Bannon, Ian, and Paul Collier, ed. 2003. *Natural Resources and Violent Conflict: Options and Actions*. Washington: World Bank.

Barefoot, Kevin B., and Raymond J. Mataloni, Jr. 2009. US Multinational Companies: Operations in the United States and Abroad in 2007. *Survey of Current Business* (August): 63–87.

Beamish, Paul W., and Andres Delios. 1997. Incidence and Propensity of Alliance Formation by US, Japanese, and European MNEs. In *Cooperative Strategies: Asian-Pacific Perspectives*, ed. Paul W. Beamish and J. Peter Killing. San Francisco: The New Lexington Press.

Belderbos, Rene, Giovanni Capanelli, and Kyoji Fukao. 2000. The Local Content of Japanese Electronics Manufacturing Operations in Asia. In *The Role of Foreign Direct Investment in East Asian Economic Development*, ed. Takatoshi Ito and Anne O. Krueger. Chicago: University of Chicago Press for the National Bureau of Economic Research.

Bell, David E., Brian Milder, and Mary Shelman. 2007. *Vegpro Group: Growing in Harmony*. Harvard Business School Case 9-508-001 (December). Cambridge, MA: Harvard Business School Publishing.

Bergsten, C. Fred, Thomas Horst, and Theodore H. Moran. 1978. *American Multinationals and American Interests*. Washington: Brookings Institution.

Bernard, Andrew B., and J. Bradford Jensen. 1999. Exceptional Exporter Performance: Cause, Effect, or Both? *Journal of International Economics* 47, no. 1: 1–25.

Bernard, Andrew B., and J. Bradford Jensen. 2007. Firm Structure, Multinationals, and Manufacturing Plant Deaths. *Review of Economics and Statistics* 89, no. 2 (May).

Bernard, Andrew B., J. Bradford Jensen, and Peter K. Schott. 2005. *Importers, Exporters and Multinationals: A Portrait of Firms in the U.S. that Trade Goods.* NBER Working Paper No. 11404. Cambridge, MA: National Bureau of Economic Research.

Bernard, Andrew B., J. Bradford Jensen, and Peter K. Schott. 2009. Importers, Exporters and Multinationals: A Portrait of Firms in the US that Trade Goods. In *Producer Dynamics: New Evidence from Micro Data,* ed. J. B., Jensen, T. Duane, and M. Roberts. Chicago: University of Chicago Press for the National Bureau of Economic Research.

Berry, Charles. 2003. Shall the Twain Meet? Finding Common Ground or Uncommon Solutions: A Broker's Perspective. In *International Political Risk Management: The Brave New World.* Washington: World Bank.

Blalock, Garrick, and Paul J. Gertler. 2004. Learning from Exporting Revisited in a Less Developed Setting. *Journal of International Economics* 75, no. 2: 397–416.

Blalock, Garrick, and Paul J. Gertler. 2005. Foreign Direct Investment and Externalities: The Case for Public Intervention. In *Does Foreign Direct Investment Promote Development?* ed. Theodore H. Moran, Edward M. Graham, and Magnus Blomström. Washington: Institute for International Economics and the Center for Global Development.

Blalock, Garrick, and Paul J. Gertler. 2008. Welfare Gains from Foreign Direct Investment through Technology Transfer to Local Suppliers. *Journal of International Economics* 74, no. 2: 402–21.

Blalock, Garrick, and Daniel H. Simon. 2009. Do All Firms Benefit Equally from Downstream FDI? The Moderating Effect of Local Suppliers' Capabilities on Productivity Gains. *Journal of International Business Studies* 40, no. 7 (September): 1075–95.

Blomström, Magnus, Ari Kokko, and Mario Zejan. 1992. *Host Country Competition and Technology Transfer by Multinationals.* NBER Working Paper 4131. Cambridge, MA: National Bureau of Economic Research.

Blomström, Magnus, Robert E. Lipsey, and K. Kulchyck. 1988. US and Swedish Direct Investment and Exports. In *Trade Policy Issues and Empirical Analysis,* ed. Robert E. Baldwin. Chicago: University of Chicago Press for the National Bureau of Economic Research.

Blonigen, Bruce A., and Alyson C. Ma. 2010. Please Pass the Catch-Up: The Relative Performance of Chinese and Foreign Firms in Chinese Exports. In *China's Growing Role in World Trade,* ed. Robert C. Feenstra and Shang-Jin Wei. Chicago: University of Chicago Press for the National Bureau of Economic Research.

Blonigen, Bruce A., and Miao Grace Wang. 2005. Inappropriate Pooling of Wealthy and Poor Countries in Empirical FDI Studies. In *Does Foreign Direct Investment Promote Development?* ed. Theodore H. Moran, Edward M. Graham, and Magnus Blomström. Washington: Institute for International Economics and the Center for Global Development.

Borensztein, E., J. de Gregorio, and J. W. Lee. 1998. How Does Foreign Direct Investment Affect Economic Growth? *Journal of International Economics* 45, no. 1 (June): 115–35.

Borga, Maria, and Robert E. Lipsey. 2009. Factor Prices, Factor Substitution and Exporting in US Manufacturing Affiliates Abroad. *World Economy* 32, no. 1 (January).

Borjas, George J. 2007. Labor Economics. Boston: McGraw-Hill. In *What Do Unions Do? A Twenty-Year Perspective* (Fourth edition), ed. James T. Bennett and Bruce E. Kaufman. New Brunswick, Canada: Transaction Publishers.

Bosworth, Barry P., and Susan M. Collins. 1999. Capital Flows to Developing Economies: Implications for Saving and Investment. *Brookings Papers on Economic Activity* 1. Washington: Brookings Institution.

Brahmbhatt, Milan, and Otaviano Canuto. 2010. *Natural Resources and Development Strategy after the Crisis.* World Bank Poverty Reduction and Economic Management Network Economic Premise Note no. 1 (February). Washington: World Bank.

Brahmbhatt, Milan, Otaviano Canuto, and Ekaterina Vostroknutova. 2010. *Dealing with Dutch Disease*. World Bank Poverty Reduction and Economic Management Network Economic Premise Note no. 16 (June). Washington: World Bank.

Brainard, S. Lael, and David A. Riker. 1997. *Are US Multinationals Exporting US Jobs?* NBER Working Paper 5958. Cambridge, MA: National Bureau of Economic Research.

Brander James A., and Barbara J. Spencer. 1981. Tariffs and the Extraction of Foreign Monopoly Rents and Potential Entry. *Canadian Journal of Economics* 14, no. 3 (August): 371–89.

Branstetter, Lee, and C. Fritz Foley. 2010. Facts and Fallacies about US FDI in China (with apologies to Rob Feenstra). In *China's Growing Role in World Trade*, ed. Robert C. Feenstra and Shang-Jin Wei. Chicago: University of Chicago Press for the National Bureau of Economic Research.

Brautigam, Deborah, Thomas Farole, and Tang Xiaoyang. 2010. *China's Investment in African Special Economic Zones: Prospects, Challenges, and Opportunities*. World Bank Poverty Reduction and Economic Management Network Economic Premise Note no. 5 (March). Washington: World Bank.

Brennan, M. J., and E. S. Schwartz. 1985. Evaluating Natural Resource Investments. *Journal of Business* 58, no. 2: 135–57.

Bucar, Maja, Matija Rojec, and Metka Stare. 2009. Backward FDI Linkages as a Channel for Transferring Technology and Building Innovation Capability: The Case of Slovenia. *European Journal of Development Research* 21, no. 1: 137–53.

Capanelli, Giovanni. 1997. Buyer-Supplier Relations and Technology Transfer: Japanese Consumer Electronics. *International Review of Economics and Business* 44, no. 3 (September): 633–62.

Carkovic, Maria, and Ross Levine. 2005. Does Foreign Direct Investment Accelerate Economic Growth? In *Does Foreign Direct Investment Promote Development?* ed. Theodore H. Moran, Edward M. Graham, and Magnus Blomström. Washington: Institute for International Economics and the Center for Global Development.

Carr, David L., James R. Markusen, and Anthony J. Venables. 1998. Multinational Firms and the New Trade Theory. *Journal of International Economics* 46, no. 1: 83–103.

CESAIS (Center for Economic and Social Applications). 2002. Workers' Voices: A Study of the Assets and Needs of Factory Workers in Vietnam. University of Ho Chi Minh, Vietnam (now Truong Doan).

Center for Global Development. 2010. Report of the Working Group on Combating Corrupt Payments in International Business Transactions. Presentation to the US House of Representatives Financial Services Committee staff, Washington.

Chaney, Thomas. 2008. Distorted Gravity: The Intensive and Extensive Margins of International Trade. *American Economic Review* 98, no. 4: 1707–721.

Chen, Huiya, and Deborah L. Swenson. 2007. Multinational Firms and New Chinese Export Transactions. *Canadian Journal of Economics* 121, no. 1: 199–218.

Choe, Jong II. 2003. Do Foreign Direct Investment and Gross Domestic Investment Promote Economic Growth? *Review of Development Economics* 7, no. 1 (February): 44–57.

Chong, Alberto, and Florencio López de Silanes. 2005. *Privatization in Latin America: Myths and Reality*. Stanford, CA: Stanford University Press.

Choudhri, Ehsan U., and Dalia S. Kakura. 2000. International Trade and Productivity Growth: Exploring the Sectoral Effects for Developing Countries. *IMF Staff Papers* 47, no. 1: 30–53.

Christian Aid. 2007. *A Rich Seam: Who Benefits from Rising Commodity Prices?* London: Christian Aid.

Clarke, George R. G., and Scott J. Wallsten. 2002. *Universal(ly) Bad) Service: Providing Infrastructure Services to Rural and Poor Urban Consumers*. Washington: World Bank.

Clerides, Sofronis K., Saul Lach, and James R. Tybout. 1998. Is Learning by Exporting Important? Micro-Dynamic Evidence from Colombia, Mexico, and Morocco. *Quarterly Journal of Economics* 113, no. 3: 903–47.

Cline, William R. 1987. *Informatics and Development: Trade, and Industrial Policy in Argentina, Brazil, and Mexico*. Washington: Economics International.

Cline, William R. 2004. *Trade Policy and Global Poverty*. Washington: Institute for International Economics.

Cline, William. 2010. *Financial Globalization, Economic Growth, and the Crisis of 2007–09*. Washington: Peterson Institute for International Economics.

Collins, Susan M., ed. 2008. *Brookings Trade Forum 2007: Foreign Direct Investment*. Washington: Brookings Institution.

Collier, Paul. 2007. *The Bottom Billion: Why the Poorest Countries Are Failing, and What Can Be Done About It*. New York: Oxford University Press.

Collier, Paul, and Benedikt Goderis. 2007. *Commodity Prices, Growth and the Natural Resources Curse: Reconciling a Conundrum*. Centre for the Study of African Economies Working Paper 276 (August). Oxford, UK: Oxford University.

Cosbey, Aaron. 2009. *A Sustainable Development Roadmap for the WTO*. Winnipeg, Canada: Institute for Sustainable Development.

Criscuolo, Alberto. 2007. Driving Growth: How did Botswana, Mauritius, Cape Verde, and Taiwan Overcome Institutional Capacity Constraints? World Bank Foreign Investment Advisory Service. Photocopy.

Davis, Graham A., and John E. Tilton. 2005. The Resource Curse. *Natural Resources Forum* 29, no. 3: 233–42.

Davis, Graham A. 1995. Learning to Love the Dutch Disease: Evidence from the Mineral Economies. *World Development* 23, no. 10: 1765–779.

de la Cruz, Justino, Robert B. Koopman, Zhi Wang, and Shang-Jin Wei. 2009. Domestic and Foreign Value-added in Mexico's Manufacturing Exports. Photocopy (May 9).

de la Cruz, Justino, Robert B. Koopman, Zhi Wang, and Shang-Jin Wei. 2010. *Estimating Foreign Value-Added in Mexico's Manufacturing Exports*. Working Paper. US International Trade Commission and National Bureau of Economic Research.

De Mello, Luiz. 1999. Foreign Direct Investment-Led Growth: Evidence from Time Series and Panel Data. *Oxford Economic Papers* 51, no. 1 (January): 133–51.

Dean, Judith, K. C. Fung, and Zhi Wang. 2009. *Measuring Vertical Specialization: The Case of China*. USITC Working Paper 2008-9-D (September). Washington: US International Trade Commission.

Delgado, Miguel A., Jose C. Farinas, and Sonia Ruano. 2002. Firm Productivity and Export Markets: A Nonparametric Approach. *Journal of International Economics* 57, no. 2: 397–422.

Desai, Miguel, C. Fritz Foley, and James R. Hines, Jr. 2005a. Foreign Direct Investment and the Domestic Capital Stock. *American Economic Review* 95, no. 2 (May): 33–38.

Desai, Miguel, C. Fritz Foley, and James R. Hines, Jr. 2005b. *Foreign Direct Investment and Domestic Economic Activity*. NBER Research Paper 11717. Cambridge, MA: National Bureau of Economic Research.

Dixit, Avinash K., and Robert S. Pindyck. 1994. *Investment under Uncertainty*. Princeton, NJ: Princeton University Press.

Dixit, Avinash K., and Joseph E. Stiglitz. 1977. Monopolistic Competition and Optimum Product Diversity. *American Economic Review* 67, no. 3: 297–308.

Doms, Mark E., and J. Bradford Jensen. 1998. Comparing Wages, Skills, and Productivity between Domestic and Foreign Owned Manufacturing Establishments in the United States. In *Geography and Ownership as Bases for Economic Accounting*, ed. Robert E. Baldwin, Robert E. Lipsey, and J. David Richardson. Cambridge, MA: National Bureau of Economic Research and University of Chicago Press.

Donnelly, Roger, and Benjamin Ford. 2008. *Into Africa: How the Resource Boom is Making Sub-Saharan Africa More Important to Australia*. Lowy Institute Paper 24. New South Wales, Australia: The Lowy Institute for International Policy.

Drabek, Zdenek, ed. 2010. *Is the World Trade Organization Attractive Enough for Emerging Economies?* Critical Essays on the Multilateral Trading System. London: Palgrave Macmillan.

Dunning, John H., ed. 1993. *The Theory of Transnational Corporations*. New York: Routledge.

Durand, Cedrick. 2007. Externalities from Foreign Direct Investment in the Mexican Retailing Sector. *Cambridge Journal of Economics* 31, no. 3: 393–411.

Easterly, William, and Luis Servén. 2003. *The Limits of Stabilization: Infrastructure, Public Deficits, and Growth in Latin America*. Stanford, CA: Stanford University Press.

Easterly, William. 2001. *The Elusive Quest for Growth: Economists' Adventures and Misadventures in the Tropics*. Cambridge, MA: MIT Press.

Eastman, H., and S. Stykolt. 1970. A Model for the Study of Protected Oligopolies. *Economic Journal* 70: 336–47.

Eaton, Jonathan, Samuel Kortum, and Francis Kramarz. 2008. *An Anatomy of International Trade: Evidence from French Firms*. NBER Working Paper 14610. Cambridge, MA: National Bureau of Economic Research.

Edwards, Lawrence, and Robert Z. Lawrence. 2010. *Do Developed and Developing Countries Compete Head to Head in High Tech?* Working Paper 10-8 (June). Washington: Peterson Institute for International Economics.

Edwards, Lawrence, and Robert Z. Lawrence. Forthcoming. *Rising Tide: Is Growth in Emerging Economies Good for the United States?* Washington: Peterson Institute for International Economics.

Encarnation, Dennis J., and Louis T. Wells, Jr. 1986. Evaluating Foreign Investment. In *Investing in Development: New Roles for Private Capital?* ed. Theodore H. Moran. Washington: Overseas Development Council.

Estache, Antonio. 2006. PPI Partnerships vs. PPI Divorces in LDCs. *Review of Industrial Organization* 29, no. 1: 3–26.

Feenstra, Robert C. 2004. *Advanced International Trade: Theory and Evidence*. Princeton: Princeton University Press.

Feenstra, Robert C., and Gordon Hanson. 1997. Foreign Direct Investment and Relative Wages: Evidence from Mexico's Maquiladoras. *Journal of International Economics* 42: 371–94.

Feenstra, Robert C., and Shang-Jin Wei, ed. 2010. Introduction. *China's Growing Role in World Trade*. Chicago: University of Chicago Press for the National Bureau of Economic Research.

Feinberg, Susan E., and Michael P. Keane. 2005. Intrafirm Trade of US MNCs: Findings and Implications for Models and Politics Toward Trade and Investment. In *Does Foreign Direct Investment Promote Development?* ed. Theodore H. Moran, Edward M. Graham, and Magnus Blomström. Washington: Center for Global Development and Institute for International Economics.

Feinberg, Susan E., and Michael P. Keane. 2006. Accounting for the Growth of MNC-Based Trade Using a Structural Model of U.S. MNCs. *American Economic Review* 96, no. 5 (December): 1515–558.

Ferrantino, Michael, Robert Koopman, Zhi Wang, Falan Yiung, Ling Chen, Fengjie Que, and Haifend Wang. 2010. *Classification and Statistical Reconciliation of Trade in Advanced Technology Products: The Case of China and the United States*. Joint Working Paper on US-China Trade in Advanced Technology Products. Washington: US International Trade Commission.

Figlio, David N., and Bruce A. Blonigen. 2000. The Effects of Foreign Direct Investment on Local Communities. *Journal of Urban Economics* 48, no. 2 (September): 338–63.

Foreign Investment Advisory Service. 2008. *Special Economic Zones: Performance, Lessons Learned, and Implications for Zone Development.* World Bank Working Paper 45869. Washington: World Bank.

Freund, Caroline, and Nadia Rocha. 2010. What Constrains Africa's Exports? *World Bank Research Digest* 4, no. 3: 1.

Gallagher, Kevin P. 2010. US-China Investment Treaty: A Threat to Stability and Growth in China. Tufts University GDAE Program. Photocopy (June 15).

Gallagher, Kevin P., and Daniel Chudnovsky. 2009. *Rethinking Foreign Investment for Sustainable Development: Lessons from Latin America.* London: Anthem Press.

Gallagher, Kevin P., and Lyuba Zarsky. 2007. *The Enclave Economy: Foreign Investment and Sustainable Development in Mexico's Silicon Valley.* Boston, MA: MIT Press.

Geishecker, Ingo, Holger Görg, and Daria Taglioni. 2009. Characterizing Euro Area Multinationals. *The World Economy* 32, no. 1 (January): 49–76.

Girma, Sourafel, and Yundan Gong. 2008. FDI, Linkages and the Efficiency of State-Owned Enterprises in China. *Journal of Development Studies* 44, no. 5: 728–49.

Giroud, Axèle, and Hafiz Mirza. 2006. Factors Determining Supply Linkages between Transnational Corporations and Local Suppliers in ASEAN. *Transnational Corporations* 15, no. 3 (December).

Glassburner, Bruce. 1988. Indonesia: Windfalls in a Poor Rural Economy. In *Oil Windfalls: Blessing or Curse?* ed. Alan Gelb et al. New York: Oxford University Press for World Bank.

Global Witness. 2006. *Heavy Mittal? A State with a State: The Inequitable Mineral Development Agreement between the Government of Liberia and Mittal Steel Holdings NV.* Washington: Global Witness.

Global Witness. 2007. *Update on the Renegotiation of the Mineral Development Agreement between Mittal Steel and the Government of Liberia* (August). Washington.

Gomes-Casseres, Benjamin. 1989. Ownership Structures of Foreign Subsidiaries: Theory and Evidence. *Journal of Economic Behavior and Organization* 11, no. 1 (January): 1–25.

Good, Kenneth. 1992. Interpreting the Exceptionality of Botswana. *Journal of Modern African Studies* 30, no. 1: 69–95.

Good, Kenneth. 1994. Corruption and Mismanagement in Botswana: A Best-Case Example? *Journal of Modern African Studies* 32, no. 3: 499–521.

Görg, Holger, and David Greenaway. 2004. Much Ado About Nothing? Do Domestic Firms Really Benefit from Foreign Direct Investment? *World Bank Research Observer* 19, no. 2: 171–97.

Görg, Holger, and Eric Strobl. 2005. Spillovers from Foreign Firms though Worker Mobility: An Empirical Investigation. *Scandinavian Journal of Economics* 107, no. 4: 693–709.

Graham, Edward M. 2000. *Fighting the Wrong Enemy: Antiglobal Activists and Multinational Enterprises.* Washington: Institute for International Economics.

Graham, Edward M., and David M. Marchick. 2006. *US National Security and Foreign Direct Investment.* Washington: Peterson Institute for International Economics.

Grossman, Gene M., and Elhanan Helpman. 1991. *Innovation and Growth in the Global Economy.* Cambridge, MA: MIT Press.

Guasch, J. Luis. 2004. *Granting and Renegotiating Infrastructure Concessions: Doing It Right.* Washington: World Bank.

Haddad, Mona, and Ann Harrison. 1993. Are There Positive Spillovers from Direct Foreign Investment? Evidence from Panel Data for Morocco. *Journal of Development Economics* 42, no. 1 (October): 51–74.

Haddad, Mona, Jamus Jerome Lim, and Christian Saborowski. 2010. *Trade Openness Reduces Growth Volatility When Countries Are Well Diversified.* Policy Research Working Paper 5222. Washington: World Bank.

Haddon, Jonathan. 2004. A Partial Solution. *Project Finance* (April). www.projectfinancemagazine. com (by subscription) (accessed on February 1, 2011).

Hanson, Gordon. 2001. *Should Countries Promote Foreign Direct Investment?* G-24 Discussion Paper Series no. 9 (February). Cambridge, MA: Center for International Development, Harvard University.

Hanson, Gordon. 2005. Comment. In *Does Foreign Direct Investment Promote Development?* ed. Theodore H. Moran, Edward M. Graham, and Magnus Blomström. Washington: Institute for International Economics and the Center for Global Development.

Harding, Torfinn, and Beata Smarzynska Javorcik. 2007. *Developing Economies and International Investors: Do Investment Promotion Agencies Bring Them Together?* World Bank Policy Research Working Paper 4339. Washington: World Bank.

Harris, Clive. 2003. *Private Participation in Infrastructure in Developing Countries: Trends, Impacts, and Policy Lessons.* Washington: World Bank.

Harrison, Ann, and Jason Scorse. 2010. Multinationals and Anti-Sweatshop Activism. *American Economic Review* 100, no. 1: 247–73.

Haskel, Jonathan E., Sonia Pereira, and Matthew Slaughter. 2007. Does Inward FDI Boost the Productivity of Domestic Firms? *Review of Economics and Statistics* 89, no. 3: 482–96.

Hausmann, Ricardo, and Dani Rodrik. 2003. Economic Development as Self-Discovery. *Journal of Development Economics* 72, no. 2: 603–33.

Hausmann, Ricardo, and Dani Rodrik. 2005. Self-Discovery in a Development Strategy for El Salvador. *Economia* 6, no. 1: 43–102.

Hausmann, Ricardo, Jason Hwang, and Dani Rodrik. 2009. What You Export Matters. *Journal of Economic Growth* 12, no. 1: 1–25.

Haveman, Jon D., Vivian Lei, and Janet S. Netz. 2001. International Integration and Growth: A Survey and Empirical Investigation. *Review of Development Economics* 5, no. 2 (June): 289–311.

Head, Keith, and John Ries. 2001. Overseas Investment and Firm Exports. *Review of International Economics* 9, no. 1: 108–22.

Helpman, Elhanan. 1984. A Simple Theory of International Trade with Multinational Corporations. *Journal of Political Economy* 92, no. 3: 451–71.

Hermes, Niels, and Robert Lensink. 2003. Foreign Direct Investment, Financial Development and Economic Growth. *Journal of Development Studies* 40, no. 1 (October): 142–63.

Hijzen, Alexander. 2008. Do Multinationals Promote Better Pay and Working Conditions? In *OECD Employment Outlook.* Paris: Organization for Economic Cooperation and Development.

Hirschman, Albert O. 1958. *The Strategy of Economic Development.* New Haven, CT: Yale University Press.

Hobday, Michael. 1995. *Innovation in East Asia: The Challenge to Japan.* London: Aldershot.

Hobday, Michael. 2000. East versus Southeast Asian Innovation Systems: Comparing OEM- and TNC-led Growth in Electronics. In *Technology, Learning, & Innovation,* ed. Linsu Kim and Richard Nelson. New York: Cambridge University Press.

Hoekman, Bernard, and Joseph Francois. 2009. *Services Trade and Policy.* Economics Working Paper 2009–03 (March). Vienna: Kepler University Linz.

Hufbauer, Gary Clyde, and Jisun Kim. 2009. *US Taxation of Multinational Corporations: What Makes Sense, What Doesn't.* Policy Briefs in International Economics 09-7. Washington: Peterson Institute for International Economics.

Hufbauer, Gary Clyde, Jeffrey J. Schott, and Woan Foong Wong. 2010. *Figuring Out the Doha Round.* Washington: Peterson Institute for International Economics.

Hummels, David, and Peter J. Klenow. 2005. The Variety and Quality of a Nation's Exports. *American Economic Review* 95, no. 3: 704–23.

ICMM (International Council on Mining & Metals). 2006-07. *The Challenge of Mineral Wealth: Using Resource Endowments to Foster Sustainable Development. Synthesis of Four Country Case Studies.* London.

ICMM (International Council on Mining & Metals). 2007. *The Challenge of Mineral Wealth: Using Resource Endowments to Foster Sustainable Development. Chile: Country Case Study* (July). London.

ICMM (International Council on Mining & Metals). 2008. *Peru Phase III Spotlight Note* (August). London.

ICMM (International Council on Mining & Metals). 2009. *Minerals Taxation Regimes: A Review of Issues and Challenges in Their Design and Application* (February). London: ICMM and Commonwealth Secretariat.

ILO (International Labor Organization). 2007. *Decent Work: A Perspective from the MNE Declaration to the Present.* Geneva.

ILO (International Labor Organization). 2008. *Declaration on Social Justice for Fair Globalization* (June). Geneva.

IMF (International Monetary Fund). 2008. IMF Country Report 08/331 Morocco: Selected Issues (October). Washington.

IMF (International Monetary Fund). 2009. Morocco—Preliminary Findings of the 2009 Article IV Consultation. Rabat (November 13). Washington.

Javorcik, Beata S. 2004. Does Foreign Direct Investment Increase the Productivity of Domestic Firms? In Search of Spillovers Through Backward Linkages. *American Economic Review* 94, no. 3: 605-27.

Javorcik, Beata S., and Yue Li. 2010. *Do the Biggest Aisles Serve a Brighter Future? Global Retail Chains and Their Implications for Romania.* World Bank Development Research Group Trade Team Policy Research Working Paper 4650. Washington: World Bank.

Javorcik, Beata S., and Kamal Saggi. 2010. Technological Asymmetry among Foreign Investors and Mode of Entry. *Economic Inquiry* 48, no. 2: 415-33.

Javorcik, Beata S., and Mariana Spatareanu. 2005. Disentangling FDI Spillover Effects: What Do Firm Perceptions Tell Us? In *Does Foreign Direct Investment Promote Development?* ed. Theodore H. Moran, Edward M. Graham, and Magnus Blomström. Washington: Institute for International Economics and Center for Global Development.

Javorcik, Beata S., Wolfgang Keller, and James Tybout. 2008. Openness and Industrial Response in a Wal-Mart World: A Case Study of Mexican Soaps, Detergents and Surfactant Products. *The World Economy* 31, no. 12 (December): 1558-180.

Jefferis, Keith. 2009. The Role of TNCs in the Extractive Industry of Botswana. *Transnational Corporations* 18, no. 1 (April): 61-93.

Jensen, J. Bradford. 2011 (forthcoming). *Fear of Offshoring: The Facts about Global Services Outsourcing.* Washington: Peterson Institute for International Economics.

Jensen, J. Bradford, and Lori G. Kletzer. 2008. *"Fear" and Offshoring: The Scope and Potential Impact of Imports and Exports of Services.* Policy Briefs in International Economics 08-1. Washington: Peterson Institute for International Economics.

Jun, Y. W., and S. G. Kim. 1990. *The Korean Electronics Industry-Current Status Perspectives and Policy Options.* OECD Report 22-23. Paris: Organization for Economic Cooperation and Development.

Kalotay, Kalman. 2008. FDI in Bulgarian and Romania in the Wake of EU Accession. *Journal of East-West Business* 14, no. 1.

Katz, Jorge M., ed. 1987. *Technology Generation in Latin American Manufacturing Industries.* New York: St. Martin's Press.

Keane, Michael P., and Susan E. Feinberg. 2007. Advances in Logistics and the Growth of Intra-firm Trade: The Case of Canadian Affiliates of U. S. Multinationals, 1984–1995. *The Journal of Industrial Economics* 60, no. 4 (December): 571–632.

Keane, Michael P., and Susan E. Feinberg. 2009. Tariff Effects on MNC Decisions to Engage in Intra-Firm and Arms-Length Trade. *Canadian Journal of Economics* 42, no. 3 (August).

Keller, Wolfgang, and Stephen R. Yeaple. 2009. Multinational Enterprises, International Trade, and Productivity Growth: Firm-Level Evidence from the United States. *Review of Economics and Statistics* 91, no. 4: 821–31.

Kenny, Charles. 2006. *Measuring and Reducing the Impact of Corruption in Infrastructure.* World Bank Policy Research Working Paper 4099. Washington: World Bank.

Kenny, Charles, and Tina Soriede. 2008. *Grand Corruption in Utilities.* World Bank Policy Research Working Paper 4805. Washington: World Bank.

Kessides, Ioannis N. 2004. *Reforming Infrastructure: Privatization, Regulation, and Competition.* Washington: World Bank and Oxford University Press.

Kessides, Ioannis N. 2005. Infrastructure Privatization and Regulation. *World Bank Research Observer* 20, no. 1: 81–108.

Khan, Mohsin, ed. Forthcoming. *The Future of the Moroccan Economy.* Washington: Peterson Institute for International Economics.

Kimura, Fukumari. 2009. *The Spatial Structure of Production/Distribution Networks and Its Implication for Technology Transfers and Spillovers.* ERIA Discussion Paper Series DP-2009-02 (updated in 2010). Jakarta: Economic Research Institute for ASEAN and East Asia.

King, Cary, Robert O. Keohane, and Sidney Verba. 1994. *Designing Social Inquiry: Scientific Inference in Qualitative Research.* Princeton, NJ: Princeton University Press.

Klein, Karen. 1995. *General Motors in Hungary: The Corporate Strategy Behind Szentgotthard.* Washington: Georgetown University, Pew Economic Freedom Fellows Program.

Kletzer, Lori G., James Levinsohn, and David Richardson. 2007. Responses to Globalization: US Textile and Apparel Workers. Unpublished draft. Washington: Peterson Institute for International Economics.

Kohpaiboon, Archanun. 2007. *Multinational Enterprises and Industrial Transformation: Evidence from Thailand.* Cheltenham, UK: Edward Elgar.

Kohpaiboon, Archanun. 2009. *Global Integration of Thai Automotive Industry.* Thammasat University Discussion Paper 0016. Bangkok: Thammasat University.

Kohpaiboon, Archanun. 2010. *Hard Disk Drive Industry in Thailand: International Production Networks versus Industrial Clusters.* Thammasat University Discussion Paper 23. Bangkok: Thammasat University.

Kokko, Ari, Ruben Tansini, and Mario C. Lejan. 1996. Local Technological Capability and Productivity Spillovers from FDI in the Uruguayan Manufacturing Sector. *Journal of Development Studies* 32 (April): 602–11.

Kokko, Ari. 1994. Technology, Market Characteristics, and Spillovers. *Journal of Development Economics* 43, no. 4 (April): 279–93.

Koopman, Robert, Zhi Wang, and Shang-Jin Wei. 2008. *How Much of Chinese Exports is Really Made in China? Assessing Domestic Value-Added when Processing Trade Is Pervasive.* NBER Working Paper 14109. Cambridge, MA: National Bureau of Economic Research.

Koopman, Robert, Zhi Wang, and Shang-Jin Wei. 2009. *A World Factory in Global Production Chains: Estimating Imported Value-Added in Chinese Exports.* CEPR Discussion Paper 7430. London: Centre for Economic Policy Research.

Krueger, Anne O. 1975. *The Benefits and Costs of Import Substitution in India: A Microeconomic Study.* Minneapolis, MN: University of Minnesota Press.

Krugman, Paul R., ed. 1986. *Strategic Trade Policy and the New International Economics.* Cambridge, MA: MIT Press.

Kumar, Nagash. 2002. *Globalization and the Quality of Foreign Direct Investment.* New Delhi: Oxford University Press.

Lall, Sanjaya, and Paul Streetan. 1977. *Foreign Investment, Transnationals, and Developing Countries.* Boulder, CO: Westview Press.

Lardy, Nicholas R. 2002. *Integrating China into the Global Economy.* Washington: Brookings Institution.

Larraín, Felipe, Luis F. López-Calva, and Andrés Rodríguez-Clare. 2001. Intel: A Case Study of Foreign Direct Investment in Central America. In *Economic Development in Central America,* vol. 1, *Growth and Internationalization,* ed. Felipe Larrain. Cambridge, MA: Harvard University Press.

Lawrence, Robert. 1996. *Single World, Divided Nations?* Paris: Organization for Economic Cooperation and Development.

Le Billon, Philippe. 2005. *Fuelling War: Natural Resources and Armed Conflict.* New York: Routledge for the International Institute for Strategic Studies.

Lederman, Daniel, and William Maloney. 2003. *Trade Structure and Growth.* World Bank Working Paper (November). Washington: World Bank.

Leigland, James. 2008. *The Rise and Fall of Brownfield Concessions: But Some Signs of Recovery After a Decade of Decline.* World Bank Public-Private Infrastructure Advisory Facility Working Paper no. 6. Washington: World Bank.

Lensink, Robert, and Oliver Morrisey. 2006. Foreign Direct Investment: Flows, Volatility and the Impact on Growth. *Review of International Economics* 14, no. 3: 478–93.

Lewis, III, Howard, and J. David Richardson. 2001. *Why Global Commitment Really Matters!* Washington: Institute for International Economics.

Lewis, Jr., Stephen R. 1989. Primary Exporting Countries. In *Handbook of Development Economics* (Volume II), ed. Hollis Chenery and T. N. Srinivasan. Amsterdam: Elsevier Science Publishers.

Likosky, Michael. 2009. Contracting and Regulatory Issues in the Oil and Gas and Metallic Minerals Industries. *Transnational Corporations* 18, no. 1 (April): 1–43.

Lim, Linda Y. C., and Pang Eng Fong. 1982. Vertical Linkages and Multinational Enterprises in Developing Countries. *World Development* 10, no. 7: 585–95.

Limão, Nuno, and Anthony Venables. 1999. *Infrastructure, Geographical Disadvantage and Transport Costs.* World Bank Policy Research Working Paper 2257. Washington: World Bank.

Linden, Greg, Kenneth L. Kraemer, and Jason Dedrick. 2007. *Who Captures Value in a Global Innovation System? The Case of Apple's iPod.* Personal Computing Industry Center Working Paper (June). Irvine, CA: University of California.

Lipsey, Robert. 2006. *Measuring the Impacts of FDI in Central and Eastern Europe.* NBER Working Paper 12808. Cambridge, MA: National Bureau of Economic Research.

Lipsey, Robert E., and Fredrik Sjöholm. 2004a. FDI and Wage Spillovers in Indonesian Manufacturing. *Review of World Economics* 140, no. 2: 287–310.

Lipsey, Robert E., and Fredrik Sjöholm. 2004b. Foreign Direct Investment, Education, and Wages in Indonesian Manufacturing. *Journal of Development Economics* 75, no. 1: 415–22.

Lipsey, Robert, and Fredrik Sjöholm. 2005. The Impact of Inward FDI on Host Countries: Why Such Different Answers? In *Does Foreign Direct Investment Promote Development?* ed. Theodore H. Moran, Edward M. Graham, and Magnus Blomström. Washington: Institute for International Economics and the Center for Global Development.

Lipsey, Robert E., and Merle Yahr Weiss. 1981. Foreign Production and Exports in Manufacturing Industries. *Review of Economics and Statistics* 63, no. 4: 448–94.

Lipsey, Robert E., and Merle Yahr Weiss. 1984. Foreign Production and Exports of Individual Firms. *Review of Economics and Statistics* 66, no. 2: 304–08.

Lipsey, Robert E., Eric D. Ramsterrer, and Magnus Blomström. 2000. *Outward FDI and Parent Exports and Employment: Japan, the United States, and Sweden.* NBER Working Paper 7623. Cambridge, MA: National Bureau of Economic Research.

Liu, Xiaming, Chengang Wang, and Yinqi Wei. 2009. Do Local Manufacturing Firms Benefit from Transactional Linkages with Multinational Enterprises in China? *Journal of International Business Studies* 40, no. 7 (September): 1113–131.

Long, Guoqiang. 2005. China's Policies on FDI: Review and Evaluation. In *Does Foreign Direct Investment Promote Development?* ed. Theodore H. Moran, Edward M. Graham, and Magnus Blomström. Washington: Institute for International Economics and the Center for Global Development.

Mansfield, Edwin, and J.-Y. Lee. 1996. Intellectual Property Protection and US Foreign Direct Investment. *Review of Economics and Statistics* 78, no. 2: 181–86.

Mansfield, Edwin, and Anthony Romeo. 1980. Technology Transfer to Overseas Subsidiaries by US-based Firms. *Quarterly Journal of Economics* 95, no. 4: 737–50.

Markusen, James. 2002. *Multinational Firms and the Theory of International Trade.* Cambridge, MA: MIT Press.

Markusen, James. 2005. Modeling the Offshoring of White-Collar Services: From Comparative Advantage to the New Theories of Trade and FDI. In *Brookings Trade Forum 2005: Offshoring White-Collar Work,* ed. S. Lael Brainard and Susan Collins. Washington: The Brookings Institution.

Markusen, James R., and Keith E. Maskus. 2001. Estimating the Knowledge-Capital Model of the Multinational Enterprise. *American Economic Review* 91, no. 3: 693–708.

Markusen, James R., and Keith E. Maskus. 2003. General-Equilibrium Approaches to the Multinational Enterprise: A Review of Theory and Evidence. In *Handbook of International Trade,* ed. E. Kwan Choi and James C. Hartigan. London: Blackwell.

Martin, Julie A., and Pamela A. Bracey. 2001. OPIC Modified Expropriation Coverage Case Study: MidAmerica's Projects in Indonesia—Dieng and Patuha. In *International Political Risk Management: Exploring New Frontiers,* ed. Theodore H. Moran. Washington: World Bank Multilateral Investment Guarantee Agency.

Maskus, Keith. Forthcoming. *The Globalization of Intellectual Property Rights: Getting the International Incentives Right.* Washington: Peterson Institute for International Economics.

Mattoo, Aaditya, Randeep Rathindran, and Arvind Subramanian. 2006. Measuring Services Trade Liberalization and Its Impact on Economic Growth: An Illustration. *Journal of Economic Integration* 21, no. 1: 64–98.

McKendrick, David G., Richard F. Donner, and Stephan Haggard. 2000. *From Silicon Valley to Singapore: Location and Competitive Advantage in the Hard Disk Drive Industry.* Stanford, CA: Stanford University Press.

McKinsey Global Institute. 2006. *New Horizons: Multinational Company Investment in Developing Economies.* New York: McKinsey & Company.

McKinsey Global Institute. 2010. *Growth and Competitiveness in the United States: The Role of Its Multinational Companies.* Washington: McKinsey & Company.

Melitz, Marc J. 2003. The Impact of Trade on Intra-Industry Reallocations and Aggregate Industry Productivity. *Econometrica* 71, no. 6: 1695–725.

Melitz, Marc J., and Gianmarco I. P. Ottaviano. 2008. Market Size, Trade, and Productivity. *The Review of Economic Studies* 75, no. 1: 295–316.

Meyer, Klaus E., and Evis Sinani. 2009. When and Where Does Foreign Direct Investment Generate Positive Spillovers? A Meta-Analysis. *Journal of International Business Studies* 40, no. 7: 1075-094.

Michelson, Hope. 2010. Welfare Impacts of Supermarkets on Developing World Farmer Suppliers: Evidence from Nicaragua. Photocopy (March 8).

Monitor Institute. 2009. *Investing for Social and Environmental Impact: A Design for Catalyzing an Emerging Industry.* Available at www.monitorinstitute.com.

Moran, Theodore H. 1998. *Foreign Direct Investment and Development.* Washington: Institute for International Economics.

Moran, Theodore H. 2001. *Parental Supervision: The New Paradigm for Foreign Direct Investment and Development.* Washington: Institute for International Economics.

Moran, Theodore H. 2002. *Beyond Sweatshops: Foreign Direct Investment and Globalization in Developing Countries.* Washington: Brookings Institution.

Moran, Theodore H. 2003. *Reforming OPIC for the 21st Century.* Washington: Institute for International Economics.

Moran, Theodore H. 2006. *Harnessing Foreign Direct Investment for Development: Policies for Developed and Developing Countries.* Washington: Center for Global Development.

Moran, Theodore H. Forthcoming. *Foreign Multinational Manufacturing Investors Are "Transforming" the Chinese Economy—Or Are They?* Washington: Peterson Institute for International Economics.

Moran, Theodore H., Edward M. Graham, and Magnus Blomström, ed. 2005. *Does Foreign Direct Investment Promote Development?* Washington: Institute for International Economics.

Morriset, Jacques, and Kelly Andrews-Johnson. 2003. *The Effectiveness of Promotion Agencies at Attracting Foreign Direct Investment.* Foreign Investment Advisory Service Occasional Paper 16. Washington: Foreign Investment Advisory Service.

Mutti, John. 2003. *Taxation and Foreign Direct Investment.* Washington: Institute for International Economics.

Mutti, John, and Harry Grubert. 2004. Empirical Asymmetries in Foreign Direct Investment and Taxation. *Journal of International Economics* 62, no. 2: 337-58.

Nellis, John, Rachel Menezes, and Sarah Lucas. 2004. *Privatization in Latin America: The Rapid Rise, Recent Fall, and Continuing Puzzle of a Contentious Economic Policy.* Inter-American Dialogue/Center for Global Development Policy Brief 3, no. 1.

Nelson, Roy C. 2009. *Harnessing Globalization: The Promotion of Nontraditional Foreign Direct Investment in Latin America.* University Park, PA: Pennsylvania State University Press.

Ngo, H., and D. Conklin. 1996. *Mekong Corporation and the Viet Nam Motor Vehicle Industry.* Working Paper 96-H002. University of Western Ontario, Richard Ivey School of Business.

Norberg, Helene, and Magnus Blomström. 1992. *Dutch Disease and Management of Windfall Gains in Botswana.* Stockholm: Handelshögskolan i Stockholm, Ekonomiska Forskningsinstitutet.

Nuñez, Wilson Peres. 1990. *Foreign Direct Investment and Industrial Development in Mexico.* Paris: Organization for Economic Cooperation and Development.

OECD (Organization for Economic Cooperation and Development). 2007. *Corruption: A Glossary of International Criminal Standards.* Paris.

OECD (Organization for Economic Cooperation and Development). 2008. Consultation Paper: Review of the OECD Instruments on Combating Bribery of Foreign Public Officials in International Business Transactions Ten Years after Adoption. Paris (January).

Olley, S., and A. Pakes. 1996. The Dynamics of Productivity in the Telecommunications Equipment Industry. *Econometrica* 64: 1263-98.

Oshikoya, T. W., A. Jerome, M. N. Hussain, and K. Mlambo. 1999. Closing the Infrastructure Deficit. Background paper prepared for Africa in the 21st Century Project. World Bank, Washington.

O'Sullivan, Robert C. 2005. Learning from OPIC's Experience with Claims and Arbitration. In *International Political Risk Management: Looking to the Future,* ed. Theodore H. Moran and Gerald West. Washington: World Bank.

Otto, James, Craig Andrews, Fred Cawood, Michael Doggett, Pietro Guj, Frank Stermole, John Stermole, and John Tilton. 2006. Taxation of the Mineral Section. In *Mining Royalties: A Global Study of Their Impact on Investors, Government, and Civil Society,* ed. James Otto et al. Washington: World Bank.

Pack, Howard. 1997. The Role of Exports in Asian Development. In *Pathways to Growth: Comparing East Asia and Latin America,* ed. Nancy Birdsall and Frederick Jaspersen. Baltimore: Johns Hopkins University Press.

Perry, Guillermo. 2010. *MDB's Direct Support to Private Firms: Growing Business or Development Priority?* Washington: Center for Global Development.

Pindyck, Robert. 2009. *Sunk Costs and Risk-Based Barriers to Entry.* NBER Working Paper 14755. Cambridge, MA: National Bureau of Economic Research.

Preeg, Ernest H. 2008. *India and China: An Advanced Technology Race and How the United States Should Respond.* Washington: Manufacturers Alliance/MAPI.

Radelet, Steven. 1999. *Manufactured Exports, Export Platforms, and Economic Growth.* Harvard Institute for International Development CAER II Discussion Paper No. 43 (November). Cambridge, MA: Harvard University.

Ramachandran, V. 1993. Technology Transfer, Firm Ownership, and Investment in Human Capital. *Review of Economics and Statistics* 75, no. 4: 64–70.

Ramondo, Natalia, and Andrés Rodríguez-Clare. 2009. Trade, Multinational Production, and the Gains from Openness. Photocopy (June 2).

Rasiah, Rajah. 1994. Flexible Production Systems and Local Machine-Tool Subcontracting: Electronics Components Transnationals in Malaysia. *Cambridge Journal of Economics* 18, no. 3 (June): 279–98.

Rasiah, Rajah. 1995. *Foreign Capital and Industrialization in Malaysia.* New York: St. Martin's Press.

Ravat, Anwar, and Andre Ufer. 2010. *Toward Strengthened EITI Reporting—Summary Report and Recommendations.* Extractive Industries for Development Series no. 14 (January). Washington: World Bank.

Razafindrakoto, Mireille, and François Roubaud. 1995. Les Entreprises Franches à Madagascar: Economie d'enclave ou promesse d'une nouvelle prospérité? Nouvel esclavage ou opportunité pour le développement du pays? *Economie de Madagascar,* no. 2.

Reisen, Helmut, and Marcelo Soto. 2001. Which Types of Capital Inflows Foster Developing-Country Growth? *International Finance* 4, no. 1 (Spring): 1–14.

Reuber, Grant L., with H. Crookell, M. Emerson, and G. Gallias-Hamonno. 1973. *Private Foreign Investment in Development.* Oxford, UK: Clarendon Press.

Rhee, Yung Whee, Katharina Katterback, and Jeanette White. 1990. *Free Trade Zones in Export Strategies.* Washington: World Bank Industry Development Division.

Richardson, J. David. 2005a. Uneven Gains and Unbalanced Burdens? Three Decades of American Globalization. In *The United States and the World Economy: Foreign Economic Policy for the Next Decade,* ed. C. Fred Bergsten. Washington: Institute for International Economics.

Richardson, J. David. 2005b. Global Forces, American Faces: US Economic Globalization at the Grass Roots. Unpublished draft. Washington: Institute for International Economics.

Riskin, Leonard L., James E. Westbrook, Chris Guthrie, Richard Reuben, Jennifer Robbennolt, and Nancy A. Welsh. 2009. *Dispute Resolution and Lawyers.* Fourth Edition. New York: Westgroup.

Rodríguez-Clare, Andrés. 1996. Multinationals, Linkages, and Economic Development. *American Economic Review* 86, no. 4: 852–73.

Rodrik, Dani. 1992. The Limits of Trade Policy Reform in Developing Countries. *Journal of Economic Perspectives* 6, no. 1: 87–105.

Rodrik, Dani. 1999. *The New Global Economy and Developing Countries: Making Openness Work*. Baltimore: Johns Hopkins University Press for the Overseas Development Council.

Rodrik, Dani. 2007. *One Economics, Many Recipes: Globalization, Institutions, and Economic Growth*. Princeton, NJ: Princeton University Press.

Rodrik, Dani. 2009. *Growth After the Crisis*. CEPR Discussion Paper 7480. London: Centre for Economic Policy Research.

Rodrik, Dani. 2010. The Return of Industrial Policy. Project Syndicate (April 12). Available at www.project-syndicate.org (accessed on February 1, 2011).

Roemer, Michael. 1985. Dutch Disease in Developing Countries: Swallowing Bitter Medicine. In *The Primary Sector in Economic Development*, ed. Mats Lundahl. London: Croom Helm.

Romer, Paul. 1990. Endogenous Technological Change. *Journal of Political Economy* 98, no. 5: S71–102.

Romer, Paul. 1992. Two Strategies for Economic Development: Using Ideas and Producing Ideas. In *Proceedings of the World Bank Annual Conference on Development Economics*. Washington: World Bank.

Romer, Paul. 1994. New Goods, Old Theory, and the Welfare Costs of Trade Restrictions. *Journal of Development Economics* 43, no. 1: 5–38.

Rugman, Alan M. 2005. *The Regional Multinationals*. Cambridge, UK: Cambridge University Press.

Rutherford, Thomas F., and David G. Tarr. 2002. Trade Liberalization, Product Variety and Growth in a Small Open Economy: A Quantitative Assessment. *Journal of International Economics* 56, no. 2: 247–72.

Sachs, Jeffrey. 2005. *The End of Poverty: Economic Possibilities for Our Time*. New York: Penguin Books.

Sachs, Jeffrey D., and Andrew M. Warner. 2001. Natural Resources and Economic Development: The Curse of Natural Resources. *European Economic Review* 45, no. 4–6: 827–38.

Samuelson, Paul. 2004. Why Ricardo and Mill Rebut and Confirm Arguments of Mainstream Economists Supporting Globalization. *Journal of Economic Perspectives* 18, no. 3: 135–46.

Sauvant, Karl P., and Geraldine McAllister, with Wolfgang A. Maschek. 2010. *Foreign Direct Investments from Emerging Markets: The Challenges Ahead*. New York: Palgrave Macmillan.

Schelling, Thomas. 1966. *Arms and Influence*. New Haven, CT: Yale University Press.

Schott, Peter K. 2004. Across-Product Versus Within-Product Specialization in International Trade. *Quarterly Journal of Economics* 119, no. 2: 647–78.

Seagate Technology. 2008. Annual Report, Form 10K. Scotts Valley, CA.

Sefton, Darby. 2009. *The Case for Company-by-Company Reporting of Data in the Extractive Industries Transparency Initiative (EITI)* (June). New York: Revenue Watch Institute.

Shah, Manju Kedia. 2006. *Subcontracting in Sub-Sahara Africa*. World Bank Working Paper (February). Washington: World Bank.

Shah, Manju Kedia, James Habyarimana, Linda Cotton, Vijaya Ramachandran, and Ivan Rossignol. 2005. *Madagascar Investment Climate Assessment: Technical Report*. World Bank Africa Private Sector Group (June). Washington: World Bank.

Shaxson, Nicholas. 2007. *Poisoned Wells: The Dirty Politics of African Oil*. New York: Palgrave Macmillan.

Slaughter, Matthew J. 2010. *How US Multinational Companies Strengthen the US Economy: Revised Update* (May). Washington: US Council for International Business.

Spar, Debora. 1998. *Attracting High Technology Investment: Intel's Costa Rican Plant*. Foreign World Bank Group Investment Advisory Service Occasional Paper 11. Washington: World Bank.

Spar, Debora. 2006. *The Impact of Intel in Costa Rica: Nine Years After the Decision to Invest*. Washington: World Bank Foreign Investment Advisory Group and Multilateral Investment Guarantee Agency.

Stevens, Paul. 2003. Resource Impact: Curse or Blessing? A Literature Survey. *Journal of Energy Literature* 9, no. 1: 3–42.

Straub, Stephane. 2008. *Infrastructure and Growth in Developing Countries: Recent Advances and Research Challenges*. Policy Research Working Paper 4460 (January). Washington: World Bank.

Swenson, Deborah L. 2008. Multinationals and the Creation of Chinese Trade Linkages. *Canadian Journal of Economics* 41, no. 2 (May): 596–618.

te Velde, Dirk Willem, and Oliver Morrissey. 2003. Do Workers in Africa Get a Wage Premium if Employed in Firms Owned by Foreigners? *Journal of African Economies* 12, no. 1: 41–73.

Thomas, Kenneth. 2010. *The Political Economy of Investment Incentives: Competition for Investment on a Global Scale*. Basingstoke, UK: Palgrave Macmillan.

Transparency International. 2009. *Global Corruption Report 2009*. Berlin.

UNCTAD (United Nations Conference on Trade and Development). 2001. *World Investment Report 2001: Promoting Linkages*. Geneva.

UNCTAD (United Nations Conference on Trade and Development). 2003. *World Investment Report 2003*. Geneva.

UNCTAD (United Nations Conference on Trade and Development). 2007a. *Investment Policy Review of Morocco*. TD/B/Com.2/76. Geneva.

UNCTAD (United Nations Conference on Trade and Development). 2007b. *Elimination of TRIMs: The Experience of Selected Developing Countries*. Geneva.

UNCTAD (United Nations Conference on Trade and Development). 2008. *World Investment Report 2008: Transnational Corporations and the Infrastructure Challenge*. New York.

UNCTAD (United Nations Conference on Trade and Development). 2009. *World Investment Report 2009*. New York.

UNCTAD (United Nations Conference on Trade and Development). 2010a. *Report on the UNCTAD Survey of Infrastructure Services Regulators*. Geneva.

UNCTAD (United Nations Conference on Trade and Development). 2010b. *Investor-State Disputes: Prevention and Alternatives to Arbitration*. New York.

UNCTAD (United Nations Conference on Trade and Development). 2010c. *World Investment Report 2010*. New York.

UNIDO (United Nations Industrial Development Organization). 2009. *Industrial Development Report 2009. Breaking In and Moving Up: New Industrial Challenges for the Bottom Billion and the Middle-Income Countries*. Vienna.

Urata, Shujiro, and Hiroki Kawai. 2000. Intrafirm Technology Transfer by Japanese Manufacturing Firms in Asia. In *The Role of Foreign Direct Investment in East Asian Economic Development*, ed. Takatoshi Ito and Anne O. Krueger. Chicago: University of Chicago Press for the National Bureau of Economic Research.

USAID (US Agency for International Development). 2008. The Role of Labor-Related Issues in the Foreign Assistance Framework: Bangladesh Labor Assessment. Photocopy (November).

USAID (US Agency for International Development). 2010. *The Role of the Labor Sector in the Foreign Assistance Framework: Honduras Labor Assessment* (July). Washington: USAID.

US Senate. 2004. Money Laundering and Foreign Corruption: Enforcement and Effectiveness of the Patriot Act: Case Study Involving Riggs Bank. Report prepared by the Minority Staff of the Permanent Subcommittee on Investigations (July 15).

Van Harten, Gus. 2010. Thinking Twice about a Gold Rush: Pacific Rim v. El Salvador. Vale Columbia Center for Sustainable International Investment: *Columbia FDI Perspectives,* no. 23 (May 24).

Vernon, Raymond. 1971. *Sovereignty at Bay.* New York: Basic Books.

Vienna Institute for International Economic Studies. 2008. Foreign Direct Investment in Central, East and South East Europe 2007–2008: Decline to Follow Uneven Growth. (June 30). Available at www.wiiw.ac.at (accessed on February 1, 2011).

Wang, Miao Grace. 2010. Foreign Direct Investment and Domestic Investment in the Host Country: Evidence from Panel Study. *Applied Economics* (forthcoming).

Wasow, Bernard. 2010. The Benefits of Foreign Direct Investment in the Presence of Price Distortions: The Case of Kenya. Photocopy.

Wells, Jr., Louis T. 1997. Enron Development Corporation: The Dabhol Power Project in Maharashtra, India. *Harvard Business Review* (February 4).

Wells, Jr., Louis T., and Rafiq Ahmed. 2007. *Making Foreign Investment Safe: Property Rights and National Sovereignty.* New York: Oxford University Press.

Wells, Jr., Louis T., and Alvin G. Wint. 2000. *Marketing a Country: Promotion as a Tool for Attracting Foreign Investment* (Revised Edition). Washington: International Finance Corporation, Multilateral Investment Guarantee Agency, and the World Bank.

Williamson, John. 1990. What Washington Means by Policy Reform. In *Latin American Adjustment: How Much Has Happened?* ed. John Williamson. Washington: Institute for International Economics.

Williamson, Oliver E. 1985. *The Economic Institutions of Capitalism.* New York: The Free Press.

Woodhouse, Erik J. 2008. Managing International Political Risk: Lessons from the Power Sector. In *International Political Risk Management: Needs of the Present, Challenges for the Future,* ed. Theodore H. Moran, Gerald T. West, and Keith Martin. Washington: World Bank Multilateral Investment Guarantee Agency.

Working Group on Development and Environment in the Americas. 2008. *Foreign Investment and Sustainable Development: Lessons from the Americas.* Washington: Heinrich Boll Foundation North America.

World Bank. 2002. *Global Economic Prospects and the Developing Countries 2002: Making Trade Work for the World's Poor.* Washington.

World Bank. 2006. *Kingdom of Morocco: Country Economic Memorandum,* two volumes. Washington (March 14).

World Bank. 2010. *Implementation of the Management Response to the Extractive Industries Review* (February). Washington.

World Bank Group Advisory Services. 2009. *Global Investment Promotion Benchmarking 2009: Summary Report.* Washington: World Bank.

Wright, Gavin, and Jesse Czelusta. 2004. The Myth of the Resource Curse. *Challenge* 47, no. 2: 6–38.

Zarsky, Lyuba, and Kevin P. Gallagher. 2008. Mexico: Sustainable FDI in Mexico's IT Sector: Missing Links, Dashed Hopes. In *Foreign Investment and Sustainable Development: Lessons from the Americas.* Working Group on Development and the Environment in the Americas. Washington: Heinrich Boll Foundation North America.

Abbreviations

ADB	Asian Development Bank
AfDB	African Development Bank
AMDI	Agence Marocaine de Développement des Investissements (Morocco)
ATP	advanced technology products
BEA	US Bureau of Economic Analysis
BIT	bilateral investment treaty
CEADEL	Center for Education and Support for Local Development
CINDE	La Coalición Costarricense de Iniciativas de Desarrollo (Costa Rica)
EBRD	European Bank for Reconstruction and Development
EDB	Economic Development Board (Singapore)
EITI	Extractive Industries Transparency Initiative
FCPA	US Foreign Corrupt Practices Act of 1977
FDI	foreign direct investment
FLA	Fair Labor Association
IASB	International Accounting Standards Board
ICMM	International Council on Mining & Metals
ICSID	International Centre for Settlement of Investment Disputes
IDB	Inter-American Development Bank
IFC	International Finance Corporation
ILO	International Labor Organization
IMF	International Monetary Fund
LIUP	Local Industry Upgrading Program
MIGA	Multilateral Investment Guarantee Agency
MNCs	multinational corporations

NAFTA	North American Free Trade Agreement
NBER	National Bureau of Economic Research
NGOs	nongovernmental organizations
NLC	National Labor Committee
OECD	Organization for Economic Cooperation and Development
OPIC	Overseas Private Investment Corporation
PLN	Perusahaan Listrik Negara (Indonesia)
PPIAF	Public-Private Infrastructure Advisory Fund
SEC	Securities and Exchange Commission
SOEs	state-owned enterprises
TRIMs	Agreement on Trade Related Investment Measures
UNCITRAL	United Nations Commission on International Trade Law
UNCTAD	United Nations Conference on Trade and Development
UNIDO	United Nations Industrial Development Organization
USAID	US Agency for International Development
WRC	Worker Rights Consortium

Index

Hewlett-Packard, 78, 79, 115
high-technology sector
   China, 119–21
   cluster formation, 45–46, 69–70, 78–80, 95
Hitachi, 45
home economy
   capital loss by, 111–13
   employment composition in, 112–14
   MNC operations in, 123–24
   outward FDI and, 102–17, 128
   wages in, 112
Honda, 77
Honduras, 61
Hong Kong stock exchange, 16
Hong Kong World Trade Organization
   Ministerial (2005), 68
horizontal (market-seeking) FDI, 34, 37,
   41–42, 50–51, 82, 122
hostage effect, 19
host-country development, 1–2. *See also specific*
   country
   extractive industries (*See* extractive sector
      FDI)
   infrastructure (*See* infrastructure FDI)
   manufacturing (*See* manufacturing FDI)
   principal channels of, 5, 6b, 81, 138
   structural transformation, 7, 81–98
host-country revenues, distribution of, 22–23
host-country supplier networks, development
   of, 44–47, 67
Huawei, 120
human capital, 3–4
human rights, 135
Hyundai, 70, 77

IBM, 39, 45, 78, 79
idea gaps, 5, 63, 81, 84–87
import substitution
   manufacturing FDI used for, 36–38, 48
   trade liberalization and, 83
incentives, 87–92, 127
India
   auto sector liberalization in, 76, 77
   manufacturing FDI, 36, 48
   services FDI, 74
Indonesia
   corruption, 13
   extractive sector FDI, 11
   infrastructure FDI, 29, 31
   manufacturing FDI, 51–52
      wage premium, 54, 55, 57, 59
industry, globalization of, impact on
   developed world, 7–8, 99–124, 128

industry analyses, 36–41. *See also specific*
   industry
informatics policy, 36, 39, 48, 78
information asymmetries, 131
information technology (IT) sector, 78–80,
   89–90
infrastructure
   effect on economic outcome, 25
   state- versus privately-owned, 25–26
infrastructure FDI, 1, 25–31
   commercial and political risk, 28–30
   contract stability, 27–31
   developed countries, 99–101
   developing countries, 3, 3t (*See also specific*
      country)
   externalities, 4–5
   moral hazard, 30–31
   policy, 5, 26–27, 125–26
insurance
   breach-of-contract, 19, 31
   political-risk, 19–20, 27, 29–30, 129–30
intangible assets, 34, 116
Intel, 64, 76, 78, 89–90
intellectual property rights, 71
intensive margin, versus extensive margin, 87,
   95–98
Inter-American Development Bank (IDB), 15,
   19, 30, 131
Interior Department (US), 17
intermediates, new varieties of, 95–98
internalization of intangible assets, 34
International Accounting Standards Board
   (IASB), 16–17
International Centre for Settlement of
   Investment Disputes (ICSID), 14, 28
international economic crisis (2008-10), 92
International Finance Corporation (IFC), 19,
   30, 132–33
International Labor Organization (ILO), 55,
   62
international labor organizations, 134–35
International Trade and Investment Program
   (NBER), 141
investment
   domestic, crowding in/crowding out
      debate, 7, 50–51, 75–80
   foreign direct (*See* foreign direct
      investment)
   socially responsible, 18, 132
investor-state arbitrations
   extractive sector FDI, 14–15, 23–24, 131
   infrastructure FDI, 28–31
InvestPenang (Malaysia), 95
Ireland, 68

Read-Rite, 39
"reform, reform" formula, 67, 88, 127
reform champions, 142
regulatory environment, 126, 131–33
rent-gathering hypothesis, 116–17
reporting requirements, 16–18
research and development (R&D), 105–106,
    122n, 128
resource curse, 1, 9–11, 83
retail services industry, 73–74
revenue-sharing formulas, 22–23
Revenue Watch Institute, 15, 17, 134
risk
    commercial, 28–30
    currency, 28–30
    political, 28–31
Rodrik, Dani, 47, 84–85, 87–89, 94, 130, 130n
Romania, 73, 92–93
Romer, Paul, 56, 85–86, 92
royalties, 20–22
Russell Corporation, 60

Sachs, Jeffrey, 10
Samsung, 70
Samuelson, Paul, 7–8, 100–102
    abandonment hypothesis, 102–107
    rent-gathering hypothesis, 116–17
    substitution hypothesis, 107–15
Sanmina-SCI, 79
Schumpeterian cycles of creative destruction,
    76, 80
Seagate, 39, 45, 114
second generation research, 1
    externalities, 140
    lessons and conclusions, 139–42
    manufacturing FDI, 5–7, 41, 50–53
    methodological approaches, 139–41
    need for, 5–7
    policy implications, 8, 125
    services FDI, 7, 73–74
sectoral analyses, 36–41. See also specific industry
Securities and Exchange Commission (SEC),
    13, 16–18
self-discovery, 63, 81, 84–85, 87
semiconductor industry, 42–43, 89–90
Senegal, 44, 67
sensitive sector investments, 129
services FDI, 2
    externalities, 4–5
    policy, 125
    second generation research, 7, 73–74
services sector
    liberalization, 73–74
    multinationals, 106

Shanghai Automotive Industry Group, 119,
    121
Singapore, 39, 42–43, 45
Sirleaf, Ellen Johnson, 21
skill intensity, 4n
    development of, 67
    domestic value-added, 121–22
    FDI flows by, 62t, 62–65, 64t, 65t
    labor market spillover and, 55
    rent-gathering and, 117
Slovakia, 92–93
Slovenia, 45
socially responsible investment, 18, 132
social rate of return, 35
Société Camerounaise de Mobiles (Cameroon),
    30
Solectron, 79
Somboon Group, 43
Sony, 115
special partnerships, 12–13, 27
spillovers. See externalities
Sri Lanka, 76
state-owned enterprises (SOE), 50–51
state-owned infrastructure, 25–26
Statoil, 17
strategic trade theory, 116–17
structural transformation, 7, 81–98
    China, 118–23
    externalities, 4–5, 87–92, 122
    trade liberalization, 83, 92–95
subcontracting, 44, 44n
subsidies (incentives), 87–92, 127
substitution hypothesis, 107–15
Suharto, President, 13
Summers, Lawrence, 7–8, 100–101
    rent-gathering hypothesis, 116–17
    substitution hypothesis, 107–15
supplier networks, development of, 44–47, 67
survey research, 5, 17, 47, 52–58, 139–40
sustainable development goals, 23–24, 137–38
sweatshops, 59–61, 116–17
Sweden, 110

take or pay contracts, 28–31
talent scouts, 45, 142
Talisman Energy, 17
Tanzania, 10, 44, 67
tariff jumping FDI, 37
Tata Motors, 92
taxation
    backward linkages and, 44
    in extractive sector FDI, 18–23
    territorial system, 123, 124
TCL, 120

technology-sharing requirements, 37–38, 70–71, 96
technology upgrades, continuous real-time, 95–98
telecommunications industry, 42–43
territorial tax system, 123
Texas Instruments, 39, 64
Thailand
    backward linkages, 79
    manufacturing FDI, 38, 39, 43–46, 69
ThyssenKrupp, 92
total factor productivity, 73, 81, 96–97, 104
Toyota, 92
trade-and-FDI modeling, 95–98
trade-balancing mandates, 69
trade liberalization, 83, 92–95
trade unions, 61
traditional trade theory, 101
transfer pricing, 21
transparency, 12, 15–18, 131, 132
Transparency International, 15, 134
    Bribe Payer's Index, 12
    Global Corruption Perceptions Index, 11
TRIMs (Agreement on Trade-Related Investment Measures), 68–69, 130, 134
Tunisia, 11
TVP Technology, 119–20

UK Export Credits Guarantee Department, 19
United Auto Workers, 114
United Nations Commission on International Trade Law (UNCITRAL), 14, 28
United Nations Conference on Trade and Development (UNCTAD), 47, 68–69, 119
United Nations Global Compact, 135–36
United States
    BIT model, 130, 134
    goods trade, 106–107
    impact of globalization on, 7–8, 99–124, 128
    multinationals (*See* multinational corporations)
    regional shifts in manufacturing in, 100–102, 105, 107
    tax policy, 124, 124n
US Census Bureau, Manufacturing Technology Survey, 104

US Dodd-Frank Wall Street Reform and Consumer Protection Act, 16–18
US Foreign Commercial Service, 129
US Foreign Corrupt Practices Act (FCPA), 5, 12, 18, 27, 126, 131
US Interior Department, 17
US Securities and Exchange Commission (SEC), 13, 16–18
Unocal, 31
Uruguay, 44

value capture, 120, 123
Vegpro, 59
vendor development programs, 45–46, 127
Venezuela, 47–48
vertical (efficiency-seeking) FDI, 34, 42–53, 82, 122
Vietnam, 44, 69
vocational training programs, 58, 67, 89–90

wage(s)
    in home economy, 112
    minimum, 134, 134n
wage premium, 54–59, 117
Wallach, Lori, 123
Wal-Mart, 76–78
Walmex, 77–78
Washington Consensus, 125
welfare benefits, 96–97
Worker Rights Consortium (WRC), 60, 61
Working Group on Investment Issues (UNCTAD), 68–69
work-outs, 30–31, 133
World Bank, 19, 132, 133
    Ease of Doing Business Index, 26, 44, 66
    EITI++, 15, 126, 131–33
    Global Gas Flaring Reduction Partnership, 23
    Group Advisory Services, 94
    infrastructure and law website, 27
    labor market externalities study, 58
    role of, 131–33, 142
    trade liberalization studies, 96–97
World Investment Report (UNCTAD), 47
World Trade Organization, 68, 130

Other Publications from the
Peterson Institute for International Economics

WORKING PAPERS

Subsidies in International Trade*
Gary Clyde Hufbauer and Joanna Shelton Erb
1984   ISBN 0-88132-004-8
International Debt: Systemic Risk and Policy
Response*   William R. Cline
1984   ISBN 0-88132-015-3
Trade Protection in the United States: 31 Case
Studies*   Gary Clyde Hufbauer,
Diane E. Berliner, and Kimberly Ann Elliott
1986   ISBN 0-88132-040-4
Toward Renewed Economic Growth in Latin
America*   Bela Balassa, Gerardo M. Bueno,
Pedro Pablo Kuczynski, and Mario Henrique
Simonsen
1986   ISBN 0-88132-045-5
Capital Flight and Third World Debt*
Donald R. Lessard and John Williamson, eds.
1987   ISBN 0-88132-053-6
The Canada-United States Free Trade
Agreement: The Global Impact*
Jeffrey J. Schott and Murray G. Smith, eds.
1988   ISBN 0-88132-073-0
World Agricultural Trade: Building a
Consensus*   William M. Miner and
Dale E. Hathaway, eds.
1988   ISBN 0-88132-071-3
Japan in the World Economy*   Bela Balassa and
Marcus Noland
1988   ISBN 0-88132-041-2
America in the World Economy: A Strategy
for the 1990s*   C. Fred Bergsten
1988   ISBN 0-88132-089-7
Managing the Dollar: From the Plaza to the
Louvre*   Yoichi Funabashi
1988, 2d ed. 1989   ISBN 0-88132-097-8
United States External Adjustment and the
World Economy*   William R. Cline
May 1989   ISBN 0-88132-048-X
Free Trade Areas and U.S. Trade Policy*
Jeffrey J. Schott, ed.
May 1989   ISBN 0-88132-094-3
Dollar Politics: Exchange Rate Policymaking
in the United States*   I. M. Destler and
C. Randall Henning
September 1989   ISBN 0-88132-079-X
Latin American Adjustment: How Much Has
Happened?*   John Williamson, ed.
April 1990   ISBN 0-88132-125-7
The Future of World Trade in Textiles and
Apparel*   William R. Cline
1987, 2d ed. June 1999   ISBN 0-88132-110-9
Completing the Uruguay Round: A Results-
Oriented Approach to the GATT Trade
Negotiations*   Jeffrey J. Schott, ed.
September 1990   ISBN 0-88132-130-3
Economic Sanctions Reconsidered (2 volumes)
Economic Sanctions Reconsidered:
Supplemental Case Histories
Gary Clyde Hufbauer, Jeffrey J. Schott, and
Kimberly Ann Elliott
1985, 2d ed. Dec. 1990   ISBN cloth 0-88132-115-X
                          ISBN paper 0-88132-105-2

Economic Sanctions Reconsidered: History
and Current Policy   Gary Clyde Hufbauer,
Jeffrey J. Schott, and Kimberly Ann Elliott
December 1990   ISBN cloth 0-88132-140-0
                          ISBN paper 0-88132-136-2
Pacific Basin Developing Countries: Prospects
for the Future*   Marcus Noland
January 1991   ISBN cloth 0-88132-141-9
                          ISBN paper 0-88132-081-1
Currency Convertibility in Eastern Europe*
John Williamson, ed.
October 1991   ISBN 0-88132-128-1
International Adjustment and Financing: The
Lessons of 1985-1991*   C. Fred Bergsten, ed.
January 1992   ISBN 0-88132-112-5
North American Free Trade: Issues and
Recommendations*   Gary Clyde Hufbauer and
Jeffrey J. Schott
April 1992   ISBN 0-88132-120-6
Narrowing the U.S. Current Account Deficit*
Alan J. Lenz
June 1992   ISBN 0-88132-103-6
The Economics of Global Warming
William R. Cline
June 1992   ISBN 0-88132-132-X
US Taxation of International Income:
Blueprint for Reform   Gary Clyde Hufbauer,
assisted by Joanna M. van Rooij
October 1992   ISBN 0-88132-134-6
Who's Bashing Whom? Trade Conflict in High-
Technology Industries   Laura D'Andrea Tyson
November 1992   ISBN 0-88132-106-0
Korea in the World Economy*   Il SaKong
January 1993   ISBN 0-88132-183-4
Pacific Dynamism and the International
Economic System*   C. Fred Bergsten and
Marcus Noland, eds.
May 1993   ISBN 0-88132-196-6
Economic Consequences of Soviet
Disintegration*   John Williamson, ed.
May 1993   ISBN 0-88132-190-7
Reconcilable Differences? United States-Japan
Economic Conflict*   C. Fred Bergsten and
Marcus Noland
June 1993   ISBN 0-88132-129-X
Does Foreign Exchange Intervention Work?
Kathryn M. Dominguez and Jeffrey A. Frankel
September 1993   ISBN 0-88132-104-4
Sizing Up U.S. Export Disincentives*
J. David Richardson
September 1993   ISBN 0-88132-107-9
NAFTA: An Assessment
Gary Clyde Hufbauer and Jeffrey J. Schott, rev. ed.
October 1993   ISBN 0-88132-199-0
Adjusting to Volatile Energy Prices
Philip K. Verleger, Jr.
November 1993   ISBN 0-88132-069-2
The Political Economy of Policy Reform
John Williamson, ed.
January 1994   ISBN 0-88132-195-8
Measuring the Costs of Protection in the
United States   Gary Clyde Hufbauer and
Kimberly Ann Elliott
January 1994   ISBN 0-88132-108-7

How Ukraine Became a Market Economy and
Democracy   Anders Åslund
March 2009   ISBN 978-0-88132-427-3
Global Warming and the World Trading
System   Gary Clyde Hufbauer,
Steve Charnovitz, and Jisun Kim
March 2009   ISBN 978-0-88132-428-0
The Russia Balance Sheet   Anders Åslund and
Andrew Kuchins
March 2009   ISBN 978-0-88132-424-2
The Euro at Ten: The Next Global Currency?
Jean Pisani-Ferry and Adam S. Posen, eds.
July 2009   ISBN 978-0-88132-430-3
Financial Globalization, Economic Growth, and
the Crisis of 2007–09   William R. Cline
May 2010   ISBN 978-0-88132-4990-0
Russia after the Global Economic Crisis
Anders Åslund, Sergei Guriev, and Andrew
Kuchins, eds.
June 2010   ISBN 978-0-88132-497-6
Sovereign Wealth Funds: Threat or Salvation?
Edwin M. Truman
September 2010   ISBN 978-0-88132-498-3
The Last Shall Be the First: The East European
Financial Crisis, 2008–10   Anders Åslund
October 2010   ISBN 978-0-88132-521-8
Witness to Transformation: Refugee Insights
into North Korea   Stephan Haggard and
Marcus Noland
January 2011   ISBN 978-0-88132-438-9
Foreign Direct Investment and Development:
Launching a Second Generation of Policy
Research, Avoiding the Mistakes of the First,
and Reevaluating Policies for Developed and
Developing Countries   Theodore H. Moran
April 2011   ISBN 978-0-88132-600-0

SPECIAL REPORTS

1   Promoting World Recovery: A Statement
    on Global Economic Strategy*
    by 26 Economists from Fourteen Countries
    December 1982   ISBN 0-88132-013-7
2   Prospects for Adjustment in Argentina,
    Brazil, and Mexico: Responding to the
    Debt Crisis*   John Williamson, ed.
    June 1983   ISBN 0-88132-016-1
3   Inflation and Indexation: Argentina, Brazil,
    and Israel*   John Williamson, ed.
    March 1985   ISBN 0-88132-037-4
4   Global Economic Imbalances*
    C. Fred Bergsten, ed.
    March 1986   ISBN 0-88132-042-0
5   African Debt and Financing*
    Carol Lancaster and John Williamson, eds.
    May 1986   ISBN 0-88132-044-7
6   Resolving the Global Economic Crisis:
    After Wall Street*   by Thirty-three
    Economists from Thirteen Countries
    December 1987   ISBN 0-88132-070-6
7   World Economic Problems*
    Kimberly Ann Elliott and John Williamson,
    eds.
    April 1988   ISBN 0-88132-055-2

Reforming World Agricultural Trade*
by Twenty-nine Professionals from
Seventeen Countries
    1988   ISBN 0-88132-088-9
8   Economic Relations Between the United
    States and Korea: Conflict or Cooperation?*
    Thomas O. Bayard and Soogil Young, eds.
    January 1989   ISBN 0-88132-068-4
9   Whither APEC? The Progress to Date and
    Agenda for the Future*
    C. Fred Bergsten, ed.
    October 1997   ISBN 0-88132-248-2
10 Economic Integration of the Korean
    Peninsula   Marcus Noland, ed.
    January 1998   ISBN 0-88132-255-5
11 Restarting Fast Track*   Jeffrey J. Schott, ed.
    April 1998   ISBN 0-88132-259-8
12 Launching New Global Trade Talks: An
    Action Agenda   Jeffrey J. Schott, ed.
    September 1998   ISBN 0-88132-266-0
13 Japan's Financial Crisis and Its Parallels to
    US Experience   Ryoichi Mikitani and
    Adam S. Posen, eds.
    September 2000   ISBN 0-88132-289-X
14 The Ex-Im Bank in the 21st Century: A
    New Approach   Gary Clyde Hufbauer and
    Rita M. Rodriguez, eds.
    January 2001   ISBN 0-88132-300-4
15 The Korean Diaspora in the World
    Economy   C. Fred Bergsten and
    Inbom Choi, eds.
    January 2003   ISBN 0-88132-358-6
16 Dollar Overvaluation and the World
    Economy   C. Fred Bergsten and
    John Williamson, eds.
    February 2003   ISBN 0-88132-351-9
17 Dollar Adjustment: How Far? Against
    What?   C. Fred Bergsten and
    John Williamson, eds.
    November 2004   ISBN 0-88132-378-0
18 The Euro at Five: Ready for a Global Role?
    Adam S. Posen, ed.
    April 2005   ISBN 0-88132-380-2
19 Reforming the IMF for the 21st Century
    Edwin M. Truman, ed.
    April 2006   ISBN 978-0-88132-387-0
20 The Long-Term International Economic
    Position of the United States
    C. Fred Bergsten, ed.
    May 2009   ISBN 978-0-88132-432-7

WORKS IN PROGRESS

China's Energy Evolution: The Consequences
of Powering Growth at Home and Abroad
Daniel H. Rosen and Trevor Houser
Global Identity Theft: Economic and Policy
Implications   Catherine L. Mann
Globalized Venture Capital: Implications
for US Entrepreneurship and Innovation
Catherine L. Mann
Forging a Grand Bargain: Expanding Trade and
Raising Worker Prosperity   Lori G. Kletzer,
J. David Richardson, and Howard F. Rosen

DISTRIBUTORS OUTSIDE THE UNITED STATES

Australia, New Zealand,
and Papua New Guinea
D. A. Information Services
648 Whitehorse Road
Mitcham, Victoria 3132, Australia
Tel: 61-3-9210-7777
Fax: 61-3-9210-7788
Email: service@dadirect.com.au
www.dadirect.com.au

India, Bangladesh, Nepal, and Sri Lanka
Viva Books Private Limited
Mr. Vinod Vasishtha
4737/23 Ansari Road
Daryaganj, New Delhi 110002
India
Tel: 91-11-4224-2200
Fax: 91-11-4224-2240
Email: viva@vivagroupindia.net
www.vivagroupindia.com

Mexico, Central America, South America,
and Puerto Rico
US PubRep, Inc.
311 Dean Drive
Rockville, MD 20851
Tel: 301-838-9276
Fax: 301-838-9278
Email: c.falk@ieee.org

Asia (*Brunei, Burma, Cambodia, China,*
Hong Kong, Indonesia, Korea, Laos, Malaysia,
Philippines, Singapore, Taiwan, Thailand,
and Vietnam)
East-West Export Books (EWEB)
University of Hawaii Press
2840 Kolowalu Street
Honolulu, Hawaii 96822-1888
Tel: 808-956-8830
Fax: 808-988-6052
Email: eweb@hawaii.edu

Canada
Renouf Bookstore
5369 Canotek Road, Unit 1
Ottawa, Ontario KlJ 9J3, Canada
Tel: 613-745-2665
Fax: 613-745-7660
www.renoufbooks.com

Japan
United Publishers Services Ltd.
1-32-5, Higashi-shinagawa
Shinagawa-ku, Tokyo 140-0002
Japan
Tel: 81-3-5479-7251
Fax: 81-3-5479-7307
Email: purchasing@ups.co.jp
For trade accounts only. Individuals will find
Institute books in leading Tokyo bookstores.

Middle East
MERIC
2 Bahgat Ali Street, El Masry Towers
Tower D, Apt. 24
Zamalek, Cairo
Egypt
Tel. 20-2-7633824
Fax: 20-2-7369355
Email: mahmoud_fouda@mericonline.com
www.mericonline.com

United Kingdom, Europe
(*including Russia and Turkey*), **Africa,**
and Israel
The Eurospan Group
c/o Turpin Distribution
Pegasus Drive
Stratton Business Park
Biggleswade, Bedfordshire
SG18 8TQ
United Kingdom
Tel: 44 (0) 1767-604972
Fax: 44 (0) 1767-601640
Email: eurospan@turpin-distribution.com
www.eurospangroup.com/bookstore

Visit our website at:
www.piie.com
E-mail orders to:
petersonmail@presswarehouse.com

Pat has written an engaging and informative guide for those who wish to consider living lighter on the land and lighter on their budgets, with step by step instructions and documented case studies. We are challenged to examine our own values as part of the design process.
Our perfect home may not resemble the one constructed in our mind by our preconceived notions.
This book clearly demonstrates that we can indeed live large on a small footprint.

Whether the right size house for you is a tiny house or something larger, this book will guide you through the critical steps to create a dwelling that is exactly what you need … nothing more, nothing less … a perfect home.

— Heidi Louisa Schweizer,
architect & general contractor,
LEED AP – BD&C